# Logo! 4 Rot

Teacher's Guide

Oliver Gray • Sarah Provan

Heinemann

Heinemann Educational,
Halley Court, Jordan Hill, Oxford OX2 8EJ

Heinemann is a registered trademark of Reed Educational & Professional Publishing Ltd

OXFORD   MELBOURNE   AUCKLAND
JOHANNESBURG   BLANTYRE   GABORONE
IBADAN   PORTSMOUTH (NH) USA   CHICAGO

All rights reserved. No part of this publication may be reproduced in any material form (including photocopying or storing it in any medium by electronic means and whether or not transiently or incidentally to some other use of this publication) without the written permission of the copyright owner, except in accordance with the provisions of the Copyright, Designs and Patents Act 1998 or under the terms of a licence issued by the Copyright Licensing Agency, 90 Tottenham Court Road, London W1P 9HE. Applications for the copyright owner's written permission to reproduce any part of this publication should be addressed to the publisher.

© Oliver Gray and Sarah Provan

First published 2001

02 03 04 05 06   10 9 8 7 6 5 4 3 2

A catalogue record is available for this book from the British Library on request.

ISBN 0 435 36727 7

Produced by **AMR** Ltd

Cover photo by Arcaid (Richard Bryant).

Printed in Great Britain by Athenaeum Press Ltd, Gateshead, Tyne and Wear

Tel: 01865 888058   www.heinemann.co.uk

Contents

	page
Introduction	iv
Coverage of AQA themes and topics in *Logo! 4 Rot*	vii
Coverage of Edexcel topic areas in *Logo! 4 Rot*	viii
Coverage of OCR contexts in *Logo! 4 Rot*	ix
Coverage of WJEC topic areas in *Logo! 4 Rot*	x
Logo! 4 Rot for Scotland	xi

1 Hallo! Ich bin's! 12
Workbook: solutions 27

2 Schulstress 29
Kursarbeit: Schule 43
Workbook: solutions 44

3 Wir haben frei! 46
Workbook: solutions 60

4 Urlaub 62
Kursarbeit: Die Ferien 76
Workbook: solutions 77

5 Meine Stadt 80
Kursarbeit: Marburg wartet auf Sie! 94
Workbook: solutions 95

6 Einkaufen 98
Workbook: solutions 114

7 Freizeit und Urlaub 117
Kursarbeit: Freizeit 133
Workbook: solutions 134

8 Mein Leben zu Hause 136
Workbook: solutions 147

9 Die Arbeit 150
Kursarbeit: Betriebspraktikum 164
Workbook: solutions 165

10 Teenies! 168
Workbook: solutions 178

Lesen / Schreiben 180
Solutions to *Grammatik* exercises 187
Photocopiable grids 190

Introduction

Logo! offers a lively, communicative approach, underpinned by clear grammatical progression.

The course is suitable for a wide range ability range and includes differentiated materials in the Pupil's Books and differentiated workbooks in *Logo! 1* and *Logo! 2*.

Logo! 3 offers differentiated Pupil's Books and workbooks.

In *Logo! 4*, the Student's Books are differentiated to cater for the two examination tiers: *Logo! 4 Rot* is for the Higher Level and *Logo! 4 Grün* is for the Foundation Level. The workbooks also reflect the examination tiers. *Logo! 4* is specifically designed to continue from *Logo! 1, 2* and *3*, but is also suitable for students who have followed a different introductory course prior to opting to study German at GCSE or Standard Grade level.

The components

Logo! 4 Rot consists of:
Student's Book
Cassettes or CDs
Teacher's Guide
Higher Workbook

Three different assessment packs are available to accompany *Logo! 4 Grün* and *Logo! 4 Rot* (AQA, OCR, Edexcel).

Student's Book
The Student's Book is designed to last for two years (Years 10 and 11 in England and Wales and S3 and S4 in Scotland) and contains all the language required for the preparation of the GCSE or Standard Grade examination. There are ten chapters or *Kapitel*, and it is expected that the first six will be completed in the first year of the course and four in the second.

At the end of each chapter is a summary of the vocabulary covered, arranged into subject groups. These pages, entitled *Wörter*, will serve as a valuable examination revision tool. At the end of alternate chapters there is a double-page spread entitled *Sprechen*. These pages are designed to help the student prepare for the Speaking Examination, and contain example role-plays and conversations from the two preceding chapters.

At the back of the Student's Book there are four sections of further practice and reference. The *Kursarbeit* sections contain guidelines for students preparing coursework or extended pieces of writing, the *Lesen / Schreiben* pages provide further differentiated reading and writing practice and the *Grammatik* explains and practises grammar points introduced in *Logo! 4 Rot* – see separate section of this introduction for further information. Finally, there is a comprehensive German–English word list and a shorter English–German word list (*Wortschatz*).

Recorded material
There are three cassettes or CDs for *Logo! 4 Rot*. They contain listening material for both presentation and practice. The material includes passages, dialogues and interviews recorded by native speakers.

Workbooks
There are two parallel workbooks to accompany *Logo! 4*, one for Foundation Level and one for Higher Level. The Foundation Workbook is designed to be used alongside *Logo! 4 Grün*, while the Higher Workbook accompanies *Logo! 4 Rot*. The workbooks provide self-access reading and writing tasks and are ideal for homework. The pages of activities are cross-referenced to the units of the Student's Book that they accompany. At the end of each chapter there is a page of Grammar revision and a page for Speaking preparation. All workbook pages are referred to at the appropriate place in the Teacher's Guide, with a miniature version of the page and solutions to the activities.

Teacher's Guide
The *Teacher's Guide* contains:
– general overview of *Logo! 4 Rot*
– overview grids for each chapter or *Kapitel*
– clear teaching notes for all activities
– solutions for activities
– full transcript of recorded material
– mapping charts for UK examinations
– photocopiable grids for selected listening activities in the Student's Book

Coursework sections (*Kursarbeit*)

The coursework section in *Logo! 4 Rot* gives regular, guided practice in preparing for the coursework element of the GCSE examination. It is cross-referenced to relevant sections in the core units. Each double-page spread is linked to a GCSE theme, and always starts with a model text on that theme (at a higher level than that expected by the student). This text acts as a stimulus to give students ideas about what they might include in their own piece of work. Students are encouraged to look at the detail of the text through the structured reading activities. They are gradually guided to produce good German sentences in the various activities, through to the final task in which they are asked to produce an extended piece of writing.

The *Hilfe* column is a feature on all the spreads. It reminds students of language they might include and particular structures that will raise the level of their writing. Remind students who are capable of achieving a Higher grade that they should always include examples of two or three tenses in their writing.

Reading/Writing pages (*Lesen/Schreiben*)

These pages are designed to give students extra practice in reading and structured writing. They allow for differentiation, *Lesen und Schreiben A* being easier than *Lesen und Schreiben B*. The intention is to provide a variety of types of authentic texts to work on. Sometimes they relate closely to the relevant chapter of the Student's Book, sometimes the link is more general. This is deliberate, to avoid the impression of all the language tasks being too tightly controlled and over-prescriptive.

Teachers may feel it is useful to work with students on the exercises, but it should also be possible for most students to work independently on them. They are not designed as GCSE tests, but rather as ways of developing the skills of reading and writing. With that in mind, teachers might still allow some judicious use of dictionaries. The writing tasks are based on the language of the reading texts and the reading tasks. It is important that students understand this – once they have completed all the reading tasks they should be able to reuse much of the language they have encountered in the writing exercises.

Grammar (*Grammatik*)

The key structures being introduced in a unit are presented in a Grammar box (*Grammatik*) on the Student's Book page, providing support for the speaking and writing activities. Structures that have already been introduced in *Logo! 4 Rot* sometimes need further revision – in these instances a similar box is used, but with the title *Wiederholung*. Both types of boxes contain page references for the comprehensive Grammar section at the end of the Student's Book where all the grammar points introduced in the core units are explained fully. There is also an alphabetical list of grammar points at the beginning of this section. Grammar practice is given within the Grammar section and in the workbook.

Skills and strategies

Many of the pages of *Logo! 4 Rot* have boxes giving students tips to improve their language-learning skills or to equip them with strategies that will enhance their performance in the forthcoming examination. These are highlighted by a symbol to make them easily recognisable. If the tip box is related to the pronunciation of German, the icon also shows a speech bubble symbol.

Tip box   Pronunciation box

Skills and strategies taught in the core units are listed in the Teacher's Guide, in the planning summary at the beginning of each chapter.

There are also two double-page spreads devoted to examination strategies for Listening, Speaking, Reading and Writing on pp. 170–173 of the Student's Book. These are entitled *Prüfungstipps*.

Progression

The first two double-page spreads or units (*Rückblick*) of each chapter are devoted to language that will already be familiar to students; the rest of the units continue to revise earlier material, but new grammar and structures are built in to the activities to ensure steady progression.

As well as the clear progression within each chapter, language is constantly recycled through all chapters in a systematic spiral of revision and extension. Clear objectives are given in the Teacher's Guide, in the planning summary at the beginning of each chapter, to help teachers plan a programme of work appropriate for the ability groups that they teach.

Assessment

There are three separate Assessment Packs available to accompany *Logo! 4*. Each pack has been written by an experienced examiner from the appropriate examination bodies (AQA, Edexcel, OCR). The design and type of questions follow the examination bodies' own papers and give much-needed regular practice in developing examination techniques.

Each pack contains assessment material at three levels, making it suitable for use with *Logo! 4 Grün* and *Logo! 4 Rot*:
– Foundation Level
– Foundation / Higher Level
– Higher Level

Each of the main assessment blocks represents two chapters. It is suggested that one assessment block is used at the end of each term of the two-year course, and that the final assessment be used at the end of the course as a pre-examination test.

The *Logo! 4* Assessment Packs include the following important features:
- Assessments have clear and concise mark schemes for Listening, Speaking, Reading and Writing.
- Each assessment contains several tasks at each level for both Listening and Reading
- Speaking assessments contain pages for students and for teachers.
- Rubrics reflect the language used by the examining bodies, familiarising students with GCSE-style questions throughout Years 10 and 11.
- Bilingual lists of rubrics are given, for reference and revision.

For information about how the **specification** of each of the above examining bodies is covered in *Logo! 4 Rot*, please refer to pp. vii–ix of this introduction. Information about coverage of the Welsh GCSE syllabuses is given on p. x. Information about coverage for Scottish Standard Grade examinations is given on p. xi. For the GCSE examinations in Northern Ireland, please refer to the Heinemann website or contact the publishers by telephone to arrange for a copy to be sent to your school.

Tel: 01865 888058   www.heinemann.co.uk

The teaching sequence

Core language can be presented using the cassettes or CDs, ensuring that students have authentic pronunciation models. Where the vocabulary and structures are unfamiliar, the text is often also given in the Student's Book so that students can read the new language and check the pronunciation at the same time. Next, students usually engage in a straightforward comprehension activity, such as a matching or true and false task, to consolidate the language taught.

Students then move on to a variety of activities in which they practise the language that has been introduced, through speaking and writing tasks. Some of the practice activities are open-ended, allowing students to work at their own pace and level. Ideas for additional practice are presented in the teaching notes for each unit.

Using the target language in the classroom

Instructions are usually given in German throughout. A page summarising these instructions is supplied for handy reference on p. 169 of the Student's Book. They have been kept as simple and as uniform as possible. A supplementary bilingual list of instructions is given in the Higher Workbook, so that students will not be in any doubt about what to do if they are working on their own. Classroom language is also recycled and extended in Chapter 2, which focuses on school. In the Assessment Booklets, the instructions are in line with those used by the appropriate examination body, and reference pages in each pack give a bilingual list of question forms that teachers may like to photocopy and give to their students for reference purposes.

Incorporating ICT

Appropriate use of Information and Communication Technology (ICT) to support modern foreign language learning is a requirement of the National Curriculum. It is an entitlement for all students.

Word processing and desktop publishing skills will be particularly useful for students who are preparing for the coursework option for the writing part of the GCSE examination. References to e-mail and websites occur throughout the course, as they do in the GCSE examination papers. Students should be encouraged to e-mail contemporaries in German-speaking countries and to research authentic information in German on the internet.

A selection of useful websites is given below, but please refer to the Heinemann website (www.Heinemann.co.uk/secondary/languages) for the most up-to-date information.

Information and organisations for teachers of German:
www.linguanet.org
www.cilt.org.uk
www.all-languages.org.uk
www.goethe.de/london
www.centralbureau.org.uk

On-line services for teachers in England, with modern languages sections:
www.standards.dfee.gov.uk
www.becta.org.uk
www.qca.org.uk

German search engines:
www.de.yahoo.com
www.web.de
www.hurra.de
www.lycos.de
www.ocr.org.uk

Examining bodies:
www.aqa.org.uk
www.edexcel.org.uk
www.wjec.co.uk
www.ccea.org.uk

Examination revision:
www.bbc.co.uk/education/gcsebitesize/ask/german

An interactive CD-ROM giving additional reading practice for GCSE is available from REVILO. This has been written by the same author as the *Logo! 4* Student's Books, and teachers and students will find it forms a useful way to complement the reading tasks in the *Logo! 4* materials, and to practise ICT skills at the same time. The CD-ROM contains 100 Foundation Level pages and 50 Higher Level pages. A free demonstration pack can be ordered from REVILO – www.revilolang.demon.co.uk

Coverage of AQA themes and topics in *Logo! 4 Rot*

For the German modular (specification B syllabus), please use the chapters and page numbers to access the material in the order of the chapters you are covering.

My world

1A Self, family and friends
Self, family and friends: Ch. 1, pp. 6–7
Greetings and introductions: Ch. 1, pp. 18–19

1B Interests and hobbies
Activities: Ch. 3, pp. 40–47
Invitations: Chs 3 & 7, pp. 48–49, 114–115

1C Home environment
House / flat and rooms: Ch. 1, pp. 12–15
Town and region: Ch. 5, pp. 74–77
Comparison of Germany and home country: Ch. 5, pp. 86–87
Advantages and disadvantages of local environment: Ch. 5, pp. 84–85

1D Daily routine
Daily routine: Ch. 8, pp. 124–125
Meals at home: Ch. 8, pp. 126–127

1E School and future plans (up to age 18)
Classroom language: Ch. 2, pp. 22–23
School routine: Ch. 2, pp. 28–29
School building: Ch. 2, pp. 24–25
School subjects: Ch. 2, pp. 26–27
Future plans: Ch. 2, pp. 32–33

Holiday time and travel

2A Travel, transport and finding the way
Travel, transport and finding the way
Travel and transport: Ch. 5, pp. 80–81
Finding the way: Ch. 5, pp. 78–79
Buying tickets: Ch. 5, pp. 82–83
Journeys: Chs 4 & 5, pp. 64–65, 80–83

2B Tourism
Weather: Ch. 4, pp. 56–57
Holidays: Ch. 4, pp. 58–69

2C Accommodation
Accommodation: Ch. 4, pp. 60–61
Problems with accommodation: Ch. 4, pp. 62–63

2D Holiday activities
Eating out: Ch. 7, pp. 110–113
Holiday activities: Ch. 4, pp. 66–69

2E Services
Postal services: Ch. 6, pp. 100–101
Money transactions: Ch. 7, pp. 108–109
Lost property: Ch. 6, pp. 102–103
Illness: Ch. 8, pp. 130–133
Breakdown and accidents: Ch. 8, pp. 134–135

Work and lifestyle

3A Home life
Meals at home: Ch. 8, pp. 126–127
Household chores: Ch. 1, pp. 16–17
Important festivals: Ch. 7, pp. 120–121

3B Healthy living
Eating healthily: Ch. 8, 128–129
Healthy / Unhealthy lifestyles: Chs 8 & 10, pp. 128–129, 162–163

3C Part-time jobs and work experience
Weekend jobs and work experience: Ch. 9, pp. 142–143, 150–151
Telephone calls: Ch. 9, pp. 148–149

3D Leisure
TV programmes, etc.: Ch. 3, pp. 42–43
Leisure facilities: Chs 3 & 7, pp. 50–51, 116–119
Arrangements to go out: Chs 3 & 7, pp. 48–49, 114–115
Sporting activities: Ch. 3, pp. 46–47
Main features of books, films, etc.: Ch. 3, pp. 52–53

3E Shopping
Shops, signs, facilities: Ch. 6, pp. 90–91
Buying things: Ch. 6, pp. 92–99
Complaints: Ch. 6, pp. 98–99

The young person in society

4A Character and personal relationships
Character: Ch. 10, pp. 158–159
Personal relationships: Ch. 10, pp. 160–161

4B The environment
Environmental issues: Ch. 10, pp. 164–167

4C Education
Issues at school: Ch. 2, pp. 30–31

4D Careers and future plans (post age 18)
Career and future plans: Ch. 9, pp. 152–155

4E Social issues, choices and responsibilities
Teenage problems: Chs 8 & 10, pp. 136–137, 162–163
Issues concerning smoking, alcohol and drugs: Ch. 10, pp. 162–163

Coverage of Edexcel topic areas in *Logo! 4 Rot*

At home and abroad

- **Things to see and do:** Ch. 5, pp. 74–77
- **Life in the town, countryside, seaside:** Ch. 5, pp. 84–87
- **Weather and climate:** Ch. 4, pp. 56–57
- **Travel, transport and directions:** Ch. 5, pp. 78–83
- **Holidays, tourist information and accomodation:** Ch. 4, pp. 58–69
- **Services and shopping abroad**
  Shopping: Ch. 6, pp. 90–99
  Post office: Ch. 6, pp. 100–101
  Money transactions: Ch. 7, pp. 108–109
  Lost property: Ch. 6, pp. 102–103
- **Customs, everyday life and traditions in target-language counties and communities:** throughout *Logo! 4*

Education, training and employment

- **School life and routine**
  School subjects, opinions, school routine and school building: Ch. 2, pp. 24–35
- **Different types of jobs:** Ch. 9, pp. 142–145
- **Job advertisements, applications and interviews:** Ch. 9, pp. 146–149
- **Future plans and work experience**
  Work experience: Ch. 9, pp. 150–151
  Future plans: Chs 2 & 9, pp. 32–33, 152–155

House, home and daily routine

- **Types of home, rooms, furniture and garden:** Ch. 1, pp. 12–15
- **Information about self, family and friends:** Chs 1 & 10, pp. 6–11, 158–161
- **Helping around the house:** Ch. 1, pp. 16–17
- **Food and drink**
  Eating at home: Ch. 8, pp. 126–127
  Eating out: Ch. 7, pp. 110–113

Media, entertainment and youth culture

- **Sport, fashion and entertainment**
  Sport: Ch. 3, pp. 46–47
  Entertainment: Chs 7 & 3, pp. 50–51, 116–117
- **Famous personalities**
- **The media:** Ch. 3, pp. 42–43, 52–53
- **Current affairs, social and environmental issues:** Ch. 10, pp. 162–167

Social activities, fitness and health

- **Free time (evenings, weekends, meeting people):** Chs 3 & 7, pp. 44–45, 48–48, 118–119
- **Special occasions:** Ch. 7, pp. 120–121
- **Hobbies, interests, sports and exercise:** Chs 3 & 8, pp. 40–41, 46–47, 128–129
- **Shopping and money matters:** Ch. 6, pp. 92–99
- **Accidents, injuries, common ailments and health issues (smoking, drugs)**
  Accidents: Ch. 8, pp. 134–135
  Ailments: Ch. 8, pp. 130–133
  Health issues: Chs 8 & 10, pp. 128–129, 162–163

Coverage of OCR contexts in *Logo! 4 Rot*

1 Everyday activities

(a) Home life
House and rooms: Ch. 1, pp. 12–17
Daily routine: Ch. 8, pp. 124–125

(b) School life
School routine, subjects and opinions: Ch. 2, pp. 22–35

(c) Eating and drinking
General likes / dislikes: Ch. 8, pp. 126–127
Eating out: Ch. 7, pp. 110–113
Problems at a restaurant: Ch. 7, pp. 112–113

(d) Health and fitness
Illness: Ch. 8, pp. 130–133
Healthy living: Ch. 8, pp. 128–129
Health matters: Ch. 10, pp. 162–163

2 Personal and social life

(a) People – the family and new contacts
Family and descriptions: Chs 1 & 10, pp. 8–11, 158–161
Invitations: Ch. 3, pp. 48–49, 114–115
Good and bad points of family life: Ch. 10, pp. 160–161

(b) Free time
Social activities: Chs 3 & 7, pp. 40–51, 116–119
Sports: Ch. 3, pp. 46–47
Personal interests: Ch. 3, pp. 40–41
Weekends: Ch. 3, pp. 44–45
Entertainment: Chs 3 & 7, pp. 50–51, 116–117

(c) Making appointments
Making arrangements: Ch. 3, pp. 48–49

(d) Special occasions
Festivals: Ch. 7, pp. 120–121

3 The world around us

(a) Local and other areas
Local town and region: Ch. 5, pp. 74–75, 84–87

(b) Shopping and public services
Shopping: Ch. 6, pp. 90–91
Buying items: Ch. 6, pp. 92–99
Complaints: Ch. 6, pp. 98–99
Post office: Ch. 6, pp. 100–101
Money transactions: Ch. 7, pp. 108–109
Telephone: Ch. 9, pp. 148–149
Lost property: Ch. 6, pp. 102–103

(c) Environment
Weather: Ch. 4, pp. 56–57
Environmental issues: Ch. 10, pp. 164–167

(d) Going places
Finding the way: Ch. 5, pp. 78–79
Transport: Ch. 5, pp. 80–81
Travel: Ch. 5, pp. 82–83
Buying tickets: Ch. 5, pp. 82–83
Accidents and car breakdown: Ch. 8, pp. 134–135

4 The world of work

(a) Jobs and work experience
General jobs: Ch. 9, pp. 144–147
Pocket money: Ch. 6, pp. 96–97
Work experience: Ch. 9, pp. 142–143, 150–151

(b) Careers and life-long learning
Work and further study: Ch. 2, pp. 32–33
Future careers: Ch. 9, pp. 152–153

5 The international world

(a) The media
TV: Ch. 3, pp. 42–43
Other media: Ch. 3, pp. 52–53

(b) World issues, events and people

(c) Tourism and holidays
Tourist area: Ch. 4, pp. 56–59, 68–69
Holidays: Ch. 4, pp. 64–67

(d) Tourist and holiday accommodation
Accommodation and facilities: Ch. 4, pp. 60–61
Problems with accommodation: Ch. 4, pp. 62–63

Coverage of WJEC topic areas in *Logo! 4 Rot*

Home life
Daily routine: Ch. 8, pp. 124–125
Meals: Ch. 8, pp. 126–127
Description of house and garden; Ch. 1, pp. 12–15
Members of the family: Chs 1 & 10, pp. 8–11, 158–161

Home town and region
Local facilities: Ch. 5, pp. 74–77
Comparisons with other towns: Ch. 5, pp. 84–87

Education
School life: Ch. 2, pp. 22–35
Future plans: Ch. 2, pp. 32–33

Environmental issues
Weather and seasons: Ch. 4, pp. 56–57
Pollution and recycling: Ch. 10, pp. 164–167

Social issues
Homelessness, crime, drugs: Ch. 10, pp. 162–163
Healthy living: Chs 8 & 10, pp. 128–129, 162–163
Injuries and accidents: Ch. 8, pp. 130–135
Religion and politics: –

Life in other countries
People and personalities abroad: –
Global issues and events: Ch. 10, pp. 162–167
Leisure time: Chs 3 & 7, pp. 40–51, 110–119
Travel: Ch. 5, pp. 78–83
Tourism: Ch. 4, pp. 58–58, 68–69

Youth culture
Fashion and music: Ch. 6, pp. 94–95
Shopping: Ch. 6, pp. 90–99
Sport: Ch. 3, pp. 46–47
Holidays: Ch. 4, pp. 58–69

New technologies
Sending messages, accessing information: Ch. 6, pp. 100–101

The world of work
Work experience: Ch. 9, pp. 142–143, 150–151
Future careers: Ch. 9, pp. 152–155

The media
Newspapers, television, film and radio: Chs 3 & 7, pp. 42–43, 52–53, 116–117
Reviews: Ch. 3, pp. 52–53

Logo! 4 Rot for Scotland

Personal information in polite / vocational context:	Ch. 1, pp. 6–7, 18–19
Members of family:	Chs 1 & 10, pp. 8–9, pp. 160–161
Friends and friendship:	Chs 1 & 8, pp. 10–11, 136–137
Physical and character description:	Chs 1 & 10, pp. 10–11, 158–159
Interpersonal problems and relationships:	Ch. 10, pp. 160–161
Parts of body, accidents and illnesses:	Ch. 8, pp. 130–135
Making appointments:	Ch. 8, pp. 132–133
Houses / room:	Ch. 1, pp. 12–15
Ideal house:	Ch. 1, pp. 14–15
Daily routine and lifestyles (compared with countries of target language):	Ch. 1, pp. 16–17; Ch. 7, pp. 120–121; Ch. 8, pp. 124–127
Life in present, past and future routines:	Ch. 7, pp. 118–119
School – compared with countries of target language:	Ch. 2, pp. 22–35
Leisure and sports:	Ch. 3, pp. 40–53
Health issues – healthy eating, exercise, drugs:	Chs 8 & 10, pp. 128–129, 162–163
TV, film and music:	Chs 3 & 7, pp. 42–43, 52–53, 116–117
Food issues:	Ch. 8, pp. 126–127
Restaurants / menus, making arrangements:	Ch. 7, pp. 110–115
Simple and complex directions:	Ch. 5, pp. 78–79
Tourist information:	Chs 4 & 5, pp. 68–69, 74–77, 86–87
Comparisons town / country:	Ch. 5, pp. 84–85
Helping the environment:	Ch. 10, pp. 164–167
Changing money:	Ch. 7, pp. 108–109
Negotiating transactional problems:	Chs 4, 5 & 6, pp. 60–65, 82–83, 92–103
Jobs / working and studying:	Ch. 9, pp. 142–155
Relative merits of jobs:	Ch. 9, pp. 154–155
Work experience:	Ch. 9, pp. 150–151
Future employment:	Ch. 9, pp. 152–153
Travel information:	Ch. 5, pp. 80–81
Travel plans:	Ch. 5, pp. 82–83
Relative merits of different means of transport:	–
Comparisons between different countries:	Ch. 5, pp. 86–87
Weather:	Ch. 4, pp. 56–57
Future holidays:	Ch. 4, pp. 58–59
Ideal holidays:	–
Past holidays:	Ch. 4, pp. 64–67

1 Hallo! Ich bin's! (Student's Book pp. 6–21)

Topic area	Key language	Grammar	Skills
1.1 Wie schreibt man das? (pp. 6–7) German alphabet Revision of personal details Numbers 1–100	Wie heißt …? Ich heiße … Wie alt ist …? Ich bin … Jahre alt. Wie schreibt man das? Wo wohnst du? Ich wohne in … am ersten Januar / elften Februar usw. Numbers 1–100; letters of the alphabet	*sein* (all parts) Ordinal numbers	German alphabet Order of German addresses *Du / Sie* forms of address Pronunciation of *ei, ie*
1.2 Das Familienspiel (pp. 8–9) Talk about family members Talk about pets	Ich habe Geschwister / einen Bruder / … Brüder / eine Schwester / … Schwestern. Ich bin ein Einzelkind. Mein Vater / Meine Mutter heißt … + all family members Er / Sie ist + age. Ich habe + pets geschieden / verheiratet Ihr / Sein Geburtstag ist am …	*Geschwister* Plurals of nouns *haben* (all forms) possessive adjectives: *mein / meine; dein / deine; sein / seine; ihr / ihre*	
1.3 So sehe ich aus (pp. 10–11) Talk about appearance	Ich habe / Er / Sie hat … braune / grüne / graue / hellbraune / dunkelbraune / braune Augen. eine Glatze / einen Bart / Schnurrbart. kurze / rote / schwarze / blonde / lange Haare + other describing words Er / Sie ist (nicht) klein / dick / schlank / groß.	Adjective endings: none for adjective following noun, *-e* for adjective with noun in accusative plural	Qualifying words: *kurz, ganz / hell- / dunkel / sehr / ziemlich* Linking words: *und, aber*
1.4 Mein Zuhause (pp. 12–13) Describe where you live	Ich wohne / Er / Sie wohnt / Wir wohnen … auf einem Bauernhof / dem Land. in einem Reihenhaus / Doppelhaus / Einfamilienhaus / Wohnblock / Bungalow / Dorf. in einer Wohnung / der Stadtmitte / am Stadtrand. Rooms and fittings in a house In der Küche / Im Wohnzimmer gibt es eine Lampe / einen Kühlschrank / ein Sofa usw. Ich wohne hier seit zwei Wochen.	*in, an, neben, auf* + dative *es gibt einen / eine / ein …* *seit …* *unser / unsere*	'Building' words
1.5 Mein Zimmer (pp. 14–15) Describe your bedroom	Mein Schlafzimmer ist ziemlich klein / sehr groß / schön / bequem / nicht sehr ordentlich. Die Wände / Gardinen sind … Der Teppich ist … blau / gelb / grün / lila / rosa / rot / weiß / bunt. In meinem Schlafzimmer habe ich / gibt es einen schönen Spiegel / eine alte Kommode / ein neues Bett usw.	*in* + dative of personal pronouns (*in meinem*, etc.) *Es gibt einen / eine / ein …* Adjective endings	Unknown vocabulary: using words you already know
1.6 Hausarbeit (pp. 16–17) Talk about household tasks	Was für Hausarbeit machst du? Ich wasche (nicht) ab / trockne (nicht) ab / sauge Staub (nicht) / kaufe (nicht) ein / räume mein Zimmer (nicht) auf / decke (nicht) den Tisch / bügle (nicht). Ich mag gern abwaschen. Ich mag nicht abtrocknen. Ich hasse einkaufen. Abwaschen finde ich furchtbar. Ich muss aufräumen.	3rd person form of verb Separable verbs + negatives of separable verbs *müssen*	Difference in meaning between *Hausarbeit* and *Hausaufgaben*

Logo! 4 1 Hallo! Ich bin's!

1.7 **Guten Tag!** (pp. 18–19) Greet people	*Guten Tag / Grüß Gott / Servus. Komm / Kommen Sie herein. Setz dich / Setzen Sie sich bitte hin. Wie geht es dir / Ihnen? Danke gut, und dir / Ihnen? Darf ich vorstellen? Vielen Dank für Ihre Gastfreundschaft. Nichts zu danken. Komm bald wieder! Gute Reise! Auf Wiedersehen / Tschüs.*		Saying hello: *Guten Tag / Grüß Gott / Servus* Greetings: *du* and *Sie* forms

- The vocabulary and structures taught in Chapter 1 are summarised on the *Wörter* pages of the Student's Book, 20–21.
- Further speaking practice on the language of this chapter is provided on p. 38.
- Further reading and writing practice on the language of this chapter is provided on pp. 186–187
- For a selection of assessment tasks for Chapters 1 and 2, please refer to the separate Assessment Pack for your chosen examination board: AQA, OCR or Edexcel.

1 Wie schreibt man das?

(pp. 6–7)

Students will learn how to:
- use the German alphabet
- give personal information

Key language
Wie heißt ...?
Ich heiße ...
Wie alt ist ...?
Ich bin ... Jahre alt.
Wie schreibt man das?
Wo wohnst du?
Ich wohne in ...
Wann hast du Geburtstag?
am ersten Januar
am elften Februar
numbers 1–100

Grammar focus
- *sein* (all parts)
- ordinal numbers

Skill focus
- German alphabet
- order of German addresses
- *du / Sie* forms of address
- pronunciation of *ei, ie*

Resources
- Cassette A, Side A
- Workbook p. 1
- Sprechen p. 38, Gespräch 1

Before starting this first spread, explain that it is concerned with revision of the basics of spelling and numbers. Students may well think that they are already infallible on these topics, so it is a good idea to remind them that it is not always as easy as they think by saying, at speed, various numbers and spellings.

1 Hör zu und beantworte die Fragen. (Listening)

Pupils listen to the extract from this "Family Fortunes"-style quiz as often as necessary to answer the questions. More able students can be asked to answer in full sentences: *Franks Vater heißt Olaf,* etc.

Answers
1 Olaf, 2 51, 3 Brigitte, 4 46, 5 Heike, 6 39

> Talkshowmoderator: Guten Abend, meine Damen und Herren, und herzlich Willkommen beim Familienspiel. Zuerst die Familie Richter. Guten Abend, Frank.
> Frank Richter: 'Abend, Christoph!
> Moderator: Wie alt sind Sie, Frank?
> Frank: Ich bin fünfundzwanzig. Hier ist mein Vater, Olaf ...
> Moderator: Wie schreibt man Olaf?
> Olaf: O.L.A.F.
> Moderator: Und wie alt sind Sie, Olaf?
> Olaf: Na ja ... ich bin einundfünfzig. Das hier ist meine Frau, Brigitte.
> Moderator: Brigitte, wie schreibt man das?
> Brigitte: B.R.I.G.I.T.T.E. Ich bin sechsundvierzig. Und zum Schluss noch, meine Schwester, Heike ...
> Moderator: ... Heike ...?
> Heike: H.E.I.K.E. Ich bin neununddreißig.

2 Hör zu und wiederhole. (Listening / Speaking)

Students listen to the letters and repeat them. There are a number of letters which can be confusing in German, especially when heard spoken at speed. Ask students to imagine they have met someone they would very much like to see again, but who is giving his / her address fast as the bus pulls away. Would they be confident of noting it down correctly?

> A ..., B ..., C ..., D ..., E ...,
> F ..., G ..., H ..., I ..., J ...,
> K ..., L ..., M ..., N ..., O ...,
> P ..., Q ..., R ..., S ..., T ...,
> U ..., V ..., W ..., X ..., Y ...,
> Z ..., ß ...

3 Hör zu! (1–6) Schreib die Tabelle ab und trag die Wörter ein. (Listening)

Students demonstrate their ability to understand German spelling and numbers by writing down the various addresses and postcodes they hear. They must first copy out the table to fill in.

Answers
1 Marseille, –, –, 2 Schwerin, Brechtallee 22, –,
3 Kronberg, Viktoriastraße 31, 61476, 4 Liverpool, –, –,
5 Berlin, Friedrichstraße, 10551, 6 Oberursel, –, –

> 1 – Die Stadt ist in Südfrankreich. Ja, M.A.R.S.E.I.L.L.E.
> 2 – Wo wohnst du? In Schwerin? Wie schreibt man das?
> – S.C.H.W.E.R.I.N.
> – Und die Adresse?
> – Brechtallee 22. B.R.E.C.H.T.A.L.L.E.E 22.
> 3 – Wie heißt die Stadt? Kronberg? K.R.O.N.B.E.R.G, ja? Und welche Straße? Viktoriastraße 31. Moment ... V.I.K.T.O.R.I.A.S.T.R.A.ß.E 31.
> Danke! Und die Postleitzahl? 61476? Danke.
> 4 – Wie schreibt man das? L.I.V.E.R.P.O.O.L? Ist das in England?
> 5 – Eine Straße in Berlin. Was? Okay. F.R.I.E.D.R.I.C.H.S.T.R.A.ß.E. Und die Postleitzahl? 10551? Danke schön.
> 6 – Wie bitte? Wie heißt die Stadt? Oberursel? Können Sie das bitte buchstabieren?
> – O.B.E.R.U.R.S.E.L.
> – Danke!

4 Partnerarbeit. Partner(in) A (▲) buchstabiert die Straße / die Stadt und nennt die Hausnummer / die Postleitzahl. Partner(in) B (●) schreibt die Informationen auf. (Speaking)

Working in pairs, students ask and answer questions about addresses. Student B should not look at the book during this. Afterwards, the pairs can make up more addresses of their own.

If you wish, give an explanation of the order in which German addresses are given. Point out in particular that the postcode comes before the town name.

5a Hör zu und schreib die Zahlen auf. (Listening)

Students practise listening to numbers from the tape (where the numbers are presented in context) and note them down.

Answers

1 5, 2 25, 3 41, 4 11, 5 36, 6 17, 7 73, 8 8.30, 9 66, 10 4, 11 52, 12 144, 13 33, 14 87, 15 2001

1 – Meine Schwester ist fünf.
2 – Ich habe fünfundzwanzig CDs.
3 – Mein Vater ist einundvierzig.
4 – Mein Bruder ist elf Jahre alt.
5 – Meine Mutter ist sechsunddreißig.
6 – Ich bin siebzehn.
7 – Mein Opa ist dreiundsiebzig.
8 – Es ist acht Uhr dreißig.
9 – Meine Oma ist sechsundsechzig.
10 – Ich habe vier Katzen.
11 – Es gibt zweiundfünfzig Wochen in einem Jahr.
12 – Wir wohnen in der Brechtstraße, Nummer hundertvierundvierzig.
13 – Dreiunddreißig ist eine Schnapszahl!
14 – Unter meinem Bett habe ich siebenundachtzig Zeitschriften.
15 – Mein Lieblingsfilm ist „Zweitausendeins".

5b Schreib die Antworten auf. (Writing)

Now students write out the numbers they have heard. If they have doubts about the spellings, help can be found on the *Wörter* pages at the end of the chapter.

Answers

1 fünf, 2 fünfundzwanzig, 3 einundvierzig, 4 elf, 5 sechsunddreißig, 6 siebzehn, 7 dreiundsiebzig, 8 acht Uhr dreißig, 9 sechsundsechzig, 10 vier, 11 zweiundfünfzig, 12 hundertvierundvierzig, 13 dreiunddreißig, 14 siebenundachtzig, 15 zweitausendeins

6 Partnerarbeit. Macht Interviews mit der du-Form. (Speaking)

In pairs, students practise mini-interviews based on the photos, using the *du* form.

Tip box

An explanation of the two forms of address: *du* and *Sie*. Please emphasise that this is not as trivial as it seems, because saying *du* inappropriately can easily cause offence, while saying *Sie* inappropriately can sound quite silly.

7 Partnerarbeit. Macht Interviews mit der Sie-Form. (Speaking)

In pairs, students practise using the *Sie* form to ask and answer questions. They can continue the activity by making up further names and ages themselves.

Grammatik: sein (the verb 'to be')

A summary of all the parts of *sein*. Point out how fundamental a complete knowledge of this verb is. Brainstorm common phrases and expressions using *sein*.

Tip box

Using the words *drei* and *vier* as a reminder of the pronunciation of *ei* and *ie*. Remind students that, even at Higher level, it is an easy mistake to get these the wrong way round. Point out how to avoid it.

8 Hör zu! Schreib die Geburtstage auf. (Listening)

Students listen to various people giving their birthdays and note down the dates.

Answers

1 12. 4., 2 20. 3., 3 8. 5., 4 21. 9., 5 1. 1., 6 25. 12.

1 – Mein Geburtstag ist am zwölften April.
2 – Anitas Geburtstag ist am zwanzigsten März.
3 – Franks Geburtstag ist am achten Mai.
4 – Herr Müllers Geburtstag ist am einundzwanzigsten September.
5 – Frau Golds Geburtstag ist am ersten Januar.
6 – Mein Geburtstag ist am fünfundzwanzigsten Dezember.

9 Partnerarbeit. Wann hast du Geburtstag? (Speaking)

Working in pairs, students dictate dates of birthdays and note them down. They should continue the exercise by making up more birthdays themselves.

Further practice of the language and vocabulary of this unit are given on the following pages.
Speaking: p. 38, Gespräch 1
Workbook: p. 1

2 Das Familienspiel (pp. 8–9)

Pupils will learn how to:
- talk about families and pets

Key language
Ich habe ...
   Geschwister.
   ... Bruder / Brüder.
   ... Schwester /
   Schwestern.
Ich bin ein Einzelkind.
Mein Vater / Meine
Mutter heißt ...
Ich habe (eine Katze).
geschieden
verheiratet
Er / Sie ist + *age*
Ihr / Sein Geburtstag ist
am ...

Grammar focus
- use of *Geschwister*
- plurals of nouns
- *haben* (all forms)
- possessive adjectives: *mein / meine; dein / deine; sein / seine; ihr / ihre*

Resources
- Cassette A, Side A
- Workbook p. 2
- Sprechen p. 38, Gespräch 2

Start this revision spread by asking students to say what they remember about how to describe their families.

1 Lies die Sätze. Wer ist wer? (Reading)
Students link up pictures to sentences in speech bubbles by writing down letters.

Answers
1 c, 2 e, 3 h, 4 b, 5 d, 6 g, 7 a, 8 f

Grammatik: Der Plural (the plural form)
The plurals of brother, sister and sibling. Point out these simple but deceptive forms. Students sometimes wrongly think that *Geschwister* means 'sisters', especially in listening tasks.

2a Hör zu! Schreib die Tabelle ab und füll sie aus. (Listening)
Students listen to a radio phone-in as often as necessary to fill in the information in the table, which must first be copied out. A photocopiable grid to accompany this exercise is available on p. 190 of this book.

Answers
Anja: Woltmershausen; 5; Rolf, 40; Petra, 36; 1 Katze
Peter: Dornhausen; nein (Einzelkind); Karl, 45; Elke, 39; nein
Sylvia: Memmingen; Bruder, 12; Hans, 37; Anita, 36; 1 Katze, 1 Hund

a Anja
Moderator: Hallo, wer ist da?
Anja: Hier spricht Anja aus Woltmershausen.
Moderator: Bitte?
Anja: Woltmershausen! W.O.L.T.M.E.R.S.H.A.U.S.E.N.
Moderator: Hast du eine große Familie?
Anja: Oh ja, ich habe fünf Geschwister, also drei Brüder und zwei Schwestern.
Moderator: Oha!
Anja: Mein Vater heißt Rolf und er ist vierzig. Meine Mutter heißt Petra und sie ist sechsunddreißig.
Moderator: Und hast du Haustiere?
Anja: Ja, wir haben eine Katze.

b Peter
Moderator: Und nun?
Peter: Hallo, hier ist Peter aus Dornhausen.
Moderator: Wo?
Peter: Dornhausen: D.O.R.N.H.A.U.S.E.N.
Moderator: Hast du Geschwister?
Peter: Nein, ich bin ein Einzelkind. Mein Vater heißt Karl und er ist fünfundvierzig.
Moderator: Und deine Mutter?
Peter: Meine Stiefmutter ... Sie heißt Elke und sie ist neununddreißig.
Moderator: Habt ihr Haustiere?
Peter: Nein, leider nicht.

c Sylvia
Moderator: Und wer ist jetzt dran?
Sylvia: Hier spricht die Sylvia aus Memmingen.
Moderator: Bitte?
Sylvia: Memmingen, das schreibt man M.E.M.M.I.N.G.E.N.
Moderator: Okay, Sylvia. Beschreib deine Familie.
Sylvia: Sie ist ganz klein. Ich habe nur einen Bruder, er heißt Manfred und er ist 12.
Moderator: Und deine Eltern?
Sylvia: Meine Mutter heißt Anita und sie ist sechsunddreißig. Mein Vater heißt Hans und er ist siebenunddreißig.
Moderator: Habt ihr Haustiere?
Sylvia: Ja, natürlich! Wir haben eine Katze und einen Hund.

2b Partnerarbeit. Lest das Interview vor. Macht dann Interviews mit Peter und Sylvia (Speaking)
Students practise an interview in preparation for the second part of the exercise.
They then interview each other, taking on the identities of Peter and Sylvia. Make sure that students realise that this pair-work activity is based on the information they noted down about the people in exercise 2a.

Grammatik: haben ('to have')
All forms of *haben*. Tell students that an accurate knowledge of this verb is essential. Brainstorm common phrases and expressions which use *haben*.

3 Welche Wörter passen in die Lücken? (Writing)
Here students practise using correct present tense forms of *haben* by copying down the sentences and filling in the gaps.

Answers

1 hast, 2 haben, 3 hat, 4 habe, 5 habt, 6 haben, 7 hat, 8 haben

4 Lies die E-Mail und beantworte die Fragen (ganze Sätze, bitte!). (Reading / Writing)

Students read an e-mail and answer questions about it in full sentences.

Answers

1 Sie heißt Manja. 2 Sie ist 15 Jahre alt. 3 Sie wohnt in Ültjen (in der Nähe von Kassel). 4 Er heißt Dirk. 5 Er ist 41 Jahre alt. 6 Sie ist 38. 7 Sie wohnt in München. 8 Er heißt Kevin. 9 Manjas Geburtstag ist am ersten Oktober. 10 Sie hat keine Haustiere.

Grammatik: Das Possessivum (possessive adjectives)

How to say 'my', 'his', 'her' and 'your'. Make sure students are confident about using these forms. More practice is available in the Grammar section.

5 Schreib eine E-Mail an Manja. (Nicht vergessen: Name, wie alt, wo du wohnst, Familie, Geburtstag.) (Writing)

Now students reply to Manja's e-mail, giving as much information as they can about themselves and their families. Encourage them to be adventurous and to write as much as they can.

Further practice of the language and vocabulary of this unit are given on the following pages.
Speaking: p. 38, Gespräch 2
Workbook: p. 2

3 So sehe ich aus (pp. 10–11)

Students will learn how to:
- talk about appearance

Key language
Ich habe ...
Er / Sie hat ...
  braune / grüne / graue /
  braune / hellbraune /
  dunkelbraune Haare.
  kurze rote / schwarze /
  blonde / lange Haare.
  eine Glatze / einen
  Bart / einen
  Schnurrbart.
Er / Sie ist ...
  ziemlich / sehr klein /
  schlank / dick / groß.

Grammar focus
- adjective ending -e in accusative plural

Skill focus
- qualifying words: *sehr, ziemlich, kurz, ganz, hell-, dunkel-*
- linking words: *und, aber*

Resources
- Cassette A, Side A
- Workbook p. 3
- Sprechen p. 38, Gespräch 2
- Lesen / Schreiben A p. 186

Start this spread by describing a few famous people, school staff or students and ask students to guess who they are. Alternatively, bring in a selection of magazine photos of people and describe them, asking students to identify which one is being described.

1 Schau die Bilder an und lies die Sätze. Richtig oder falsch? (Reading)
Pupils do a simple 'true or false' exercise based on photographs and descriptions.

Answers
1 Richtig. 2 Falsch. 3 Falsch. 4 Falsch. 5 Falsch.
6 Richtig. 7 Falsch. 8 Richtig.

2 Hör zu! Wer ist wer? Schreib Anke, Gitti, Barbara, Stefan, Alex oder Rolf. (Listening)
Students listen to people describing themselves and their families and work out who is who. They write down names.

Answers
Anke 2, Gitti, 4, Barbara 5, Stefan 1, Alex 6, Rolf 3

> a Hallo! Mein Name ist Anke. Ich habe braune Augen und braune Haare. Meine Schwester Gitti ist jünger als ich. Sie hat blonde Haare und blaue Augen. Meine Freundin Barbara hat lange schwarze Haare und grüne Augen.
>
> b Ich bin der Stefan. Ich habe graue Augen und kurze dunkelbraune Haare. Mein Freund Alex hat lange hellbraune Haare und blaue Augen. Mein Vater Rolf hat graue Haare und einen Schnurrbart.

Grammatik: Adjektive (adjective endings)
Adjectives standing on their own do not need an ending. An adjective with a noun needs an ending. The ending in the accusative plural is -e. Make sure that students realise that adjective endings are a complicated topic in German. Full details are in the Grammar section.

Tip box
Use qualifying words: *sehr, ziemlich, hell-* and *dunkel-*. Emphasise how easy it is to make your German sound so much more natural merely by using some qualifying words. This will be pointed out at various stages of this course.

3 Schreib Sätze. (Writing)
Students have practice in writing sentences using the information about adjective endings.

Answers
1 Karl hat blaue Augen und kurze schwarze Haare.
2 Tanja hat grüne Augen und ziemlich lange hellbraune Haare. 3 Elena hat blaue Augen und sehr lange blonde Haare. 4 Paul hat grüne Augen und kurze dunkelbraune Haare. 5 Petra hat braune Augen und lange blonde Haare.
6 Martin hat blaue Augen und sehr kurze rote Haare.

4 Partnerarbeit. Schaut die Bilder an. Wer ist wer? (Speaking)
Students take it in turns to choose one of the pictures to describe. The partner has to say who is being described.

5 Lies den Brief. Wer ist wer? Schreib Sonja, Freddi oder Bettina. (Reading)
Students read the letter and work out which people are being described in the sentences.

Answers
1 Sonja, 2 Bettina, 3 Freddi, 4 Sonja, 5 Bettina, 6 Sonja

Tip box
Use linking words *und* and *aber* to make longer sentences and get better marks. Simple but true! Encourage students to use *und* and *aber* when they are doing any extended pieces of writing or speaking.

**6 Jetzt du. a Beschreib dich! Nicht vergessen: deine Größe, deine Augen, deine Haare.
b Beschreib einen Freund / eine Freundin / einen Star / eine Person in deiner Familie. (Writing)**
Students write descriptions of themselves and others.

Further practice of the language and vocabulary of this unit are given on the following pages.
Speaking: p. 38, Gespräch 2
Reading and Writing A: p. 186
Workbook: p. 3

Logo! 4 1 Hallo! Ich bin's!

4 Mein Zuhause (pp. 12–13)

Students will learn how to:
- describe where they live

Key language
Ich wohne ...
Er / Sie wohnt ...
Wir wohnen ...
    auf einem Bauernhof /
    dem Land.
    in einem Reihenhaus /
    Einfamilienhaus /
    Doppelhaus /
    Wohnblock /
    Bungalow / Dorf.
    in einer Wohnung /
    der Stadtmitte.
    am Stadtrand.
rooms and fittings in a house
Unser / Mein Haus hat ...
Unsere / Meine Wohnung hat ...
    eine Küche / Toilette (ein Klo) / Treppe.
    ein Wohnzimmer / Esszimmer / Schlafzimmer.
    einen Flur.
In der Küche / Im Wohnzimmer gibt es ...
eine Badewanne / Dusche / Lampe / Spülmaschine / Waschmaschine / Heizung.
einen Kühlschrank / Herd / Tisch / Stuhl / Sessel / Fernseher / Teppich.
ein Bett / Sofa.
Ich wohne hier seit zwei Wochen.

Grammar focus
- *in, an, neben, auf* with the dative
- *es gibt einen / eine / ein ...*
- *seit ...*
- *unser / unsere*

Resources
- Cassette A, Side A
- Workbook p. 4
- Sprechen p. 38, Gespräch 3
- Lesen / Schreiben B p. 187

Before starting this spread, brainstorm house vocabulary.

1a Hör zu! Wo wohnen Peter, Sylvia, Ayse, Jürgen und Vanessa? Schreib zwei Buchstaben für jede Person. (Listening)

Students listen to the interviews and note down, in each case, two letters to indicate where the people live.

Answers

1 Peter: b, g, 2 Sylvia: a, f, 3 Ayse: e, h, 4 Jürgen: i, c, 5 Vanessa: g, d

> 1 Interviewer: Wo wohnst du, Peter?
> Peter: Ich wohne in einer Wohnung am Stadtrand.
> 2 Interviewer: Und du, Sylvia? Wohnst du auch am Stadtrand?
> Sylvia: Nee, ich wohne auf einem Bauernhof, auf dem Land.
> 3 Interviewer: Hallo, Ayse, wo wohnst du?
> Ayse: Ich? Ich wohne in einem Bungalow in einem Dorf.
> 4 Interviewer: Und du, Jürgen, wohnst du auch in einem Bungalow?
> Jürgen: Nein, gar nicht. Ich wohne in der Stadtmitte, in einem Reihenhaus.
> 5 Interviewer: Und Vanessa, wo wohnst du denn?
> Vanessa: Ach, ich wohne nicht in der Stadtmitte. Ich wohne am Stadtrand in einem Wohnblock.

1b Schreib die Informationen auf. (Writing)

Students now write down the information they gleaned in exercise 1a (in full sentences).

Answers

1 Peter wohnt in einer Wohnung am Stadtrand. 2 Sylvia wohnt auf einem Bauernhof auf dem Land. 3 Ayse wohnt in einem Bungalow in einem Dorf. 4 Jürgen wohnt in der Stadtmitte in einem Reihenhaus. 5 Vanessa wohnt am Stadtrand in einem Wohnblock.

2a Ludo Kleinmann und Dieter Frost moderieren das Fernsehquiz „Wer wohnt hier?" Hör zu und schreib auf, wo Ludo ist. (Listening / Writing)

Students listen to this episode of "Through the Keyhole" and write down where Ludo is in each case (just in note form).

Answers

1 im Wohnzimmer, 2 in der Küche, 3 im Badezimmer, 4 im Schlafzimmer, 5 im Esszimmer, 6 in der Toilette, 7 in der Garage

> 1 Dieter Frost: Hallo Ludo! Wo bist du?
> Ludo: In diesem Zimmer gibt es einen Fernseher und einen Sessel.
> 2 Dieter Frost: Aha! Und wo bist du jetzt?
> Ludo: Hier gibt es eine Spülmaschine. Neben der Spülmaschine sehe ich einen Kühlschrank.
> 3 Dieter Frost: Ludo, wo bist du?
> Ludo: In diesem Zimmer gibt es eine Badewanne und in der Ecke gibt es eine Dusche.
> 4 Dieter Frost: So! Und wo bist du nun?
> Ludo: Hier haben wir ein Bett. Neben dem Bett steht ein Nachttisch und auf dem Nachttisch steht eine Lampe.
> 5 Dieter Frost: Ach, so! Wo bist du jetzt, Ludo?
> Ludo: Hier gibt es einen Tisch und vier Stühle um den Tisch.
> 6 Dieter Frost: Wo bist du jetzt?
> Ludo: Äääh ... hier gibt's ein Klo!
> 7 Dieter Frost: Und zum Schluss, Ludo ... Wo bist du?
> Ludo: Moment ... ich mache die Tür auf ... Aha! Hier gibt's ein Auto! Also, wer wohnt in diesem Haus?

Grammatik: Präpositionen (+ Dativ) (prepositions with the dative)

in, an, neben, auf with the dative, including the contractions *im* and *am*. Make sure that students realise that the dative form after these prepositions only applies when no motion is involved.

2b Partnerarbeit. Macht Dialoge. (Speaking)
In pairs, students choose a room to pretend to be in. The partner must identify where they are, based on what is in the room. Students make up their own cues in this exercise.

Grammatik: Es gibt ... ('there is / there are')
Es gibt einen / eine / ein. Emphasise just how common and useful (yet easily forgotten) this expression is. Make sure students avoid the dreaded *da ist*.

3 Schreib Sätze. (Writing)
Students build and write sentences using *es gibt*.

Answers
1 Mein Haus hat eine Küche. In der Küche gibt es eine Waschmaschine und einen Herd. 2 Mein Haus hat ein Wohnzimmer. Im Wohnzimmer gibt es einen Sessel und einen Fernseher. 3 Mein Haus hat ein Badezimmer. Im Badezimmer gibt es eine Dusche und eine Badewanne. 4 Mein Haus hat ein Schlafzimmer. Im Schlafzimmer gibt es ein Bett und einen Schrank.

4 Lies den Text und beantworte die Fragen auf Deutsch. (Reading / Writing)
Students read a diary entry and answer German questions in full sentences.

Answers
1 Es gibt drei Schlafzimmer. 2 Die Sessel sind im Wohnzimmer. 3 In der Küche git es einen Kühlschrank, einen Herd und eine Spülmaschine. 4 Olivia findet die Spülmaschine super. 5 Die Garage ist neben dem Haus. 6 Ja, Olivia hat einen Computer in ihrem Schlafzimmer.

Grammatik: seit ('for' in expressions of time)
Seit and the present tense are used to indicate time. Point out this very un-English construction and get students to practise a few examples (how long they have been learning a subject, how long they have lived where they live, etc.).

5 Jetzt du. Beschreib dein Haus. (Writing)
Students write as detailed a description as possible of their own houses, contents of the rooms, etc. Encourage them to be adventurous and to write as much as possible. This is material which will be very useful in the exam, so it needs to be taken in and marked, then learnt by heart.

Further practice of the language and vocabulary of this unit is given on the following pages.
Speaking: p. 38, Gespräch 3
Reading and Writing B: p. 187
Workbook: p. 4

Logo! 4 I Hallo! Ich bin's!

5 Mein Zimmer (pp. 14–15)

Students will learn how to:
- describe their bedroom

Key language
Mein Schlafzimmer ist …
 ziemlich klein / sehr groß / schön / bequem / nicht sehr ordentlich.
Die Wände / Gardinen sind …
Der Teppich ist …
 blau / gelb / grün / lila / rosa / rot / weiß / bunt.
In meinem Schlafzimmer habe ich / gibt es …
 einen schönen Spiegel / modernen Nachttisch / gelben Teppich.
 einen Kleiderschrank / Schreibtisch / Wecker / Computer / Fernseher.
 eine alte Kommode / kleine Stereoanlage / rote Lampe.
 ein neues Bett / schönes Radio / grünes Regal.
 viele Kleider / Kassetten.

Grammar focus
- *in* + dative of personal pronouns (*in meinem*, etc.)
- adjective endings

Skill focus
- working out the meaning of unknown words

Resources
- Cassette A, Side A
- Workbook p. 5
- Sprechen p. 38, Gespräch 4

Start this spread by asking students to come up with as many words as they can remember which would be useful in describing their bedrooms.

1 Lies den Artikel und beantworte die Fragen auf Deutsch. (Reading / Writing)
Students read a magazine article in which a pop star describes her bedroom. They may give short answers or answer in full sentences.

Answers

1 Die Wände sind lila. 2 Die Gardinen sind rosa. 3 Der Teppich ist rot. 4 Das Bett ist gelb. 5 Lena findet bunte Farben gut. 6 Lenas Kleider sind in einem großen Kleiderschrank. 7 Sie macht ihr Make-up am Toilettentisch. 8 Die Lampe steht auf dem Nachttisch. 9 Der Fernseher ist in der Ecke. 10 Lena sieht gern fern (und liest und hört Musik).

Tip box: Vocabulary
The meanings of many words can be guessed by breaking them down into the words they are made up of. Many students enjoy working out the meanings of typically German words made up of other words put together. Ask them to give some other examples, either from their own knowledge or from leafing through the book and finding them.

2 Hör zu und schau die Bilder an. Was gibt es in diesen Schlafzimmern? (Listening)
Students listen to people describing things in their bedrooms and note down letters. Make sure they realise that there are two answers to each question.

Answers

1 d, i, 2 b, f, 3 c, e, 4 a, g, 5 h, j

Was gibt es in deinem Schlafzimmer?
1 – In meinem Schlafzimmer gibt es einen Computer und viele Poster.
2 – In meinem Schlafzimmer habe ich eine Kommode und einen Kleiderschrank.
3 – Mein Zimmer ist schön. Ich habe eine Stereoanlage und einen Fernseher.
4 – Ich habe ein bequemes Zimmer. Im Zimmer gibt es ein großes Bett und einen modernen Toilettentisch.
5 – In meinem Schlafzimmer habe ich einen Spiegel und eine Lampe.

3 Partnerarbeit. Beschreibt diese Schlafzimmer. (Speaking)
Students conduct short interviews about four illustrations of bedrooms. The first one is provided as an example. Encourage them to carry on the exercise, making up their own cues.

Afterwards, they should write down the descriptions like this: *Olafs Schlafzimmer ist klein. Die Wände sind gelb, die Gardinen sind blau und der Teppich ist rot.*

Grammatik: in + Dativ (the dative after in)
In with personal pronouns: *in meinem / deinem*, etc. and *in meiner / deiner*, etc. Remind students that they must use *ihr* for 'her' and *sein* for 'his', plus the appropriate endings as detailed.

4 Vervollständige die Sätze. (Writing)
Students copy out sentences and fill in the correct endings, based on the grammar box.

Answers

1 einen modernen Fernseher, 2 einen braunen Schreibtisch, 3 eine neue Kommode, 4 eine sehr gute Stereoanlage, 5 einen großen Spiegel, 6 einen kleinen Wecker

Grammatik: Adjektive (adjective endings)
Using the accusative after *ich habe* and *es gibt*, including examples of adjective endings. Tell students that these two expressions will be very helpful in any kind of personal descriptions, as long as the appropriate accusative endings are used.

5 Schreib einen Artikel für eine Zeitschrift. Beschreib *dein* Schlafzimmer. Wie sind die Wände, die Gardinen und der Teppich? Was gibt es in dem Zimmer?
(Writing)
Students write an article describing their bedroom. Ask them to provide as much detailed information as they can manage. This material should be taken in, marked and then learnt.

> Further practice of the language and vocabulary of this unit is given on the following pages.
> Speaking: p. 38, Gespräch 4
> Workbook: p. 5

Logo! 4 1 Hallo! Ich bin's!

6 Hausarbeit (pp. 16–17)

Students will learn how to:
- talk about household tasks

Key language
Was für Hausarbeit machst du?
Ich wasche (nicht) ab / trockne (nicht) ab / sauge Staub (nicht) / kaufe (nicht) ein / räume mein Zimmer (nicht) auf / decke (nicht) den Tisch / bügle (nicht).
Ich mag gern abwaschen.
Ich mag nicht abtrocknen.
Ich hasse einkaufen.
Abwaschen finde ich furchtbar.
Ich muss aufräumen.

Grammar focus
- 3rd person form of verbs
- separable verbs + negatives of separable verbs
- *müssen*

Skill focus
- difference in meaning between *Hausarbeit* and *Hausaufgaben*

Resources
- Cassette A, Side A
- Workbook p. 6
- Sprechen p. 38, Gespräch 5

Introduce this spread by inviting contributions, in English and / or German, on the subject of household tasks. What do students do (or not do) around the house?

1 Hör zu! Was machen Rikki, Imke, Tommy und Gabi? Notiere die Buchstaben und dann schreib die Antworten auf.
(Listening / Writing)

Students listen to four youngsters being interviewed about what they do around the house. On first hearing, they can just write down the letters, and on second hearing they should write down the information. Apart from Rikki, each person mentions two things.

Answers
1 Rikki: g Ich bügle. 2 Imke: e, b Ich räume mein Zimmer auf und trockne ab. 3 Tommy: c, a Ich sauge Staub und wasche ab. 4 Gabi: f, d Ich decke den Tisch und kaufe ein.

> 1 Interviewer: So, und nun zu unserem nächsten Thema: die Hausarbeit. Rikki, was machst du denn zu Hause?
> Rikki: Ach, ich hasse Hausarbeit. Ich muss bügeln, aber ich will es nicht. Bügeln ist schrecklich!
> 2 Interviewer: Finde ich auch. Und du, Imke, musst du auch was zu Hause tun?
> Imke: Na ja, ich räume mein Zimmer auf. Manchmal trockne ich ab, aber abtrocknen mag ich nicht gern.
> 3 Interviewer: Kein Wunder! Tommy, was für Hausarbeit machst du denn?
> Tommy: Ab und zu sauge ich Staub und am Abend wasche ich ab.
> Interviewer: Machst du das gern?
> Tommy: Nee, gar nicht.
> 4 Interviewer: Und zum Schluss noch du, Gabi. Hilfst du deinen Eltern zu Hause?
> Gabi: Ja, schon. Ich decke den Tisch für's Mittagessen. Und ich kaufe auch ein, wenn ich Zeit habe.

2 Partnerarbeit. (Speaking)

In pairs, students conduct an information gap activity. Student A asks about housework based on the grid provided. Student B chooses a person from the grid and gives the answers (including what they *don't* do). Student A can then work out who student B is.

Tip box
The difference in meaning between *Hausarbeit* and *Hausaufgaben*. Simple but often forgotten!

3 Partnerarbeit. (Speaking)

Working in pairs, students ask and answer questions based on picture prompts.

Grammatik: Das Präsens (the present tense)

Third person form of verbs including some examples of separable verbs. Refer students to the Grammar section for further details and practice. Emphasise that at Higher Level, saying *ich* all the time is not sufficient; knowledge of other persons must be demonstrated.

4 Lies Alis Tagebuch und beantworte die Fragen. (Reading / Writing)

Students read a diary entry and answer questions about it. More able students should answer in full sentences: *Nein, Ali mag nicht abtrocknen.*

Answers
1 Nein, Ali mag nicht abtrocknen. 2 Ja, Ali mag einkaufen. 3 Er hasst abtrocknen und Staub saugen. 4 Mutti mag einkaufen. 5 Ja, er muss Staub saugen. 6 Nein, er muss nicht einkaufen. 7 Er muss zu Hause bleiben und arbeiten. 8 Er findet das nicht in Ordnung.

Grammatik: Trennbare Verben (separable verbs)

Explains how the prefix goes to the end of the sentence but stays joined to the verb when another verb is also used in the sentence.

Grammatik: müssen (talking about what you have to do)

Examples of the use of *müssen*. This is just a brief introduction. More detailed information and practice with modal verbs can be found in the Grammar section.

5 Partnerarbeit. (Speaking)

In pairs, students ask and answer questions about housework. This exercise is to be done both ways round and answers must be either truthful or made up (i.e. there are no prompts.)

6 Schau Alis Tagebuch in Übung 4 an. Schreib einen Tagebuchausschnitt über die Hausarbeiten, die *du* machst. (Writing)
Based on Ali's diary entry, students write a paragraph about what tasks they and their family members do. This should be marked, learnt and kept for reference. Encourage students to include as much information and as many opinions as possible.

Further practice of the language and vocabulary of this unit is given on the following pages.
Speaking: p. 38, Gespräch 5
Workbook: p. 6

Logo! 4 1 Hallo! Ich bin's!

7 Guten Tag! (pp. 18–19)

Students will learn how to:
- meet and greet people

Key language
Guten Tag / Grüß Gott / Servus.
Komm / Kommen Sie herein.
Setz dich / Setzen Sie sich bitte hin.
Wie geht es dir / Ihnen?
Danke gut, und dir / Ihnen?
Darf ich vorstellen?
Vielen Dank für Ihre Gastfreundschaft.
Nichts zu danken.
Komm bald wieder!
Gute Reise!
Auf Wiedersehen / Tschüs.

Skill focus
- Guten Tag / Grüß Gott / Servus
- greetings: *du* and *Sie* forms

Resources
- Cassette A, Side A
- Sprechen p. 39, Rollenspiel

Introduce this spread by pointing out that, even if students don't themselves take part in an exchange visit, many exam tasks are based on exchanges and on meeting and greeting people. Point out that it is important to tread carefully, because of the *du / Sie* problem. Brainstorm the kinds of things that might be said on first meeting a family.

Tip box
An introduction to the three ways of saying 'hello' in German-speaking countries. Explain to students that the conversation provided in the book is probably rather unnatural (people would either use *Servus, Grüß Gott* or *Guten Tag,* but probably not all three). However, they are provided in order to demonstrate their use.

1a Hör zu, lies den Text und schreib die folgenden Sätze auf Deutsch.
(Listening / Writing)
Students can read the text as well as listening to it. The teacher can decide whether to use it as a 'pure' listening exercise, but this would be difficult because the task is to write down German expressions.

Answers
1 Komm herein. 2 Darf ich vorstellen? 3 Guten Tag / Grüß Gott / Servus. 4 Willkommen. 5 Wie geht's? 6 Setz dich bitte hin! 7 Wie war die Reise? 8 Hast du Hunger?

Susan Carter aus Bristol besucht ihre Brieffreundin Jessica in Hamburg.
Jessica: Komm herein, Susan. Also, Mama, Papa, darf ich vorstellen? Das ist meine Freundin Susan aus England.
Susan: Guten Tag, Frau Dresch, Guten Tag, Herr Dresch!
Frau Dresch: Grüß Gott, Susan. Herzlich Willkommen in Hamburg!
Herr Dresch: Servus, Susan! Wie geht's?
Susan: Danke, gut, und Ihnen?
Herr Dresch: Auch gut. Setz dich bitte hin!
Frau Dresch: Wie war die Reise?
Susan: Nicht schlecht, aber ich bin ein bisschen müde.
Jessica: Hast du Hunger?
Susan: Nein, aber ich möchte etwas trinken.
Frau Dresch: Gern! Eine Cola, vielleicht? Jessica, hol mal eine Cola aus dem Kühlschrank.

1b Wähle die richtige Antwort.
(Reading)
Students complete these simple sentences by choosing the correct answer. Ask them to write the sentences out.

Answers
1 Susan kommt aus England. 2 Susan geht es gut. 3 Die Reise war okay. 4 Susan ist müde. 5 Susan hat Durst. 6 Susan wohnt in Bristol. 7 Susan ist jetzt in Hamburg. 8 Jessica holt eine Cola. 9 Die Cola ist im Kühlschrank. 10 In Norddeutschland sagt man Servus.

Tip box
Du and *Sie* forms of greetings. Refer students to exercise 4, which practises deciding whether to use *du* or *Sie*.

2a Partnerarbeit. Wählt die richtigen Sätze, um die Lücken auszufüllen. (Speaking)
In pairs, students conduct a 'meeting and greeting' conversation, with partner A selecting the responses from those provided in the box. Students should take it in turns to be A and B.

2b Partnerarbeit. Wiederholt das Gespräch aus Übung 2a, aber mit „Sie / Ihnen" statt „du / dich / dir". (Speaking)
The same conversation is repeated, but using the *Sie* form. Make sure students know exactly what they are doing before they start.

3 Hör zu, lies den Text und schreib auf! Wie sagt man auf Deutsch …? (Listening / Reading)
Students now listen to and read the 'end of a visit' conversation, showing how to say thanks and goodbye. They note down the expressions in German.

Answers
1 Tschüs. 2 Komm bald wieder! 3 Auf Wiedersehen. 4 Vielen Dank für Ihre Gastfreundschaft! 5 Nichts zu danken. 6 Gute Reise!

Herr Dresch: Tschüs, Susan! Komm bald wieder!
Susan: Auf Wiedersehen, Herr Dresch. Vielen Dank für Ihre Gastfreundschaft!
Frau Dresch: Nichts zu danken, Susan.
Jessica: Tschüs, Susan! Gute Reise!

4 Wer sagt was? Schreib die Sätze auf. (Writing)

Ask students to make sure they look at the pictures carefully, to identify which form they should be using before writing the answers down.

Answers

> 1 Komm bitte herein! 2 Kommen Sie bitte herein! 3 Setzen Sie sich bitte hin! 4 Setz dich bitte hin! 5 Wie geht es Ihnen? 6 Wie geht es dir? 7 Tschüs! 8 Auf Wiedersehen! 9 Guten Tag / Grüß Gott / Servus. 10 Auf Wiederhören.

5 Partnerarbeit. Sprich mit deinem Partner / deiner Partnerin. Benutze alle Ausdrücke aus Übung 1 und Übung 3. (Speaking)

In pairs, students create their own conversations using all the new expressions.

Further practice of the language and vocabulary of this unit is given on the following page.
Speaking: p. 39, Rollenspiel

All the vocabulary and structures from this chapter are listed on the *Wörter* pages at the end (pp. 20–21). These can be used for revision by covering up either the English or the German. Students can check here to see how much they remember from the chapter.

For more speaking practice to do with this chapter, use pp. 38–39.

For futher speaking and grammar practice for the whole chapter, see pp. 7–8 of the Workbook.

Assessment materials for Chapters 1 and 2 are available after Chapter 2.

Workbook (pp. 1–8)

Logo! 4 1 Hallo! Ich bin's!

p. 1

1 1 a zweiundfünfzig, **b** zweiundfünfzig Wochen in einem Jahr, **2 a** vierundzwanzig, **b** vierundzwanzig Stunden an einem Tag, **3 a** sechzig, **b** sechzig Minuten in einer Stunde, **4 a** sieben, **b** sieben Tage in einer Woche, **5 a** dreihundertfünfundsechzig, **b** dreihundertfünfundsechzig Tage in einem Jahr
2 1 Er heißt Richard. **2** R.I.C.H.A.R.D. **3** Sie heißt Birgit. **4** Sie heißt Silvia. **5** Er ist neunzehn. **6** Er ist fünfundvierzig.
3 open-ended

p. 2

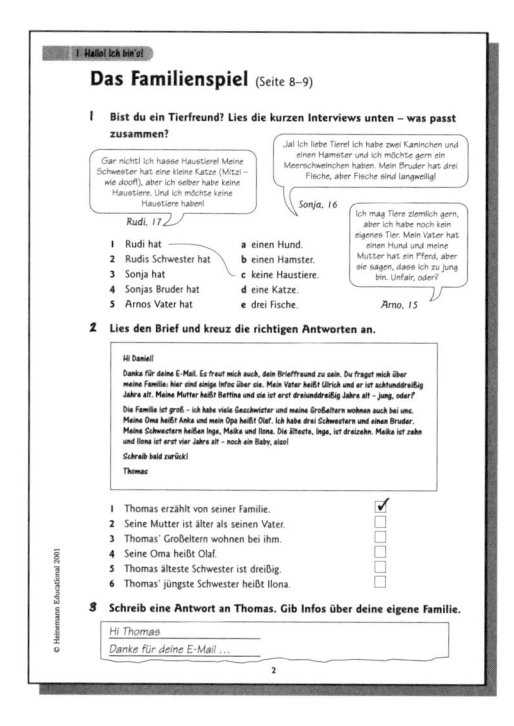

1 1 c, **2** d, **3** b, **4** e, **5** a
2 ticks for questions 1, 3, 6
3 open-ended: 1 mark per correct sentence; overlook minor errors

p. 3

1 a Dennis, **b** Manfred, **c** Andreas, **d** Magdalena, **e** Angela
2 open-ended: the information given must match the text, but can be given in any order
3 open-ended

p. 4

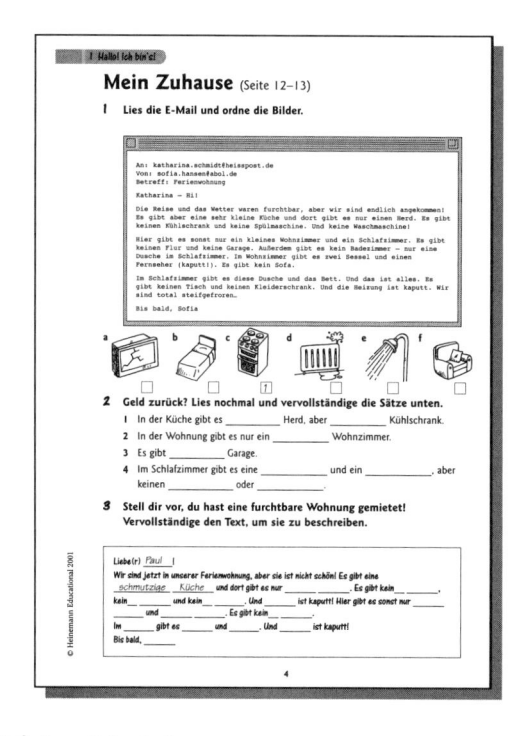

1 1 c, **2** e, **3** f, **4** a, **5** b, **6** d
2 1 In der Küche gibt es einen Herd, aber keinen Kühlschrank. **2** In der Wohnung gibt es nur ein kleines Wohnzimmer. **3** Es gibt keine Garage. **4** Im Schlafzimmer gibt es eine Dusche und ein Bett, aber keinen Tisch oder Kleiderschrank.
3 open-ended

27

p. 5

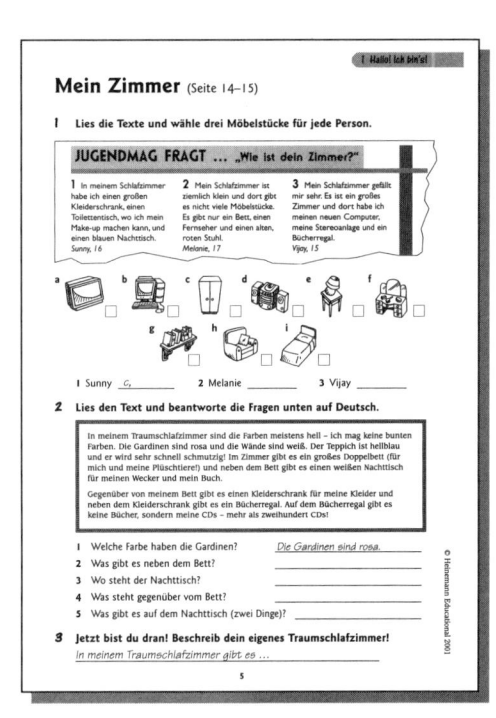

1 1 Sunny – c, f, e, 2 Melanie – i, a, h, 3 Vijay – b, d, g
2 1 Die Gardinen sind rosa. 2 Es gibt einen (weißen) Nachttisch. 3 Der Nachttisch steht neben dem Bett. 4 Ein Kleiderschrank steht gegenüber vom Bett. 5 Es gibt einen Wecker und ein Buch auf dem Nachttisch.
3 open-ended

p. 6

1 1 Claudia muss bügeln und Staub saugen. 2 Amrit muss abwaschen und abtrocknen. 3 Tommy und Tobias müssen kochen und den Tisch decken. 4 Bianca muss einkaufen. 5 Florian muss den Jungenschlafraum aufräumen. 6 Tamara muss den Mädchenschlafraum aufräumen. 7 Nadja muss nichts machen!
2 1 Claudia hasst Bügeln, aber sie mag Staub saugen. 2 Amrit mag Abwaschen und Abtrocknen nicht. 3 Tommy und Tobias mögen Kochen und den Tisch decken. 4 Bianca mag Einkaufen. 5 Florian hasst Aufräumen. 6 Tamara findet Aufräumen nicht schlecht. 7 (Nadja muss nichts machen!)   3 open-ended

p. 7

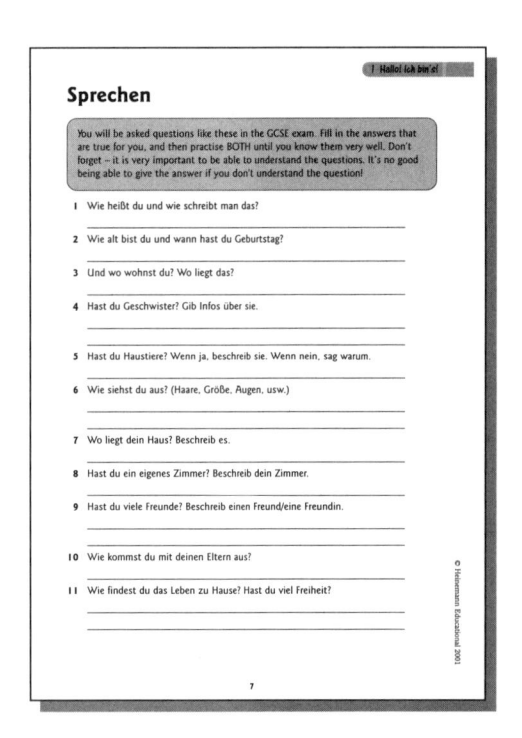

no answers – *Sprechen*

p. 8

1 1 Er ist acht Jahre alt. 2 Meine Eltern sind geschieden. 3 Wir sind alle sechzehn Jahre alt. 4 Mein Kaninchen ist so doof! 5 Ihr seid meine Freunde. (Other grammatically correct sentences which use up all the words are also acceptable.)
2 1 Mein Geburtstag ist am vierzehnten Mai. 2 Mein Geburtstag ist am siebten November. 3 Mein Geburtstag ist am dreizehnten Dezember. 4 Mein Geburtstag ist am zwölften Januar.
3 1 Ich habe blaue Augen. 2 Sie hat braune Haare. 3 Seine Haare sind grau. 4 Er hat grüne Augen. 5 Meine Mutter hat blaue Augen. 6 Meine Schwester hat blonde Haare. 4 open-ended

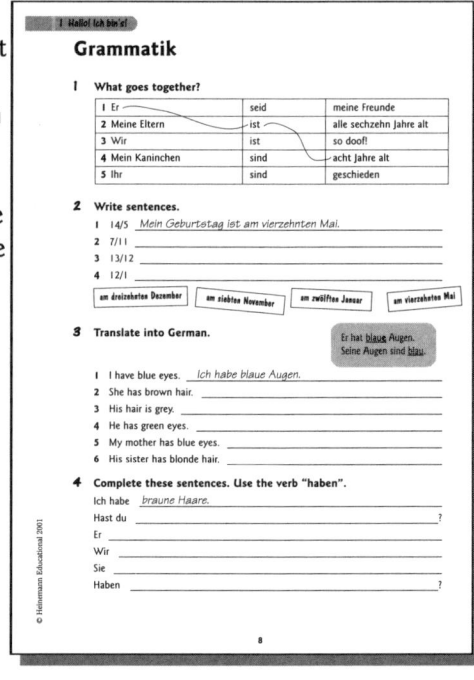

2 Schulstress (Student's Book pp. 22–29)

Topic area	Key language	Grammar	Skills
2.1 **Im Klassenzimmer** (pp. 22–23) Communicate in the classroom	*Darf ich bitte auf Toilette gehen? Kann ich bitte das Fenster aufmachen? Wie sagt man ... auf Deutsch? Ich habe vergessen, wie man ... schreibt. Kann ich bitte ein Heft haben? Was bedeutet ...? Kann ich bitte Deutsch sprechen?*	*dürfen* Imperatives: *du, ihr* and *Sie* forms	Using target language in the classroom
2.2 **Meine Schule** (pp. 24–25) Describe your school	*Meine Schule heißt die ... Schule. Sie ist ein Gymnasium / eine Gesamtschule / eine Privatschule. Sie ist groß / klein / modern / alt. Wir haben ungefähr ... Schüler und Schülerinnen / Lehrer und Lehrerinnen. Es gibt / Wir haben einen Schulhof / Informatikraum / eine Aula / Bibliothek / Turnhalle / ein Klassenzimmer / Lehrerzimmer / Labor. Ich finde die Schule / Lehrer + adjectives*	Adjective endings in the accusative	Qualifying words: *sehr, ziemlich, ganz, extrem* Writing an advert for a school
2.3 **Welche Fächer hast du?** (pp. 26–27) Talk about school subjects and give your opinion	*Meine erste / zweite / dritte / vierte / fünfte / Stunde ist ... Ich finde ... gut / interessant / langweilig / schwer / einfach / schlecht. Ich mag ... (nicht), weil der Lehrer / die Lehrerin doof / nett ist / weil ... schwer ist / weil ich sehr sportlich bin. Ich lerne seit ... Jahren ... Ich hasse ... Ich liebe ... Mein Lieblingsfach ist ...*	*weil* sends the verb to the end of the sentence	Abbreviations of school subjects Writing a letter about your school
2.4 **Der Schultag** (pp. 28–29) Talk about life at school	*Die Schule beginnt um ... Uhr: Die Schule ist um ... Uhr aus. Es gibt ... Stunden pro Tag. Eine Stunde dauert ... Minuten. Die große Pause / Mittagspause ist um ... Uhr. Ich komme zu Fuß / mit dem Auto / Bus / Rad / Zug zur Schule. Ich gehe ... nach Hause.*	Word order: verb comes second in a sentence	Two meanings of *eine Stunde* Question words: *wann, was, wie, wie lange, wie viele?*
2.5 **Meinungen über die Schule** (pp. 30–31) Give opinions about your school	*Mann muss (nicht) ... Man darf (nicht) ... einen Rock / eine Hose (usw.) tragen. Kaugummi wegwerfen / in der Freistunde nach Hause gehen. ein Handy in die Schule mitbringen. viel Englisch sprechen / ruhig sein.*	*müssen* and *dürfen* – all parts	*man darf / muss (nicht)*
2.6 **Pläne** (pp. 32–33) Talk about options after exams	*Ich will auf die Oberschule gehen / in die Oberstufe gehen / Abitur machen / die Schule verlassen / eine Lehre machen / arbeiten / Geld verdienen / Urlaub machen / einen Job finden. above expressions in the present tense*	*wollen* and *mögen* to express the future	Vocabulary for post-16 choices Using the present tense to express the future
2.7 **Ausbildung** (pp. 34–35) Talk about differences between German and British schools	*Deutsche / Britische Schüler finden die Uniform ... / tragen (k)eine Uniform / machen Ihre Hausaufgaben am Abend / Nachmittag / essen zu Mittag in der Schule / zu Hause / haben viele kleine Pausen.*		Scanning texts Advice for oral presentations

- The vocabulary and structures taught in Chapter 2 are summarised on the *Wörter* pages of the Student's Book, 36–37.
- Further speaking practice on the language of this chapter, is provided on p. 39.
- Coursework pages relating to this chapter can be found on pp. 176–177.
- Further reading and writing practice on the language of this chapter is provided on pp. 188–189.
- For a selection of assessment tasks for Chapters 1 and 2, please refer to the separate Assessment Pack for your chosen examination board: AQA, OCR or Edexcel.

1 Im Klassenzimmer (pp. 22–23)

Students will learn how to:
- communicate in the classroom

Key language	Gib mir …
Darf ich bitte auf Toilette gehen?	Zeig mir …
Kann ich bitte das Fenster aufmachen?	Sei ruhig!
Wie sagt man … auf Deutsch?	Mach … zu!
Ich habe vergessen, wie man … schreibt.	Mach … auf!
Kann ich bitte ein Heft haben?	**Grammar focus**
Was bedeutet …?	• dürfen
Kann ich bitte Deutsch sprechen?	• imperatives: *du, ihr* and *Sie* forms
Hör zu!	**Skill focus**
Steh auf!	• using the target language in the classroom
Setz dich hin!	**Resources**
Komm hierher!	• Cassette A, Side A

Before starting this spread, check how many classroom phrases students remember from earlier in the course. Provide them with a few visual cues as prompts, e.g. mime opening the window or wanting to go to the toilet.

1 Hör zu! Was passt zusammen? (Listening)
Students listen to the tape which features various students in a German classroom making requests and asking questions. They write down letters to show which sentence goes with which picture.

Answers

1 e, 2 d, 3 b, 4 f, 5 g, 6 c, 7 a

1 Kevin: Herr Schultz!
  Lehrer: Ja, Kevin?
  Kevin: Darf ich bitte auf Toilette gehen?
  Lehrer: Okay, Kevin.
2 Isabell: Herr Schultz!
  Lehrer: Ja, Isabell?
  Isabell: Hier ist es so warm. Kann ich bitte das Fenster aufmachen?
  Lehrer: Ja, Isabell.
3 Björn: Herr Schultz!
  Lehrer: Ja, Björn?
  Björn: Wie sagt man „doof" auf Englisch?
  Lehrer: „Stupid", Björn.
4 Sina: Herr Schultz!
  Lehrer: Ja, Sina?
  Sina: Ich habe vergessen, wie man „stupid" schreibt.
  Lehrer: S.T.U.P.I.D.
5 Jasmin: Herr Schultz!
  Lehrer: Ja, Jasmin?
  Jasmin: Ich habe mein Heft verloren. Kann ich bitte ein Heft haben?
  Lehrer: Hier, bitte schön, Jasmin.
6 Etta: Herr Schultz!
  Lehrer: Ja, Etta?
  Etta: Was bedeutet „freckles"?
  Lehrer: Sommersprossen!
7 Florian: Herr Schultz!
  Lehrer: Ja, Florian?
  Florian: Kann ich bitte Deutsch sprechen?
  Lehrer: Nein, Florian, das ist eine Englischstunde!

2 Verbinde die Satzteile und schreib sie auf. (Reading / Writing)
This is a writing exercise as well as a reading activity. Students link the sentence parts in order to make full sentences and write them down to help them remember.

Answers

1 f Kann ich bitte ein Heft haben? 2 e Darf ich bitte auf Toilette gehen? 3 a Wie schreibt man „stupid"? 4 b Wie sagt man „doof" auf Englisch? 5 g Kann ich bitte das Fenster aufmachen? 6 d Kann ich bitte Deutsch sprechen? 7 c Was bedeutet „freckles"? 8 i Ich weiß nicht. 9 j Können Sie die Frage wiederholen? 10 h Ich verstehe nicht.

Grammatik: dürfen (to be allowed to)
Darf ich is more polite than *Kann ich*. It goes with an infinitive which goes at the end of the sentence. Refer pupils to the Grammar section for the full paradigm of *dürfen*. Emphasise that this is a verb which they should certainly recognise and use at Higher Level.

3 Was fragst du? (Writing)
Having worked out how to say the things suggested here in English (all of which could well crop up in the Speaking Test), students write them down.

Answers

1 Was bedeutet „Jugendherberge"? 2 Können Sie die Frage wiederholen? 3 Ich verstehe nicht. 4 Wie sagt man „computer" auf Deutsch? 5 Ich weiß nicht. 6 Darf ich bitte auf Toilette gehen?

4 Hör zu! Wer ist wer? (Listening)
Students listen to the tape as often as they need to identify which person is which and to write down the names and the pictures they refer to.

Answers

Maria 4, Anton 3, Elisabeth 5, Olaf und Tim 6, Tanja 1, Karin und Birte 2

Lehrerin: Maria, sei ruhig!
Maria: Bitte?

Lehrerin: Anton, mach die Tür zu!
Anton: Aber es ist so warm hier.
Lehrerin: Elisabeth, gib mir bitte deinen Walkman!
Elisabeth: Aber ich will Musik hören!
Lehrerin: Olaf und Tim, setzt euch bitte hin!
Olaf und Tim: Okay, Frau Thomas.
Lehrerin: Tanja, komm hierher!
Tanja: Warum?
Lehrerin: Karin und Birte, zeigt mir eure Turnschuhe!
Karin und Birte: Hier, Frau Thomas.

Grammatik: Der Imperativ (the imperative form)

Examples of the *du, ihr* and *Sie* forms of the imperative. Ask students to practise saying these aloud and to learn the *du* and *Sie* forms.

5 Welche Wörter passen in die Sprechblasen? (Writing)

A reading and writing activity to practise imperative verb forms. Students link phrases to pictures and write them down.

Answers

1 Setzt euch hin! 2 Mach die Tür zu! 3 Gib mir bitte dein Heft! 4 Seid ruhig! 5 Mach das Fenster auf!

2 Meine Schule (pp. 24–25)

Students will learn how to:
- describe their school

Key language	(ziemlich) altmodisch.
Meine Schule heißt die ... Schule.	(ganz) doof / streng / nett.
Sie ist ein Gymnasium / eine Gesamtschule / eine Privatschule.	**Grammar focus**
Sie ist groß / klein / modern / alt.	• accusative adjective endings with indefinite article
Wir haben ungefähr ...	
... Schüler und Schülerinnen.	**Skill focus**
... Lehrer und Lehrerinnen.	• qualifying words: *sehr, ziemlich, ganz, extrem*
Es gibt / Wir haben ...	• writing an advert for a school
einen Schulhof / Informatikraum.	
eine Aula / Bibliothek / Turnhalle.	**Resources**
ein Klassenzimmer / Lehrerzimmer / Labor.	• Cassette A, Side A
Ich finde die Schule / Lehrer ...	• Workbook p. 9
(sehr) interessant / gut / toll / super.	• Sprechen p. 39, Gespräch 1

Start this spread by brainstorming in order to elicit as much vocabulary as students can remember about types of schools and the various buildings and rooms in a school.

1 Hör zu und lies den Text. Sind die Sätze unten richtig oder falsch? (Listening / Reading)
Students read and listen to the text about a grammar school and decide whether the sentences underneath are true or false.

Answers

1 Falsch. 2 Richtig. 3 Falsch. 4 Richtig. 5 Richtig. 6 Falsch. 7 Richtig. 8 Falsch.

> Hallo! Herzlich willkommen in meiner Schule! Ich bin Dirk und meine Schule heißt die Otto-Hahn-Schule. Sie ist ein Gymnasium und liegt in Koblenz. Ich besuche diese Schule seit zwei Jahren. Früher war ich an der Grundschule. Meine Schule ist ziemlich groß und ganz modern. Wir haben ungefähr neunhundert Schüler und Schülerinnen und sechzig Lehrer und Lehrerinnen. Wir haben viele Klassenzimmer, eine gute Bibliothek, eine große Aula, eine kleine Turnhalle, mehrere Labors und natürlich einen schönen Schulhof. Da spielen wir Fußball. Ich mag meine Schule sehr gern.

2a Korrigiere die falschen Antworten aus Übung 1 und schreib sie in ganzen Sätzen auf. (Writing)
Now students must correct the false statements in exercise 1 and write them out correctly in full sentences.

Answers

1 Die Otto-Hahn-Schule ist ein Gymnasium. 3 Die Schule hat sechzig Lehrer und Lehrerinnen. 6 Die Turnhalle ist klein. 8 Dirk geht gern in die Schule.

2b Partnerarbeit. Macht ein Interview mit Dirk über die Otto-Hahn-Schule. (Speaking)
Working in pairs, students complete a conversation about Dirk's school. Make sure that pupils take it in turns to question and answer.

2c Partnerarbeit. Macht jetzt mit den Fragen aus Übung 2b ein Interview über eure Schule. (Speaking)
Students now use the questions from exercise 2b to create a similar dialogue, but this time with real information about their own school.

Wiederholung: Adjektive (+ Akkusativ) (adjectives with the accusative)
Es gibt and *Wir haben* with the indefinite article and adjective endings: *einen ...en ...; eine ...e ...; ein ...es ...; ...e ...* Emphasise to the students that these expressions are so common that they will need to use them all the time. They must be used accurately.

3 Schreib die Sätze ab und füll die Lücken aus. Die Wörter stehen im Kästchen oben. (Writing)
Students add endings to articles and adjectives and then write out the sentences correctly. The Grammar box and the Key language box above will provide all the information they need, and they can refer to the Grammar section as well.

Answers

1 In meiner Schule gibt es eine große Aula. 2 Wir haben auch eine moderne Bibliothek. 3 Es gibt einen schönen Schulhof. 4 Wir haben eine gute Turnhalle. 5 Es gibt auch ein altes Labor. 6 Wir haben nette Lehrer. 7 Es gibt viele alte Klassenzimmer. 8 Wir haben einen modernen Informatikraum.

4 Partnerarbeit. (Speaking)
Working in pairs, students practise expressing opinions about aspects of school. Encourage them to use their imagination and to say as much as they can. Students should take it in turns to ask questions and give answers. Point out that this type of activity is

appropriate for working at Higher Level. The answers are not provided for them, they have to work things out for themselves.

Tip box
Using qualifying words: *sehr, ziemlich, ganz, extrem*. Remind students to use these words when writing and speaking, in order to give a more natural feel to their German.

5 Jetzt du. Beschreib deine Schule. (Writing)
This activity presents an ideal opportunity for practising ICT skills and can be set for homework or as a project.

Tip box
Advice for students on creating an advert for their school.

> Further practice of the language and vocabulary of this unit is given on the following pages.
> Speaking: p. 39, Gespräch 1
> Workbook: p. 9

3 Welche Fächer hast du?

(pp. 26–27)

Students will learn how to:
- talk about school subjects and give their opinions

Key language
Meine erste / zweite / dritte / vierte / fünfte / sechste Stunde ist ...
  Deutsch / Englisch / Französisch / Spanisch / Informatik / Kunst / Musik / Erdkunde / Sport / Mathe / Werken / Geschichte / Naturwissenschaften (Physik, Chemie, Biologie) / DSP (darstellendes Spiel)
Ich finde ... gut / interessant / langweilig / schwer / schlecht / einfach / super.
Ich hasse ...
Ich liebe ...
Mein Lieblingsfach ist ...
Mein bestes Fach ist ...
Ich mag ... (nicht) ...
weil der Lehrer / die Lehrerin doof / nett ist.
weil ... schwer ist.
weil ich sehr sportlich bin.

Grammar focus
- *weil* + verb at end of sentence

Skill focus
- abbreviations of school subjects
- writing a letter about your school

Resources
- Cassette A, Side A
- Workbook p. 10
- Sprechen p. 39, Gespräch 2 + 3

Before starting this spread, ask students to note down as many school subjects in German as they can remember.

1 Hör zu! Schreib die Tabelle ab und füll die Lücken aus. (Listening)
Students listen to the conversation as often as they need in order to complete the grid (which they must copy out) by writing in which subjects the speakers have in their first three lessons.

Answers
Felix: 1. Mathematik 2. Deutsch 3. Französisch.
Fatima: 1. Biologie 2. Französisch 3. Englisch

> Felix: Morgen, Fatima.
> Fatima: Morgen, Felix. Na, wie geht's?
> Felix: Na ja, es geht. Aber in der ersten Stunde habe ich Mathematik. Igitt! Herr Brinkmann! Mathe mag ich überhaupt nicht.
> Fatima: Ach, du hast Pech! In der ersten Stunde habe ich Biologie. Das ist mein Lieblingsfach.
> Felix: So? Wirklich? Ich mag Naturwissenschaften gar nicht gern. Mein bestes Fach ist Deutsch. Deutsch habe ich in der zweiten Stunde.
> Fatima: Ja? In der zweiten Stunde habe ich Französisch. Das mag ich gern.
> Felix: Ich habe Französisch in der dritten Stunde. Ich finde Französisch auch gut. Die Lehrerin, Frau Schlüter, ist toll!
> Fatima: Du hast Glück! In der dritten Stunde habe ich Englisch. Das finde ich extrem langweilig.

2a Schreib auf! Welche Stunde ist es? Um wie viel Uhr beginnt die Schule? (Writing)
Students identify the school subjects indicated by the symbols and write sentences to show what time the lessons start, based on the timetable provided.

Answers
1 Das ist Französisch. Die Stunde beginnt um 9.20.
2 Das ist Sport. Die Stunde beginnt um 11.20. 3 Das ist Deutsch. Die Stunde beginnt um 8.20. 4 Das ist Geschichte. Die Stunde beginnt um 10.15. 5 Das ist Englisch. Die Stunde beginnt um 11.20. 6 Das ist Biologie. Die Stunde beginnt um 11.20. 7 Das ist Mathe. Die Stunde beginnt um 7.30. 8 Das ist Erdkunde. Die Stunde beginnt um 9.20.

Tip box
Common abbreviations of school subjects: *Bio, Mathe*.

2b Partnerarbeit. Schaut den Stundenplan aus Übung 2a an und stellt Fragen. (Speaking)
Make sure students understand that this pair-work activity is based on the timetable in exercise 2a. This again is an open-ended activity, in which the students make up the questions. Partner B must therefore listen carefully to what partner A asks, while partner A must pay attention to whether partner B is answering correctly.

3 Lies den Brief. Du bist Kai. Schreib deine Antworten auf. (Reading / Writing)
Students read the letter from Kai and answer questions about it using *weil*. More able students can be asked to respond using full sentences: *Ich finde Englisch gut, weil ich englische Popmusik mag.*

Answers
1 Weil ich englische Popmusik mag. 2 Weil der Lehrer doof ist. 3 Weil die Lehrerin nett ist. 4 Weil Physik schwer ist. 5 Weil ich sehr sportlich bin.

4 Partnerarbeit. (Speaking)
Working in pairs, students ask and answer questions about which subjects they like and why. Various suggestions are provided, but encourage students to be as adventurous as they can with the language they use.

Grammatik: weil (because)
Weil sends the verb to the end of the sentence. Mastery of this construction is essential for a good grade at Higher Level, which is why it crops up several times in the book.

**5 Jetzt du. Schreib einen Brief an Kai.
(Writing)**
Students write a reply to Kai, including all the material suggested in the book and adding in as much extra detail as they wish.

> Further practice of the language and vocabulary of this unit is given on the following pages.
> Speaking: p. 39, Gespräch 2 + 3
> Workbook: p. 10

4 Der Schultag (pp. 28–29)

Students will learn how to:
- talk about daily life at school

Key language
Die Schule beginnt um ... Uhr.
Die Schule ist um ... Uhr aus.
Es gibt ... Stunden pro Tag.
Eine Stunde dauert ... Minuten.
Die große Pause / Mittagspause ist um ... Uhr.
Ich komme zu Fuß / mit dem Auto / Bus / Rad / Zug zur Schule.
Ich gehe ... nach Hause.

Grammar focus
- verb is second idea in a sentence

Skill focus
- *eine Stunde* – two meanings
- Question words: *wann, was, wie, wie lange, wie viele?*

Resources
- Cassette A, Side A
- Workbook p. 11
- Sprechen p. 39, Gespräch 4
- Kursarbeit pp. 176–177

Before starting this spread, ask students to provide the class with as much information as they can remember about the differences between the German school day and its UK equivalent.

1 Hör zu und beantworte die Fragen. Schreib „in England" oder „in Deutschland". (Listening)

Students listen to the interview as often as necessary in order to answer the questions with *in England* or *in Deutschland*. The text is not provided in the Student's Book, so careful listening is necessary, although the questions will give guidance as to what to listen out for.

Answers

1 in England 2 in Deutschland 3 in Deutschland 4 in England 5 in Deutschland 6 in England 7 in Deutschland 8 in England

> **Reporter:** Also, Carolin, letztes Jahr warst du in einer Schule in Bristol. Wie war die Schule in England?
> **Carolin:** Also, ich fand die Schule gut, aber alles war anders! Bei uns in Hamburg beginnt die Schule um Viertel vor acht, aber in England beginnt sie um neun Uhr. Dann gibt's eine Vollversammlung, die heißt „assembly" auf Englisch.
> **Reporter:** Wie viele Stunden gibt es pro Tag in der Schule in Bristol?
> **Carolin:** Es gibt acht Stunden. Aber eine Stunde dauert nur 35 Minuten. In Deutschland dauert eine Stunde 45 Minuten. Und in Deutschland haben wir nur fünf oder sechs Stunden pro Tag. In der Schule in Bristol haben sie acht Stunden!

Tip box
Eine Stunde means an hour as well as a lesson. This information is worth pointing out, as it is rather mysterious for English learners of German.

2 Lies den Text und beantworte die Fragen (ganze Sätze, bitte!). (Reading / Writing)

Now students read more information in Carolin's notes about the UK school she is visiting. The questions are then to be answered in full German sentences.

Answers

1 Die erste große Pause ist um 11 Uhr. 2 Die Mittagspause ist um Viertel vor eins. 3 Mann isst oft in der Schule. 4 Man isst zu Hause. 5 Die Schule in England ist um 4 Uhr aus. 6 Die Schule in Deutschland ist um 1 Uhr aus.

Grammatik: Wortfolge (word order)
The verb is always the second idea in a sentence. Make sure students appreciate this fundamental difference between English and German sentence construction.

3 Bau die Sätze um. (Writing)
Students practise using the 'verb second' concept by changing sentences and writing them out.

Answers

1 In Deutschland beginnt die Schule um acht Uhr. 2 In England gibt es eine Mittagspause. 3 In der Schule essen wir um ein Uhr. 4 Um vier Uhr gehe ich nach Hause. 5 In England kannst du in der Kantine essen. 6 Um neun Uhr gibt es eine Vollversammlung.

4a Partnerarbeit. (Speaking)
Working in pairs, students practise asking and answering typical questions which would crop up in a Speaking Test on the subject of school. Make sure students take it in turns to ask and answer questions. If wished, students can repeat the exercise, making up other information to replace the picture prompts.

Tip box
Translations of the question words *wann, was, wie, wie lange* and *wie viele* to help with activity 4a.

4b Partnerarbeit. Jetzt stellt und beantwortet die Fragen für *eure* Schule. (Speaking)
Now students do the same speaking exercise, but this time use true information about their own school.

5 Schreib einen Artikel über deinen Schulalltag. Beantworte alle Fragen in Übungen 2 und 4a. (Writing)

By answering questions from this spread, students construct written information about their own school day, to be learnt for later use in the exam. Encourage them to add in as much extra information as they confidently can.

> Further practice of the language and vocabulary of this unit is given on the following pages.
> Speaking: p. 39, Gespräch 4
> Kursarbeit: pp. 176–177
> Workbook: p. 11

Kursarbeit
The activities in this unit form an ideal introduction to coursework preparation. Specific coursework practice on this topic is provided on pp. 176–177.

5 Meinungen über die Schule (pp. 30–31)

Students will learn how to:
- talk about school

Key language
Mann muss (nicht) …
Man darf (nicht) …
  einen Rock / eine Hose (usw.) tragen.
  ein Handy in die Schule mitbringen.
  Kaugummi wegwerfen.
  in der Freistunde nach Hause gehen.
  viel Englisch sprechen.
  ruhig sein usw.

Grammar focus
- *müssen* and *dürfen* (all parts)

Skill focus
- *man darf / muss nicht*

Resources
- Cassette A, Side A
- Workbook p. 12
- Sprechen p. 39, Rollenspiel

Start the spread by asking students to list, in English, the things they are and aren't allowed to do in their school. Do they have any information about differences between UK and German schools in this respect?

1 Welche Regeln gibt es in der Schule in Bristol? Was schreibt Carolin? Schreib „ja" oder „nein". (Reading)

Students read the letter from Carolin and answer questions about it using *Ja* or *Nein*. If wished, they can be asked to write out the answers in full sentences: *Ja, die Mädchen müssen einen Rock tragen.*

Answers

1 Ja. 2 Nein. 3 Nein. 4 Nein. 5 Ja. 6 Nein. 7 Ja. 8 Nein.

Tip box
Man darf nicht / Man muss nicht. Make sure students understand that *man muss nicht* … doesn't mean 'you mustn't …'

Grammatik: Modale Verben (modal verbs)
Concentrates on all parts of the verbs *müssen* and *dürfen*.

2a Partnerarbeit. (Speaking)

Based on a notice detailing rules in a school playground, students ask and answer questions about what one may and may not do. Explain that it isn't a terrible error to say *Man darf nicht Fußball spielen*, but that the correct version should be *Man darf keinen Fußball spielen*.

2b Was darf man hier machen? Was darf man nicht machen? Schreib vier Sätze. (Writing)

Students write out what one may and may not do, based on the notice in exercise 2a.

3a Hör zu und beantworte die Fragen (kurze Antworten). (Listening)

Students listen to the conversation on tape as often as necessary in order to note down short answers to the questions.

Answers

1 um 8 Uhr, 2 den Namen ins Klassenbuch schreiben, 3 viel Englisch sprechen, 4 ruhig sein, 5 in die Kantine gehen, 6 Turnschuhe

> Martin: So, Philip, das hier ist meine Schule. Wir müssen um acht Uhr hier sein. Sonst schreibt der Lehrer unsere Namen ins Klassenbuch.
> Philip: Das Klassenbuch? Was ist das?
> Martin: Der Lehrer muss ins Klassenbuch schreiben, wenn ein Schüler zu spät ankommt oder gar nicht ankommt!
> Philip: So? Und was habt ihr in der ersten Stunde?
> Martin: Die erste Stunde ist Englisch. Wir müssen viel Englisch sprechen, wenn wir eine gute Note haben wollen. Für dich ist das kein Problem!
> Philip: Und die zweite Stunde?
> Martin: Das ist Mathe. Da muss man ruhig sein, weil der Lehrer streng ist.
> Philip: Wann ist die Pause?
> Martin: Um 9.20. Dann müssen wir in die Kantine gehen, weil man da Essen kaufen kann.
> Philip: Was machen wir dann?
> Martin: Nach der Pause haben wir Sport. Dafür müssen wir Turnschuhe anziehen.
> Philip: Gut! Ich habe meine Turnschuhe mit. Und dann?
> Martin: Dann haben wir frei. Wir können nach Hause gehen.

3b Schreib jetzt die Sätze auf. (Writing)

Now students write out the answers to exercise 3a in full sentences.

Answers

1 Sie müssen um 8 Uhr in der Schule sein. 2 Wenn ein Schüler / eine Schülerin zu spät kommt, schreibt der Klassenlehrer den Namen des Schülers / der Schülerin ins Klassenbuch. 3 Man muss viel Englisch sprechen, wenn man eine gute Note haben will. 4 Sie müssen ruhig sein. 5 Man muss in die Kantine gehen, um zu essen. 6 Er muss Turnschuhe tragen.

4 Partnerarbeit. (Speaking)

Students ask and answer questions about what is allowed in the school in Bristol which Carolin has written about. Encourage them to take it in turns to ask and answer questions and to invent further questions and answers.

5 Regeln. (Writing)
Students conclude this spread by writing down information about the rules in their own school. Make sure that answers are as detailed as possible and include their opinions about the rules.

> Further practice of the language and vocabulary of this unit is given on the following pages.
> Speaking: p. 39, Rollenspiel
> Workbook: p. 12

6 Pläne (pp. 32–33)

Students will learn how to:
- talk about what they will do after finishing their exams

Key language
Ich will ...
  auf die Oberschule gehen.
  in die Oberstufe gehen.
  Abitur machen.
  die Schule verlassen.
  eine Lehre machen.
  arbeiten / Geld verdienen.
  Urlaub machen.
  mir einen Job suchen
above expressions in the present tense

Grammar focus
- *wollen / mögen* used to express future

Skill focus
- vocabulary for options post-16
- using present tense to express future

Resources
- Cassette A, Side A
- Workbook p. 13
- Sprechen p. 39, Gespräch 5
- Lesen / Schreiben A p. 188

Before starting this spread, find out how much students know about further and higher education in the German-speaking countries.

1 Wer macht was nächstes Jahr? Schreib Dennis, Lars, Fiona oder Ines. (Reading)

Students read what the pictured students have to say about their plans for the next year and identify who is who by writing down names. More able students can write out the answers in full sentences: *Ines möchte sich einen Job suchen.*

Answers
1 Ines, 2 Fiona, 3 Lars, 4 Dennis, 5 Fiona, 6 Lars

2 Hör zu! Was machen Marcel, Jan, Jasmin, Katharina und Florian? Schreib Sätze. (Listening / Writing)

Students listen to the interviews as often as necessary to choose from the box who plans to do what. It may be best if they just jot down notes on the first hearing.

Answers
1 Marcel macht Abitur in der Oberstufe. 2 Jan geht arbeiten. 3 Jasmin macht eine Lehre. 4 Katharina macht Abitur auf der Oberschule. 5 Florian verlässt die Schule.

> Lehrerin: Was willst du nächstes Jahr machen, Marcel?
> Marcel: Ich gehe in die Oberstufe und mache Abitur.
> Lehrerin: Gut. Und du, Jan?
> Jan: Ich möchte arbeiten gehen. Ich will nicht Abitur machen. Ich will Geld verdienen!
> Lehrerin: Und du, Jasmin? Was machst du nächstes Jahr?
> Jasmin: Ach, zuerst mache ich Urlaub in der Schweiz, dann werde ich eine Lehre machen.
> Lehrerin: Und was möchtest du machen, wenn du mit dem Gymnasium fertig bist, Katharina?
> Katharina: Ich gehe auf die Oberschule und lerne für mein Abitur.
> Lehrerin: Und zum Schluss noch du, Florian?
> Florian: Ich verlasse die Schule, aber ich weiß nicht, was ich dann machen werde.

Tip box

An explanation of: *Abitur, Oberschule, Oberstufe, Lehre.* Point out to students that there is no exact equivalent of a Sixth Form College in Germany. After much consultation with native speakers in Germany, the authors have concluded that the term *Oberschule* comes close to conveying the concept of a Sixth Form College.

Tip box

How to use the present tense to talk about future plans. Make sure students realise that the present tense is by far the most usual way of expressing the future in German, but that there are other ways, including the 'real' future tense, which will have to be demonstrated in their exam.

3a Partnerarbeit. (Speaking)

Working in pairs, students ask and answer some questions about future plans, using the present tense and the prompts provided.

Grammatik: Das Futur (two more ways of expressing future intentions)

How to use *wollen* and *mögen* with the infinitive to talk about future plans. Students will almost certainly have come across this information before. Remind them that these are ways of expressing intentions, not the pure future.

3b Partnerarbeit. (Speaking)

Students ask and answer questions using *wollen*.

3c Beantworte die Fragen (ganze Sätze, bitte!). (Writing / Speaking)

This time students write their answers, but before doing so, this exercise can be used as a speaking activity if wished.

Answers
1 Ich möchte nächstes Jahr eine Lehre machen. 2 Ich möchte nach den Prüfungen arbeiten gehen. 3 Ich möchte nach den Sommerferien in die Oberstufe gehen.

**4 Lies den Artikel. Was sagen Elke, Frank, Roland, Birgit, Uli und Martha?
(Reading / Writing)**
Students read the extract from a magazine article and write down in the first person, in full sentences, what each person plans to do.

Answers

1 Elke sagt: Ich will die Schule verlassen und in Stuttgart eine Lehre machen. 2 Frank sagt: Ich will in die Oberstufe gehen und Abitur machen. 3 Roland sagt: Ich will arbeiten, weil ich Geld brauche. 4 Birgit sagt: Ich will nach Berlin fahren und dort die Oberschule besuchen. 5 Uli sagt: Ich will Abitur machen. 6 Martha sagt: Ich will Urlaub machen und dann eine Lehre machen.

5 Und du? Schreib auf: Was willst du nach den Prüfungen machen? Was möchte dein Freund / deine Freundin machen? (Writing)
Students sum up what they have practised in this spread by writing down information about their own plans and those of their friends. Encourage them to include as much detail as they confidently can.

Further practice of the language and vocabulary of this unit is given on the following pages.
Speaking: p. 39, Gespräch 5
Reading and Writing A: p. 188
Workbook: p. 13

Logo! 4 2 Schulstress

7 Ausbildung (pp. 34–35)

Students will learn how to:
- talk about differences between British and German schools

Key language	die Prüfung
Deutsche / Britische Schüler ...	die Noten
finden die Uniform ...	sitzen bleiben
tragen (k)eine Uniform.	**Skill focus**
machen Ihre Hausaufgaben am Abend / Nachmittag.	• scanning texts • advice for oral presentations
essen zu Mittag in der Schule / zu Hause.	**Resources**
haben viele kleine Pausen.	• Cassette A, Side A • Lesen / Schreiben B p. 189

Tell students that this is a largely reading-based spread summing up the content of the rest of the chapter, and thus is suitable for private study if wished. Teachers who like to tackle reading activities as a whole-class activity are welcome to do so, and can take the opportunity to teach reading and scanning skills.

1a Lies den Artikel, verbinde die Satzteile und schreib die Sätze auf. (Reading / Writing)

Students read this extract from a magazine article, link up the sentence parts and write out the complete sentences.

Answers

1 d: Anke findet die Uniform doof. 2 f: Viele britische Eltern finden die Uniform gut. 3 a: Markenkleidung ist teuer. 4 e: Paul findet die Uniform okay. 5 b: Deutsche Schüler tragen normale Kleidung. 6 g: Die meisten britischen Schüler tragen eine Uniform. 7 h: Eine Uniform ist gut, wenn man nicht viel Geld hat. 8 c: Die Lehrer in Deutschland finden die Kleidung der Schüler nicht interessant.

1b Lies den Artikel, schreib die Sätze ab und füll die Lücken aus. Schreib „britische Schüler" oder „deutsche Schüler". (Reading)

Students read the next section of the article and complete the sentences by identifying whether the sentences refer to British or German school students.

Answers

1 Britische Schüler machen ihre Hausaufgaben am Abend. 2 Britische Schüler sind am Nachmittag in der Schule. 3 Britische Schüler schlafen lange. 4 Deutsche Schüler müssen früh aufstehen. 5 Deutsche Schüler machen ihre Hausaufgaben am Nachmittag. 6 Britische Schüler essen zu Mittag in der Schule. 7 Deutsche Schüler gehen um ein Uhr nach Hause. 8 Deutsche Schüler haben viele kleine Pausen.

1c Lies den Artikel und finde die deutschen Wörter im Text. (Reading)

Students look at the final magazine extract and identify some German phrases which will probably be new to them. Also ask them to make notes in English to demonstrate that they have understood the information in the text.

Answers

1 wiederholen, 2 sitzen bleiben, 3 Prüfung, 4 Noten, 5 Tests / Klassenarbeiten, 6 komisch, 7 Trimester, 8 Semester

Tip box

Advice to scan the text for the parts that relate to the questions. Refer students also to the *Prüfungstipps* section at the end of the book for further advice on tackling reading texts.

2 Schreib einen Aufsatz über deine Meinungen über: Schuluniform oder Schule in Deutschland und in England. (Writing)

Students use the information on this spread to write short essays on either of these topics, or both. This work will need to be collected in, marked and returned.

Tip box

Advice to learn the presentation for use in the exam. This sort of topic is highly likely to come in useful in the Speaking Test and would make a good oral presentation.

Further practice of the language and vocabulary of this unit is given on the following page.
Reading and Writing B: p. 189

All the vocabulary and structures from this chapter are listed on the *Wörter* pages at the end (pp. 36–37). These can be used for revision by covering up either the English or the German. Students can check here to see how much they remember from the chapter.

For more speaking practice to do with this chapter, use p. 39.

Further grammar and speaking practice of the language of this chapter is provided on pp. 14–15 of the Workbook.

Assessment materials for Chapters 1 and 2 are available after Chapter 2.

Logo! 4 2 Schulstress

Kursarbeit

2 Schule (pp. 176–177)

The coursework spreads in *Logo! 4* give regular, guided practice in preparing for the coursework element of the GCSE exam.

The spreads always start with a model text on each theme (at a higher level than that expected by the student) which acts as a stimulus to give students ideas of what they might include in their own piece of work. Students are encouraged to look at the detail of the text through the guided reading activities. They are gradually guided to produce good German sentences in the tasks through to the final task, which is to produce an extended piece of writing. The *Hilfe* column is a feature on all the spreads. It reminds students of language they might include and particular structures that will raise the level of their writing. Remind students who are capable of achieving a Higher grade that they should always include examples of two or three tenses in their writing.

This spread guides students to produce an extended piece of writing on the topic of school

1 Lies die E-Mail. Schreib die braunen Wörter auf Deutsch und Englisch auf.

Students read the e-mail and write out all the words in brown in German and in English.

Answers

es gibt = there are; ungefähr = about / approximately; fast = almost; normalerweise = usually; nur = only; obwohl = although; entspannend = relaxing; schon = already; insgesamt = in total; anderthalb = one and a half

2 Du bist Tobias. Beantworte die Fragen.

Students answer the questions as if they were Tobias.

Answers

1 Meine Schule ist eine ziemlich große Realschule. Sie heißt „Klaus Michelsburg Realschule". 2 Es gibt ungefähr 900 Schüler. 3 Die Schule ist im Stadtzentrum. 4 Ich fahre normalerweise mit dem Rad zur Schule. 5 Ich brauche 10 Minuten, um zur Schule zu kommen. 6 Ich fahre mit dem Bus, wenn das Wetter schlecht ist. 7 Ich finde Kunst ganz interessant und entspannend. 8 Meine Lieblingsfächer sind Sport und Informatik. 9 Sie gefällt mir sehr gut / Sie ist total spitze! 10 Englisch und Informatik sind sehr wichtige und nützliche Fächer. 11 Die erste Stunde beginnt um Viertel vor acht. 12 Ich verlasse das Haus um 7.20 Uhr. 13 Ich habe 6 Stunden pro Tag. 14 Die Schule ist um 1.20 Uhr aus. 15 Normalerweise bekomme ich in zwei Fächern Hausaufgaben (anderthalb Stunden). 16 Ich sehe fern oder höre Musik.

3 Beantworte die Fragen für dich.

Students now answer the questions from exercise 2 for themselves.

4 Schreib eine E-Mail an deinen Brieffreund / deine Brieffreundin. Beschreib deine Schule.

Students now write an e-mail to a penfriend describing their school, using the tips in the *Hilfe* box as support.

Hilfe

Tips for students when writing an e-mail:
- using linking words
- saying what you like and giving your opinion
- using adjectives and giving reasons with *weil*

Workbook (pp. 9–15)

p. 9

1 1 Die Martin-Luther-Schule ist ein Gymnasium. 2 Sie existiert seit 25 Jahren. 3 Es gibt drei Labors. 4 Es gibt dreißig Klassenzimmer. 5 Fußball kann man auf dem Schulhof spielen.

2

Prospekt der Lehrer(innen)	Prospekt der Schüler(innen)
Die Schule ist nicht weit von Friedrichshafen entfernt.	Die Schule liegt 50 km von Friedrichshafen entfernt.
Die Schule ist sehr schön.	Die Schule ist hässlich.
Die Schule ist ziemlich modern.	Sie sieht sehr alt aus.
Es gibt drei neue Labors.	Es gibt drei alte Labors.
Es gibt eine moderne Bibliothek.	Es gibt eine alte Bibliothek.
Die Bibliothek hat 20 000 Bücher.	Die Bibliothek hat nur 10 000 Bücher.
Es gibt einen großen Schulhof.	Es gibt einen kleinen Schulhof.
Dort kann man Fußball spielen.	Dort kann man nichts machen.

(Alternative phrasing is acceptable as long as the meaning is conveyed accurately.)

3 open-ended

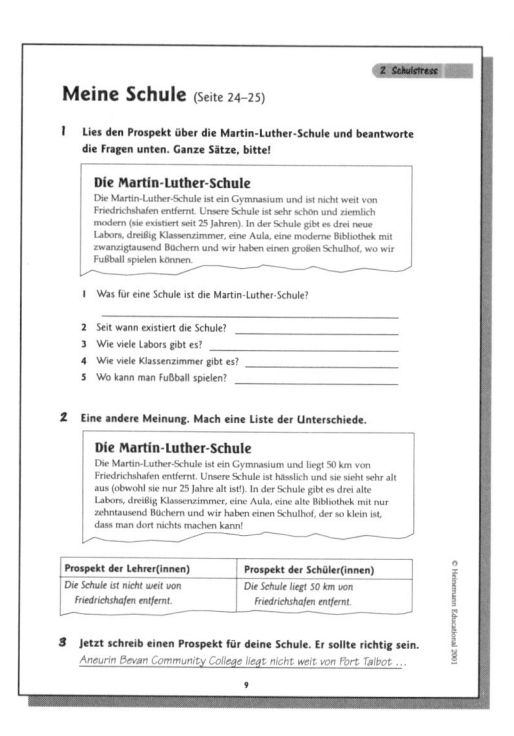

p. 10

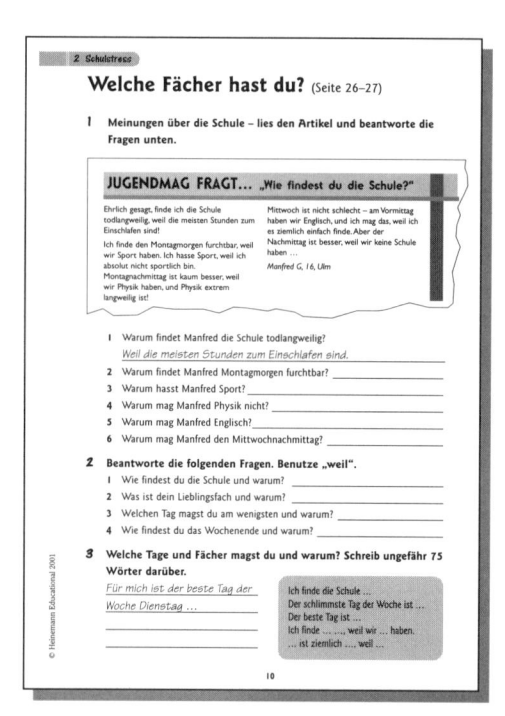

1 1 Weil die meisten Stunden zum Einschlafen sind. 2 Weil er Sport hat. 3 Weil er nicht sportlich ist. 4 Weil es extrem langweilig ist. 5 Weil er es ziemlich einfach findet. 6 Weil er keine Schule hat.

2 open-ended

3 open-ended: overlook minor errors

p. 11

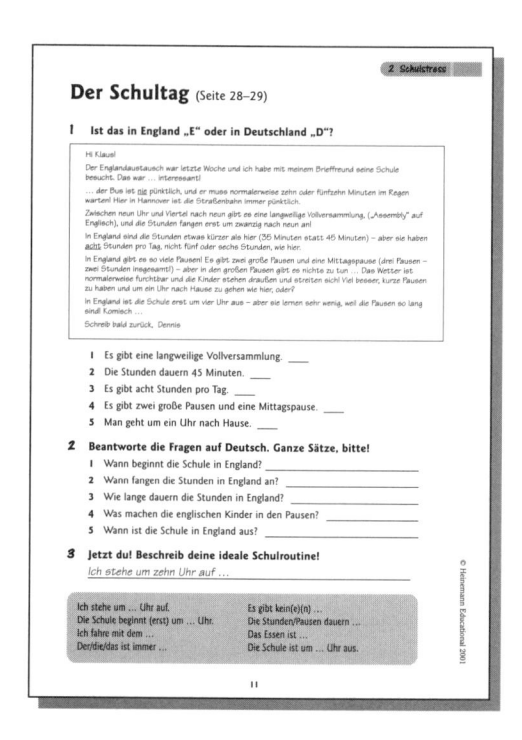

1 1 E, 2 D, 3 E, 4 E, 5 D

2 1 Die Schule in England beginnt um neun Uhr. 2 Die Stunden fangen um zwanzig nach neun an. 3 Die Stunden dauern fünfunddreißig Minuten. 4 Sie streiten sich. 5 Die Schule in England ist um vier Uhr aus.

3 open-ended: overlook minor errors

Logo! 4 2 Schulstress

p. 12

1 1 Falsch. 2 Richtig. 3 Richtig. 5 Falsch.
2 1 Sie findet die Kinder meistens freundlich. 2 Sie findet die Lehrer viel zu streng. 3 Sie müssen eine blaue Jacke, ein weißes Hemd, einen Schlips und eine graue Hose tragen. 4 Sie müssen einen grauen Rock, eine blaue Jacke, eine weiße Bluse und einen Schlips tragen. 5 Die schlimmste Regel ist, dass man kein Handy mit in die Schule bringen darf. (Alternative phrasing is acceptable if linguistically and factually correct.)
3 open-ended

p. 13

1 1 Richtig. 2 Richtig. 3 Falsch. 4 Richtig. 5 Falsch. 6 Richtig.
2 1 Sie will nicht Abitur machen. 2 Sie hofft, in die USA zu fahren. 3 Weil er die Nase voll hat. 4 Sie findet die Schule toll. 5 Er wird vielleicht eine Lehre in Berlin machen. 6 Sie will dort die Oberstufe besuchen.
3 open-ended: overlook minor errors

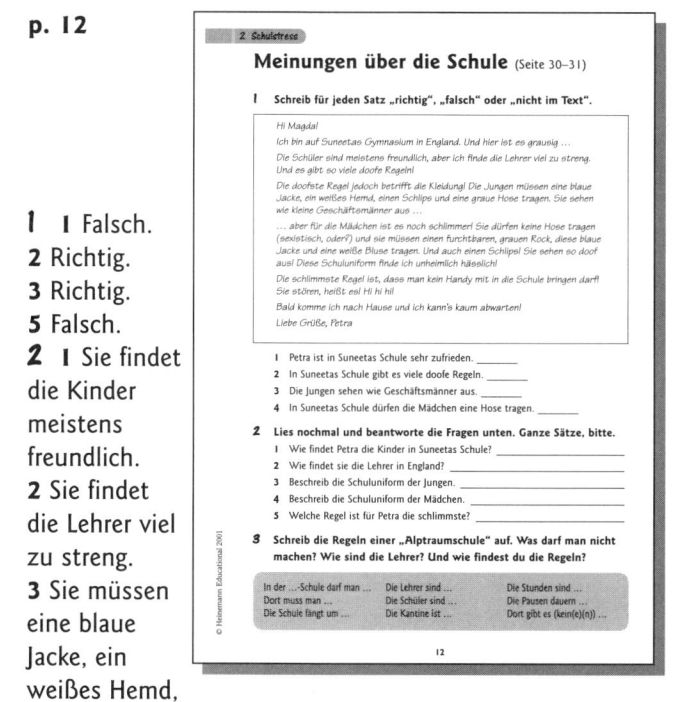

p. 14

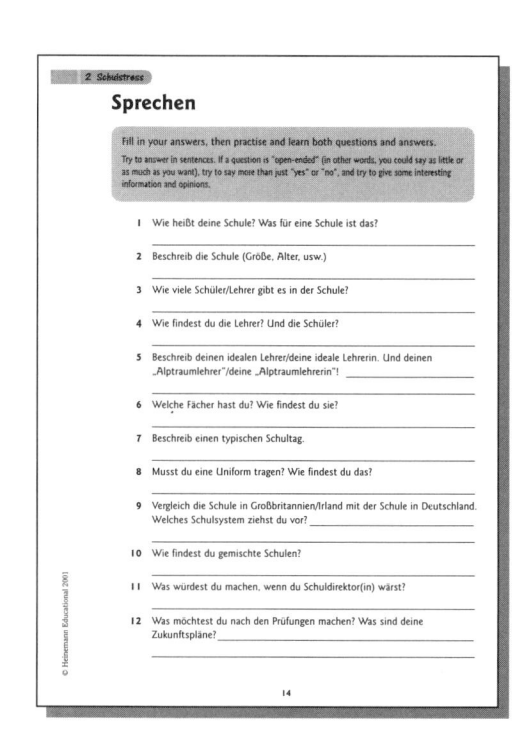

no answers – *Sprechen*

p. 15

1 open-ended
2 1 Meine Schule hat eine große Aula. 2 Es gibt auch einen großen Schulhof. 3 Wir haben einen Informatikraum. 4 Meine Schule hat eine große Turnhalle. 5 Es gibt ein neues Labor.
3 open-ended

3 Wir haben frei! (Student's Book pp. 40–55)

Topic area	Key language	Grammar	Skills
3.1 Hobbys (pp. 40–41) Talk about hobbies and interests	*Ich sammle gern Briefmarken. / Ich gehe gern in die Disco / ins Kino. Ich lese gern Bücher / Ich interessiere mich für Musik / meinen Computer. Ich spiele Geige in einer Band. Ich spiele gern klassische Musik. Ich höre gern Musik. Mein Hobby ist Fotografieren. Ich sehe gern fern. Ich treffe mich mit meinen Freunden / gehe aus.*	Present tense of *gehen, spielen, lesen, sehen, treffen* Using *gern*	Singular verb for one name, plural for two names Learning hobbies information for use in exam
3.2 Wir sehen fern (pp. 42–43) Talk about viewing and listening habits	*Ich sehe (nicht) gern …. Das ist ein Krimi / Film / eine Serie / Sendung / Musiksendung / Show / ein Quiz. Das sind die Nachrichten. Meine Lieblingssendung ist / heißt … Ich finde (Krimis) doof / interessant / langweilig / toll.*	Adjective endings: nominative with indefinite article	TV vocabulary
3.3 Was hast du gemacht? (pp. 44–45) Talk about activities in the past	*Ich habe / Wir haben (Pizza) gegessen / (Schuhe) gekauft / Karten gespielt / (einen Film) gesehen / Musik gehört. Ich bin / Wir sind (in die Stadt) gegangen / nach (Hamburg) gefahren / gewandert.* time phrases: *am Wochenende, gestern, am Abend*	Perfect tense (*haben* and *sein*)	Auxiliary verb comes second in sentence Learning text for use in exam
3.4 Sport (pp. 46–47) Describe sporting activities	*Ich treibe gern Sport. Ich bin sportlich / Ich schwimme / Ich spiele Basketball / Fußball / Tischtennis / Badminton (Federball) / Squash / Volleyball / Tennis. Ich fahre Rad / Ski. Ich gehe ins Fitnesszentrum. / Ich gehe gern angeln. Ich bin in einem (Fußball)verein. Ich mache … gern / Ich mag … Kegeln / Radfahren / Reiten / Schwimmen / Segeln / Skifahren / Rollschuhlaufen. Ich sehe gern … im Fernsehen.*	Present tense of *spielen* and *fahren*	Sports vocabulary: *Mannschaft, Verein*
3.5 Einladungen (pp. 48–49) Give and respond to invitations	*Möchtest du … in die Disco / Stadt gehen / ins Kino / Schwimmbad / Theater gehen / schwimmen / tanzen gehen? Wann treffen wir uns? Um …. Uhr. Wo treffen wir uns? Vor dem Bahnhof. In der Disco / Stadt. Im Kino / Theater / Jugendklub / Sportzentrum.* time phrases: *morgen, heute Abend, am Samstag usw.* making excuses: *Ich kann nicht, weil ich müde / krank bin / kein Geld habe / zu viele Hausaufgaben habe.*	Prepositions taking accusative or dative depending on whether motion is involved	Using *weil* when declining invitations
3.6 Wir gehen aus! (pp. 50–51) Find out about events and activities	*Was läuft heute? Wann beginnt das Stück / Spiel? Um wie viel Uhr macht das Schwimmbad / Stadion auf? Was kostet der Eintritt für Erwachsene / Kinder? Ich nehme eine / zwei Karte(n). Was für ein Stück / Spiel ist es?*		Use *Um wie viel Uhr?* as well as *Wann?*
3.7 Rezensionen (pp. 52–53) Describe films, books and programmes	*Die Sendung heißt … Sie läuft am (Dienstag). Der Film / Das Buch / Die Sendung war zu lang / langweilig / spannend / gut. Gestern / Letzte Woche habe ich einen Film / eine Sendung gesehen / ein Buch gelesen.*	Perfect tense	Talk about films and programmes: use the perfect tense and give opinions

- The vocabulary and structures taught in Chapter 3 are summarised on the *Wörter* pages of the Student's Book, 54–55.
- Further speaking practice on the language of this chapter is provided on p. 72.
- Further reading and writing practice on the language of this chapter is provided on pp. 190–191.

Logo! 4 3 Wir haben frei!

1 Hobbys (pp. 40–41)

Students will learn how to:
- talk about hobbies and interests

Key language
Ich sammle gern Briemarken.
Ich gehe gern in die Disco / ins Kino / Theater / zum Jugendklub.
Ich lese gern Bücher / Zeitschriften.
Ich interessiere mich für Rockmusik / meinen Computer.
Ich spiele Geige / Gitarre / Klavier / Schlagzeug in einer Band / Gruppe / in einem Orchester.
Ich spiele gern klassische Musik.
Ich höre gern Musik / Popmusik.
Mein Hobby ist Fotografieren.
Ich sehe gern fern.
Ich sammle gern Briefmarken / Münzen usw.
Ich treffe mich mit meinen Freunden / gehe aus.

Grammar focus
- present tense of *gehen, spielen, lesen, sehen, treffen*
- *(nicht) gern*

Skill focus
- singular verb for one name; plural for two names
- learn hobbies information for use in the exam

Resources
- Cassette A, Side B
- Workbook p. 16

Start this unit by inviting students to recall as many hobbies and interests as possible in German, based on their past experience.

1a Hör zu! Wer ist wer? Schreib die Namen auf (1–10). (Listening)

Students listen to the tape as often as they need in order to find out who is speaking and write down the names. Warn them that there are distracting elements in what is said, but that they should listen out for the essential information (just like in real life).

Answers
1 Tina, 2 Jana, 3 Adrian, 4 Vincent, 5 Morten, 6 Ben, 7 Angela, 8 Udo, 9 Wiebke, 10 Silke

1 – Ich sammle gern Briefmarken aus aller Welt! Ich habe achthundert Briefmarken in meiner Sammlung.
2 – Ach nee, Briefmarken, wie langweilig! Ich gehe lieber in die Disco. Ich tanze so gern!
3 – So? Ich nicht. Ich lese lieber. Ich mag Bücher, aber auch Zeitschriften wie „Bravo".
4 – Lesen mag ich nicht. Ich interessiere mich für Musik. Ich spiele Gitarre in einer Band.
5 – So? Ich bin nicht in einer Gruppe. Aber ich höre gern Musik, meistens Rockmusik. Ich habe einen CD-Spieler und einen CD-Walkman.
6 – Ich habe keine Zeit für Musik! Ich interessiere mich nur für meinen Computer. Ich spiele oft damit, aber ich programmiere meinen Computer auch.
7 – Ich nicht. Computer finde ich doof. Mein Hobby ist Fotografieren. Ich mache Fotos von meiner Familie.
8 – Gut, aber das ist nichts für mich. Ich habe ein Klavier zu Hause und ich spiele gern klassische Musik, vor allem Bach und Beethoven.
9 – Igitt, klassische Musik! Wie schrecklich! Nee, ich sehe gern fern. Ich mag Talkshows und Quizsendungen. Ich sehe jeden Tag fern.
10 – Echt? Ich hasse so was. Ich gehe gern ins Kino. Ich mag Filme aus Amerika. Ich gehe ein- oder zweimal im Monat.

1b Lies die Sätze. Schreib „richtig" oder „falsch". (Reading)

Students read the statements and note down whether they are true or false. Make sure they realise that this exercise is based on the same material as exercise 1a.

Answers
1 Falsch. 2 Richtig. 3 Richtig. 4 Falsch. 5 Falsch. 6 Falsch. 7 Falsch. 8 Falsch. 9 Richtig. 10 Falsch.

2 Gruppenarbeit. Was sind deine Hobbys? Was machst du in deiner Freizeit? Stell Fragen und notiere die Antworten. (James mag / spielt / hört ... usw.) (Speaking)

Encourage students to give detailed answers as they ask as many classmates as possible about their hobbies and interests. They should note down the responses in the *er / sie* form.

Grammatik: Das Präsens (the present tense)

All forms of the following regular verbs: *gehen* and *spielen* plus the following irregular verbs: *lesen, sehen, treffen*. Make sure students are completely confident in the use of these fundamental verbs. Other verbs are to be found in the Grammar section (pp. 206–227).

Tip box

Use of the singular verb with the name of one person and the plural verb for names of two or more people. Point this out to students, because even the more able tend to say things like *Tim er geht ...*

Grammatik: gern (like)

How to use *(nicht) gern* to express liking or disliking an activity. Get students to give a few oral examples.

3 Beantworte Vanessas Brief. (Writing)
Students reply to a letter with information about their own hobbies and interests. Encourage them to write as informatively as they can. If they feel confident about using *weil* and the perfect tense, they should do so.

Tip box
The tip box gives advice on learning the information from students' own letters for possible use in the Speaking or Writing Test.

> Further practice of the language and vocabulary of this unit is given on the following page.
> Workbook: p. 16

Logo! 4 3 Wir haben frei!

2 Wir sehen fern (pp. 42–43)

Students will learn how to:
- talk about viewing and listening habits

Key language
Ich sehe (nicht) gern …
Das ist …
　ein Krimi / Film.
　eine Serie /
　Musiksendung /
　Sportsendung.
　ein Quiz.
Das sind die
Nachrichten.
Im (ersten) Programm
läuft …
Meine Lieblingssendung
ist / heißt …
Ich finde (Krimis) doof /
interessant / langweilig /
toll.

Grammar focus
- adjective endings: nominative after indefinite article

Skill focus
- TV vocabulary

Resources
- Cassette A, Side B
- Workbook p. 17
- Lesen / Schreiben A p. 190

Before starting this spread, ask students whether they know any German TV shows. Recommend those with satellite or cable TV to tune in to some German channels, of which plenty are available. They will find that many UK shows have German equivalents. Find out how many hours of TV they watch each week.

1 Hör zu und beantworte die Fragen. (Listening)

Students listen to a family discussing what to watch on TV. They answer the questions by choosing from the answers provided. There is no printed support on the page, so they may have to listen to the tape a few times. Afterwards, encourage them to write out the answers in sentences: 1 *Gabi will „Liebe im Krankenhaus" sehen.*

Answers

1 „Liebe im Krankenhaus", 2 eine Serie, 3 „Wer wird Millionär?" 4 eine Quizsendung, 5 „Tatort", 6 ein Krimi, 7 ein Schauspieler, 8 die Nachrichten

> **Mutter:** Also, was gucken wir heute Abend? Was meinst du, Gabi?
> **Gabi:** Ich weiß, Mutti! Um 21 Uhr im ersten Programm läuft eine neue Serie, „Liebe im Krankenhaus".
> **Hans:** Ach nee, nicht schon wieder eine blöde Serie! Ich hasse Soaps. Die sind doch sooo langweilig.
> **Gabi:** Ach, Hans, du bist doof. Was willst du denn gucken?
> **Hans:** Es gibt doch eine tolle Sendung bei RTL: „Wer wird Millionär?" Das ist eine neue Quizsendung mit Günter Jauch.
> **Mutter:** Nein, Hans, du weißt, so was mag ich nicht gern. Ich möchte lieber einen schönen Krimi sehen. Schau mal! Im zweiten Programm gibt es um zwanzig Uhr „Tatort" mit Ulrich Meyer. Der ist doch ein toller Schauspieler. Was meinst du, Vati?
> **Vater:** Ja, also, Pech für alle. Ich habe die Fernbedienung und ich will um acht Uhr die Nachrichten sehen.
> **Alle:** [sighs, boos, sounds of dissent]
> **Nachrichtensprecher:** Guten Abend, meine Damen und Herren. Und jetzt die Nachrichten …

Tip box

Explanations of the following vocabulary: *das Programm, eine Sendung, die Tagesschau, gucken.* Point out that this information could help them to avoid falling into traps when doing the Reading or Listening exam.

2 Partnerarbeit. (Speaking)

Students use the prompts provided to help them construct dialogues about TV viewing habits. Afterwards, they can make up their own conversations along the same lines.

3 Lies die Sätze. Wie heißt die Sendung? Wann beginnt sie? (Reading)

Students read an extract from a TV listings magazine and write down what the programmes are and when they begin. This can be done as classwork or for homework. They could have some fun making up their own listings for an imaginary German TV station.

Answers

1 Die Sendung heißt „Top Pop". Sie beginnt um 21 Uhr. 2 Die Sendung heißt „Liebe im Krankenhaus". Sie beginnt um 21 Uhr. 3 Die Sendung heißt „Wer wird Millionär?". Sie beginnt um 20 Uhr. 4 Die Sendung heißt „Susi". Sie beginnt um 18 Uhr. 5 Die Sendung heißt „Tatort". Sie beginnt um 20 Uhr. 6 Die Sendung heißt „Fawlty Towers". Sie beginnt um 18 Uhr.

Wiederholung: Adjektive (+ Nominativ) (adjectives + nominative)

A reminder of the adjective endings used with the indefinite article in the nominative. Point out that this is an area which is very different from English and therefore likely to cause difficulty.

4 Schreib die Sätze ab und füll die Lücken aus. (Writing)

Students practise using adjectives as shown in the *Wiederholung* box.

Answers

1 „Tatort" ist ein spannender Krimi. 2 „Tiger Tiger" ist eine schöne Sendung. 3 „Wer wird Millionär?" ist ein neues Quiz. 4 „Susi" ist eine blöde Talkshow. 5 „Liebe im Krankenhaus" ist eine langweilige Serie.

5 Was siehst du gern im Fernsehen? Schreib einen Artikel über die Sendungen, die du magst und die Sendungen, die du nicht gut findest. (Writing)
Students write an article about their viewing habits, based on the example provided.

> Further practice of the language and vocabulary of this unit is given on the following pages.
> Reading and Writing A: p. 190
> Workbook: p. 17

Logo! 4 3 Wir haben frei!

3 Was hast du gemacht?

(pp. 44–45)

Students will learn how to:
- talk about activities in the past

Key language
time phrases: am Wochenende, am Samstag, gestern, am Abend
Ich habe … / Wir haben …
  (Pizza) gegessen.
  (Schuhe) gekauft.
  (einen Film) gesehen.
  Musik gehört / Karten gespielt.
Ich bin … / Wir sind …
  in die Stadt / ins Kino / ins Restaurant gegangen.
  nach (Hamburg) gefahren.
  gewandert.

Grammar focus
- perfect tense (with *haben* and *sein*)

Skill focus
- auxiliary verb comes second in sentence
- learning text for use in the exam

Resources
- Cassette A, Side B
- Workbook p. 18
- Sprechen p. 72, Gespräch 1

Start this spread by emphasising (probably not for the first or last time!) that students can only attain a high grade if they include information about the past. They will probably remember quite a lot from their earlier studies. Invite them to contribute information about what they did yesterday / last week / last weekend, etc.

1 Lies den Artikel aus „Jugend heute". Wer hat was gemacht? Beantworte die Fragen (ganze Sätze, bitte!). (Reading)

Students read a magazine article and answer questions about it in full sentences. Ask them to find examples of use of the perfect tense and jot them down / read them out.

Answers

1 Timo hat einen Film gesehen. 2 Linda hat einen Techno-DJ gesehen. 3 Timo hat eine Show im Fernsehen gesehen. 4 Werner hat italienisch gegessen. 5 Timo hat Schularbeiten gemacht. 6 Werner hat lange geschlafen. 7 Linda ist zum Jugendklub gegangen. 8 Linda ist nach Hamburg gefahren.

Grammatik: Das Perfekt (the perfect tense)

An explanation of the perfect tense (with *haben* and *sein*). Remind students of the general principle that verbs of motion (plus the honourable exceptions *bleiben* and the more macabre *sterben*) take *sein*. This information is presented all together on the assumption that students will remember quite a lot from their previous studies.

2a Hör zu und bring die Bilder in die richtige Reihenfolge. (Listening)

Tell students that putting pictures or sentences into order is a type of task favoured by GCSE examiners. This can be irritatingly difficult, so ask them to concentrate hard while listening.

Answers

1 e, 2 h, 3 c, 4 a, 5 g, 6 d, 7 f, 8 b

> Ich bin um zwei Uhr nach Hause gekommen. Dann habe ich ferngesehen. Von vier bis fünf habe ich Hausaufgaben gemacht und am Abend bin ich zu einer Party gegangen. Da habe ich eine Bratwurst gegessen und viel Bier getrunken. Ich habe mit Freunden getanzt. Das war gut, aber um Mitternacht war ich müde. Ich bin nach Hause gegangen und bin ins Bett gegangen.

2b Partnerarbeit. Macht ein Interview mit Carla. (Speaking)

In pairs, students construct a conversation with Carla, based on the results of the previous activity.

2c Schreib die Geschichte in der richtigen Reihenfolge auf. (Writing)

Finally, they must write out the story in the correct order. Sentences are provided for them. If wished, teachers can ask students to write out the story in the *ich* form, as if they were Carla.

Answers

Carla ist um zwei Uhr nach Hause gekommen. Dann hat sie ferngesehen. Von vier bis fünf hat sie Hausaufgaben gemacht. Am Abend ist sie zu einer Party gegangen. Da hat sie eine Bratwurst gegessen und viel Bier getrunken. Sie hat mit Freunden getanzt. Um Mitternacht war sie müde. Sie ist nach Hause gegangen und ist ins Bett gegangen.

Ich bin um zwei Uhr nach Hause gekommen. Dann habe ich ferngesehen. Von vier bis fünf habe ich Hausaufgaben gemacht. Am Abend bin ich zu einer Party gegangen. Da habe ich eine Bratwurst gegessen und viel Bier getrunken. Ich habe mit Freunden getanzt. Um Mitternacht war ich müde. Ich bin nach Hause gegangen und bin ins Bett gegangen.

Tip box

The auxiliary verb comes second in the sentence, whether the tense is present or perfect. Students will be aware of this in the present tense, but should be alert when using the perfect. Give them a few sentences plus a time expression to add in, so that they get practice in altering the word order.

3 Interview. (Speaking)
Students practise using the perfect tense with the expression of time first and the verb second. Assure them that, if they use this format in their Speaking Test, they will sound very natural!

4 Jetzt du. Was hast du am Wochenende gemacht? Wohin bist du gefahren? (Writing)
Emphasise to students that a narrative using the perfect tense is adaptable to various uses in the Speaking or Writing exams, and that it is vital to have plenty of detailed, accurate information at their fingertips. Make sure they include as much extra information and opinions as they can. This work will have to be marked and returned for reference.

Tip box
A reminder for students that the text for exercise 4 may be useful in their Speaking and Writing Tests.

Further practice of the language and vocabulary of this unit is given on the following pages.
Speaking: p. 72, Gespräch I
Workbook: p. 18

Logo! 4 3 Wir haben frei!

4 Sport (pp. 46–47)

Students will learn how to:
- describe their sporting activities

Key language
Ich treibe gern Sport.
Ich bin sportlich.
Ich schwimme.
Ich spiele Basketball / Fußball / Tischtennis / Badminton (Federball) / Squash / Volleyball / Tennis.
Ich fahre Rad / Ski.
Ich gehe ins Fitnesszentrum.
Ich gehe gern angeln.
Ich bin in einem (Fußball)verein.
Ich mache ... gern.
Ich mag ...
    Kegeln / Radfahren / Reiten / Schwimmen / Segeln / Skifahren / Rollschuhlaufen.
Ich sehe gern ... im Fernsehen.

Grammar focus
- Present tense of *spielen* and *fahren*

Skill focus
- Sports vocabulary: *Mannschaft*, *Verein*

Resources
- Cassette A, Side B
- Workbook p. 19
- Sprechen p. 72, Gespräch 2
- Lesen / Schreiben B p. 191

Start the spread by asking students to contribute as many types of sporting activity in German as they can remember. Also: how many famous German, Austrian or Swiss sports stars (past and present) do they know?

1a Hör zu! Wer macht was? (Listening)
Tell students that studio talk shows such as this one are extremely common and popular in Germany on stations like RTL and SAT 1. Some channels have nothing else all day. That is why this format is featured several times in *Logo! 4*.

Students listen to the conversations and study the pictures, then note down which types of sport the three people participate in. Make sure they understand that there are three answers for Jan and Mehmet and two for Vanessa.

Answers
1 Jan: h, c, d. 2 Vanessa: b, g. 3 Mehmet: a, e, f

> **Fernsehmoderatorin:** Hallo Leute! Herzlich Willkommen bei „Sport für junge Leute!" Die Umfrage heute ist „Bist du sportlich?" Hallo! Wie heißt du?
> **Jan:** Ich bin der Jan.
> **Fernsehmoderatorin:** Und bist du sportlich, Jan?
> **Jan:** Jawohl! Sehr sportlich! Ich schwimme jeden Dienstag im Hallenbad. Ich spiele auch einmal in der Woche Basketball und ich fahre auch gern Rad. Ich fahre jeden Tag in die Schule.
> **Fernsehmoderatorin:** Super! Vielen Dank. Und du?
> **Vanessa:** Hallo, Uwe! Ich bin Vanessa und ich bin auch sportlich. Ich gehe am Wochenende ins Fitnesszentrum und im Sommer schwimme ich jeden Tag im Freibad.
> **Fernsehmoderatorin:** Danke, Vanessa. Hallo!
> **Mehmet:** Hallo, Uwe! Also, mein Name ist Mehmet und ich bin nicht besonders sportlich. Im Winter fahre ich gern Ski und am Samstag sehe ich gern ein Fußballspiel im Stadion. Ich spiele auch Fußball, aber nicht oft. Ich kann nicht gut spielen!

1b Wer sagt was? Hör nochmal zu und vervollständige die Sätze. (Writing)
Now students write out the answers to exercise 1a. Encourage them to include as much as they have understood.

Answers
1 **Jan:** Ich schwimme, ich spiele Basketball und ich fahre Rad. 2 **Vanessa:** Ich gehe ins Fitnesszentrum und ich schwimme. 3 **Mehmet:** Ich fahre Ski, ich sehe ein Fußballspiel im Stadion und ich spiele Fußball. (Students can add in more detail if they wish.)

Wiederholung: Das Präsens (the present tense)
Explain that the verb *fahren* has been singled out because it is so common and useful. *Spielen* is not included because it is regular.

2 Partnerarbeit. (Speaking)
Working in pairs, students ask and answer simple questions about sport. Each student should try and ask several classmates, who should give true answers. This activity can be expanded into a full-scale class survey, if wished, providing an opportunity to use ICT for creating graphs.

Tip box
The Tip box suggests trying exercise 2 as a guessing game. This approach can often be used in speaking tasks. It gives an opportunity for lots of practice in asking the questions until the correct answer is found.

3 Lies die Texte und schau die Poster an. Wer ist zu welcher Veranstaltung gegangen? (Reading)
Students study some statements and link them to posters advertising sporting events. Then they write out who went to each one, using the perfect tense. Variations are possible.

Answers
1 Otto ist zum Segelwettbewerb gegangen. 2 Marcel hat Tennis gespielt. 3 Peter hat im Sportverein Basketball gespielt. 4 Kati ist reiten gegangen. 5 Sabine ist schwimmen gegangen.

Tip box
How to say you go to a sports club or play in a team.
Point out to students that this information will be useful
if the topic of sport comes up in the Speaking or Writing
Test, especially if they play sport for a team or club.

4 Schreib eine Anzeige für einen Brieffreund / eine Brieffreundin für *dich*. (Writing)
Based on an example provided, students write a small ad
asking for a penfriend with similar sporting interests.

5 Was für Sport hast du in diesem Jahr gemacht? Schreib es auf. (Writing)
Here, students are invited to display their ability to write
about sporting activities in the past. Remind them that
what they put doesn't necessarily have to be true!

Further practice of the language and vocabulary of this
unit is given on the following pages.
Speaking: p. 72, Gespräch 2
Reading and Writing B: p. 191
Workbook: p. 19

Logo! 4 3 Wir haben frei!

5 Einladungen (pp. 48–49)

Students will learn how to:
- give and respond to invitations

Key language
time phrases: morgen, heute Abend, am Samstag
Möchtest du …
   in die Disco / Stadt gehen?
   ins Kino / Schwimmbad / Theater gehen?
   schwimmen / tanzen gehen?
Wann treffen wir uns?
Um … Uhr.
Wo treffen wir uns?
Vor dem Bahnhof / der Disco.
In der Disco / Stadt.
Im Kino / Theater / Jugendklub / Sportzentrum.

making excuses: Ich kann nicht, weil … ich müde / krank bin / kein Geld habe / zu viele Hausaufgaben habe.

Grammar focus
- prepositions taking accusative / dative depending on whether motion is involved

Skill focus
- using *weil* when declining invitations

Resources
- Cassette A, Side B
- Workbook p. 20
- Sprechen p. 72, Rollenspiel 1

Before starting this spread, revise telling the time. Students may well be shocked to find that they have forgotten some of the details, such as the half past / twenty-five past / to problem. Try them out with some times spoken quickly and just once. Make sure they realise that if they misunderstand, they may well miss a train or be an hour late for a date (not to mention losing a mark in an exam).

1 Wann treffen wir uns? Schreib die Antwort auf. (Writing)

Students look at the times on the clocks and write sentences suggesting meetings at the various times.

Answers

1 Treffen wir uns um sechs Uhr. **2** Treffen wir uns um Viertel nach sechs. **3** Treffen wir uns um halb sieben. **4** Treffen wir uns um Viertel vor sieben. **5** Treffen wir uns um sieben Uhr. **6** Treffen wir uns um Viertel nach sieben. **7** Treffen wir uns um halb acht.

2a Hör zu und lies das erste Gespräch zwischen Birgit und Rosita. Schreib die Tabelle ab und füll sie für alle vier Gespräche aus. (Listening)

Students copy out the grid and fill in the information gleaned from four phone conversations. Make sure that they realise that only the first conversation is provided on the page. The other three are 'pure' listening activities. A photocopiable grid to accompany this exercise is available on p. 190 of this book.

Answers

Birgit / Rosita: ins Kino; um acht Uhr; vor dem Kino
Robert / Uli: ins Schwimmbad; um drei Uhr; im Sportzentrum
Petra / Felix: in die Stadt; um ein Uhr; bei Petra
Isabell / Michael: in die Disco / um 22 Uhr / vor dem Jugendklub

1 Birgit: Müller!
   Rosita: Hallo, Birgit. Sag mal, möchtest du heute Abend ins Kino gehen?
   Birgit: Was läuft?
   Rosita: Ich glaube, ein Krimi.
   Birgit: Und um wie viel Uhr?
   Rosita: Um acht.
   Birgit: Okay. Wo treffen wir uns?
   Rosita: Vor dem Kino?
   Birgit: Ist gut. Bis dann!
2 Robert: Hallo, Uli!
   Uli: Hi, Robert. Was willst du denn?
   Robert: Wollen wir heute ins Schwimmbad?
   Uli: Gute Idee! Um wie viel Uhr?
   Robert: Um drei?
   Uli: Okay. Wo treffen wir uns?
   Robert: Im Sportzentrum.
   Uli: Alles klar.
3 Petra: Ist das Felix?
   Felix: Ja, wer spricht denn?
   Petra: Ich bin's, Petra.
   Felix: Hallo, Petra, wie geht's?
   Petra: Gut. Sag mal, Felix, ich gehe heute in die Stadt. Kommst du mit?
   Felix: Wann denn?
   Petra: Um ein Uhr.
   Felix: Okay. Wo treffen wir uns?
   Petra: Bei mir.
4 Isabell: Hi, Michael! Hier spricht Isabell.
   Michael: Grüß dich, Isabell.
   Isabell: Michael, was sagst du? Möchtest du am Freitag mit mir in die Disco gehen?
   Michael: Aber gern! Wann beginnt die denn?
   Isabell: Um 22 Uhr.
   Michael: Ist gut! Wo treffen wir uns?
   Isabell: Vor dem Jugendklub.
   Michael: Toll! Bis dann!

2b Schreib die Sätze aus Übung 2a auf. (Writing)

Based on a provided example, students write four sentences giving the information gained from the phone conversations in exercise 2a.

Answers

1 Birgit und Rosita gehen heute Abend ins Kino und treffen sich um acht Uhr vor dem Kino. **2** Robert und Uli gehen heute Nachmittag um drei Uhr ins Schwimmbad und treffen sich im Sportzentrum.

55

3 Petra und Felix gehen heute Nachmittag um ein Uhr in die Stadt und treffen sich bei Petra. **4** Isabell und Michael gehen heute Abend um 22 Uhr in die Disco und treffen sich vor dem Jugendklub.

Grammatik: Präpositionen (prepositions)

The following prepositions take the accusative where motion is involved and the dative where there is no motion: *in, an, auf, hinter, unter, neben, über, zwischen, vor*. *In* is used to describe a place inside a building; *vor* is used to describe being outside (i.e. in front of) a building.

Explain to students that this is one of the most vexed aspects of German for English-speaking learners. The teacher may well wish to go into detail here with explanations in English, extra activities using OHTs, blackboard and classroom objects. More practice is available in the Grammar section as well as in the book *German Grammar 11–14* (Gray and Stevens, *Heinemann*).

3 Partnerarbeit. Schaut die Bilder an und macht Gespräche. (Speaking)

Working in pairs, students make arrangements to meet. Before starting, they should plan carefully, consulting the Grammar box to ensure that what they say will be linguistically accurate. Tell them that approximation may be acceptable at Foundation Level, but that at Higher Level, examiners are looking for accuracy.

Tip box

How to use *weil* when declining invitations. This is another opportunity to practise using *weil*.

4 Partnerarbeit. Schaut die Bilder an und macht Gespräche. (Speaking)

In pairs, students practise declining invitations and explaining why.

5 Lies die Einladung und schreib drei weitere Einladungen an deine Klassenkameraden. Schreib Antworten auf die Einladungen. (Writing / Reading)

Students write three invitations to give to classmates. Then everyone should write replies to the invitations they receive, saying whether they can come or not. If not, what is the reason?

Further practice of the language and vocabulary of this unit is given on the following pages.
Speaking: p. 72, Rollenspiel 1
Workbook: p. 20

Logo! 4 3 Wir haben frei!

6 Wir gehen aus! (pp. 50–51)

Students will learn how to:
- find out about events and activities

Key language	Was kostet der Eintritt für Erwachsene / Kinder?
Was läuft im Theater / Stadium / Freizeitzentrum / in der Stadthalle?	Ich nehme eine / zwei Karte(n).
Was für ein Stück / Spiel ist es?	**Skill focus**
Wann / Um wie viel Uhr …	• *Wann? Um wie viel Uhr?*
beginnt das Stück / Spiel?	**Resources**
macht das Schwimmbad / Stadion auf?	• Cassette A, Side B
	• Sprechen p. 72, Rollenspiel 2

1 Lies die Anzeigen und beantworte die Fragen auf Deutsch (ganze Sätze, bitte!). (Reading / Writing)

Point out to students that in the Higher Level exam, they will often be asked to write reasonably accurate answers in German. For this reason, they will now increasingly find that they are required to do this in *Logo! 4*. Here, they study five newspaper advertisements for events and write answers to questions in order to demonstrate that they have understood.

Answers

1 a Es gibt ein Fußballspiel. b Borussia Dortmund und Eintracht Frankfurt spielen. c Das Spiel beginnt um 14 Uhr. d Der Eintritt kostet €15,00. e Man kommt am besten mit dem Bus hin. 2 a Es gibt ein Handballspiel. b Der Turnier beginnt um 15 Uhr. c Man muss nichts zahlen (Eintritt ist frei). 3 a Das Schwimmbad macht am Montag um 8 Uhr auf. b Das Schwimmbad ist am Sonntag nicht geschlossen. c Peter zahlt €1,75. d Sein Vater zahlt €2,50. 4 a Shakespeare hat das Theaterstück geschrieben. b Es beginnt um 19.30 Uhr. c Der Eintritt kostet weniger als das Fußballspiel. 5 a Es gibt eine Computerausstellung. b Die Aufstellung macht um 9 Uhr auf. c Sie findet im März statt. d Man muss nichts zahlen (Eintritt ist frei).

2 Hör zu! Schreib die Anzeigen ab und trag die Informationen ein. (Listening)

Students copy the advertisements for events and fill in the information based on what they hear on the tape. The tape may need to be played several times.

Answers

1 Sport: Schwimmen; Beginn: 10 Uhr; Preis: €3,50 Erwachsene, €1,75 Kinder. 2 Titel: „Cats"; Typ: Musical; Beginn: 2.30 Uhr; Preis: €12,50. 3 Sport: Fußball; München gegen: Hertha Berlin; Beginn: 15 Uhr; Preis: €12,50

1 – Guten Tag. Freizeitbad Kronberg.
 – Guten Tag. Wann macht das Schwimmbad heute auf?
 – Um 10 Uhr.
 – Und wann macht es wieder zu?
 – Um 21 Uhr.
 – Und was kostet der Eintritt?
 – Für Erwachsene €3,50 und für Kinder €1,75.
 – Danke schön!
2 – Königstheater, Guten Tag.
 – Guten Tag. Welches Stück läuft im Moment?
 – „Cats" von Andrew Lloyd Webber.
 – Aha, und was für ein Stück ist das?
 – Das ist ein Musical.
 – Um wie viel Uhr beginnt das Stück?
 – Um 2.30.
 – Und was kostet der Eintritt?
 – €12,50.
3 Guten Tag. Hier spricht der Telefondienst vom Fußballverein Bayern München. Leider ist im Moment unser Büro geschlossen. Unser nächstes Spiel ist am kommenden Samstag um 15 Uhr, gegen Hertha Berlin. Die Karten kosten €12,50. Danke schön.

Tip box

Use *Um wie viel Uhr?* to replace *Wann?* to add variety. In general, advise students to avoid being too repetitive if they can, for stylistic reasons.

3a Partnerarbeit. A (▲) möchte ins Kino / Theater gehen. Er / Sie ruft an. B (●) antwortet. Macht *drei* Telefongespräche. (Speaking)

Working in pairs, students now create phone conversations finding out information about events. Partner B makes up the information. Students should take it in turns to ask and answer questions. Students need to note down the information for use in exercise 3b.

3b Schreib die Informationen aus Übung 3a auf. (Writing)

Using the information provided by partners in the previous speaking activity, students now write out the venue, time and price of the events.

Further practice of the language and vocabulary of this unit is given on the following page.
Speaking: p. 72, Rollenspiel 2

7 Rezensionen (pp. 52–53)

Students will learn how to:
- describe films, books and programmes

Key language	Grammar focus
Die Sendung heißt …	• perfect tense
Sie läuft am (Dienstag).	
Der Film / das Buch / die Sendung war …	**Skill focus**
zu lang / langweilig / spannend / gut.	• use perfect tense and opinions when describing films and programmes
Gestern / Letzte Woche habe ich …	
einen Film / eine Sendung gesehen.	**Resources**
ein Buch gelesen.	• Cassette A, Side B

The main purpose of this spread is extended reading practice, but introduce the theme by finding out (in English or German) what books, TV programmes and shows students have experienced recently. Can they tell you anything about them in German?

1a Lies den Text rechts. Wie heißt die Sendung? An welchem Tag läuft sie? (Reading / Writing)
Students read extracts from a TV listings magazine and demonstrate that they have understood which programmes are being referred to in the exercise by naming the programmes and what days they are on, as in the example.

Answers

1 Die Sendung heißt „Wer verliert?". Sie läuft am Donnerstag. 2 Die Sendung heißt „Radiohead Live in Berlin". Sie läuft am Samstag. 3 Die Sendung heißt „Urlaub in Frankreich". Sie läuft am Dienstag. 4 Die Sendung heißt „Elefanten im Zirkus". Sie läuft am Freitag. 5 Die Sendung heißt „Fußball: Europameisterschaft". Sie läuft am Sonntag.

1b Beschreib die Sendungen aus Übung 1a. Schreib im Perfekt. (Writing)
Students now use their imagination to pretend that they have seen the programmes in exercise 1a. They must describe them using the perfect tense. This is a challenging activity but should be fun. It can be set for homework.

Answers

A variety of responses are acceptable here. Teachers should mark using their own discretion.

2 Lies den Text auf Seite 53 und beschreib die Bücher. Schreib im Perfekt. (Writing / Reading)
Students descibe the books reviewed by putting the descriptions into the perfect tense. Actually, this is just an old-fashioned grammar exercise, but students don't need to be told that!

Answers

A variety of responses are acceptable here. Teachers should mark using their own discretion. Here are some suggested answers.

Das letzte Buch, das ich gelesen habe, war „Harry Potter und die Kammer des Schreckens" von J. K. Rowling. Der junge Zauberer hat gegen ein Tier gekämpft. Er hat gewonnen und hat seine Freunde gerettet.

Das letzte Buch, das ich gelesen habe, war „Einsatz in Kopenhagen" von Anton Becker. Der Privatdetektiv Ulrich Meisel ist nach Dänemark gefahren und hat einen Drogendealer aus Hamburg gesucht. Aber in Kopenhagen hat er nur ein junges, hübsches Mädchen gefunden. War sie auch in der Drogengang?

Das letzte Buch, das ich gelesen habe, war „Der Dschungelkönig" von Anni Huber. In diesem Kinderbuch hat der Löwe Goldi mit seiner Familie im Dschungel gelebt. Aber es gab / hat ein Problem gegeben. Die Menschen haben den Dschungel zerstört und haben Häuser und Fabriken gebaut. Die Tiere haben um ihre Heimat gekämpft.

Das letzte Buch, das ich gelesen habe, war „Welcher Computer ist am besten?" von Dr. Emil Obermeier. Ein Computerexperte hat die besten Computer, Scanner und Monitore beschrieben. Dies war ein interessantes Werk. Dr. Obermeier hat mit 82 Computern gearbeitet und hat die besten vorgestellt.

3a Hör zu! Der Rap-Star Wilko Wunderlich beschreibt seinen Lieblingsfilm. Wähle die beste Antwort. (Listening)
Students listen to a German rap star talking about his favourite film and answer multiple-choice questions about it. They may have to listen several times.

Answers

1 b, 2 b, 3 a, 4 c, 5 c

> **Mein bester Film**
> *Der Rap-Star Wilko Wunderlich beschreibt seinen Lieblingsfilm:* Mein Lieblingsfilm ist *Blair Witch Project*. Das ist ein amerikanischer Gruselfilm. Er ist toll, aber auch grausam! Vier junge Studenten gehen in den Wald und suchen eine Hexe, die „Blair Witch" heißt. Aber auf einmal wissen sie nicht mehr, wo sie sind. Es ist dunkel und sie haben Angst. Eine Studentin filmt alles mit ihrer Videokamera …

Logo! 4 3 Wir haben frei!

3b Beschreib den Film aus Übung 3a im Perfekt. (Writing)

Now students write down as much detail as they can remember about the *Blair Witch Project*. Teachers can offer assistance with vocabulary and information.

Suggested answer

Mein Lieblingsfilm war „Blair Witch Project". Das war ein Gruselfilm aus den USA. Die Studenten sind in den Wald gegangen und haben eine Hexe gesucht. Auf einmal haben sie nicht mehr gewusst, wo sie waren. Eine Studentin hat alles mit ihrer Videokamera gefilmt.

4 Jetzt du. Beschreib einen Film, den du gesehen hast, eine Fernsehsendung, die du gesehen hast und ein Buch, das du gelesen hast. (Writing)

Students use the Tip box at the bottom of the page to help them to construct information about films, books and TV shows they have enjoyed. This is a favourite question in Speaking Tests, so they need to be well prepared.

All the vocabulary and structures from this chapter are listed on the *Wörter* pages at the end (pp. 54–55). These can be used for revision by covering up either the English or the German. Students can check here to see how much they remember from the chapter.

For more speaking practice to do with this chapter, use p. 72.

Further grammar and speaking practice of the language of this chapter is provided on pp. 21–22 of the Workbook.

Assessment materials for Chapters 3 and 4 are available after Chapter 4.

Workbook (pp. 16–22)

p. 16

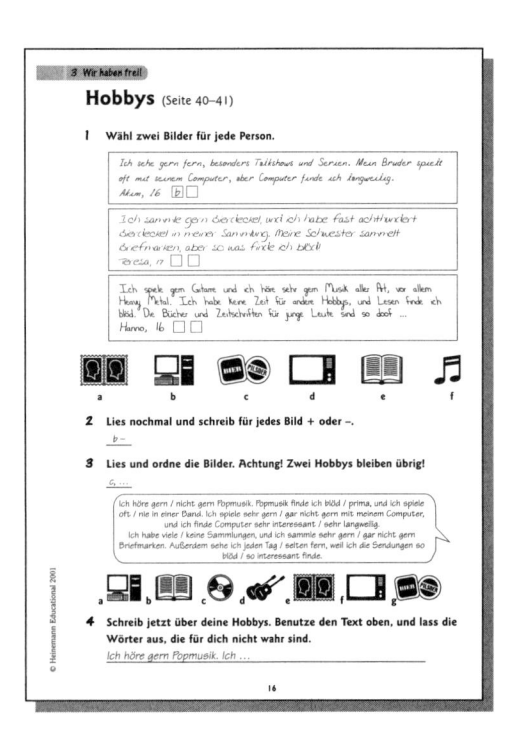

p. 17

1 Akim: b, d; Teresa: a, c; Hanno: e, f
2 b –, d +; a –, c +; e –, f +
3 c, d, a, e, f: b and g are left over
4 open-ended

1 18.00 Bedrohte Tiere, 18.30 Popeye, 19.00 Komm rein, 20.00 Hits der Woche
(These are the *only* programmes to which no family members object.)
2 open-ended: overlook minor errors

p. 18

1 Lieber Manfred!

Wie war dein Wochenende? Mein Wochenende war **so-o-o-o langweilig**! Am Freitagabend habe ich also nur ferngesehen. Das Programm war aber **furchtbar** – zwei doofe Quizsendungen und die Lotto. Ich bin <u>um zehn Uhr</u> ins Bett gegangen und am Samstagmorgen bin ich spät aufgestanden.

<u>Um zwei Uhr</u> bin ich mit dem Bus in die Stadtmitte gefahren, aber es gab in den Geschäften nichts Neues und ich habe nichts gekauft. Die Geschäfte hier sind **langweilig**. <u>Um halb sechs</u> bin ich nach Hause gefahren und habe Abendbrot gegessen. Danach habe ich wieder ferngesehen – aber das Programm war wieder **furchtbar**!

Sonntag war **kaum besser**. Am Morgen bin ich bis <u>elf Uhr</u> im Bett geblieben und habe gelesen (das Wetter war schon wieder **furchtbar**). <u>Um elf Uhr</u> bin ich aufgestanden, und ich habe mit meinem Computer gespielt. Um <u>zwei Uhr</u> bin ich nach Georgs Haus gegangen. <u>Um sechs Uhr</u> bin ich nach Hause gekommen und habe Abendbrot gegessen. Danach habe ich mein Buch gelesen und bin wiederum früh ins Bett gegangen. Nach so einem Wochenende war es **spannend** am Montag in die Schule zu gehen!

Was hast du am Wochenende gemacht? Schreib bald wieder!

Bis bald, Rainer

(Opinions in bold type; times underlined.)

2 1 Er hat ferngesehen. **2** Das Programm war furchtbar. **3** Nein, er ist spät aufgestanden. **4** Er hat nichts gemacht. **5** Er ist in die Stadtmitte gefahren.
3 open-ended

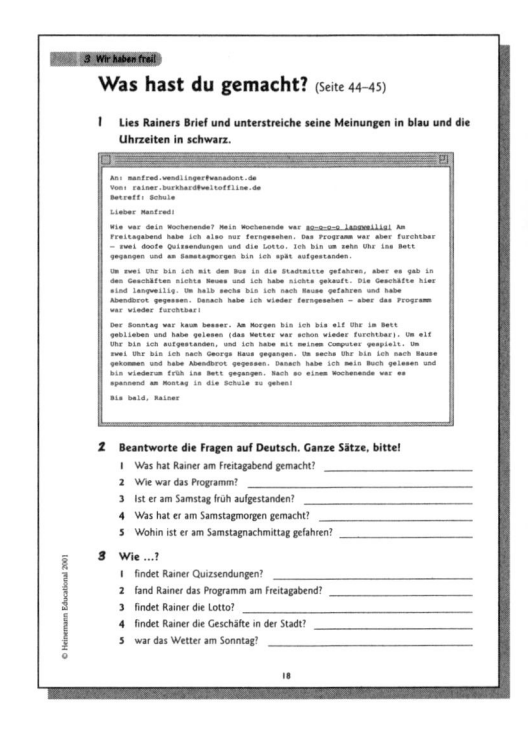

Logo! 4 3 Wir haben frei!

p. 19

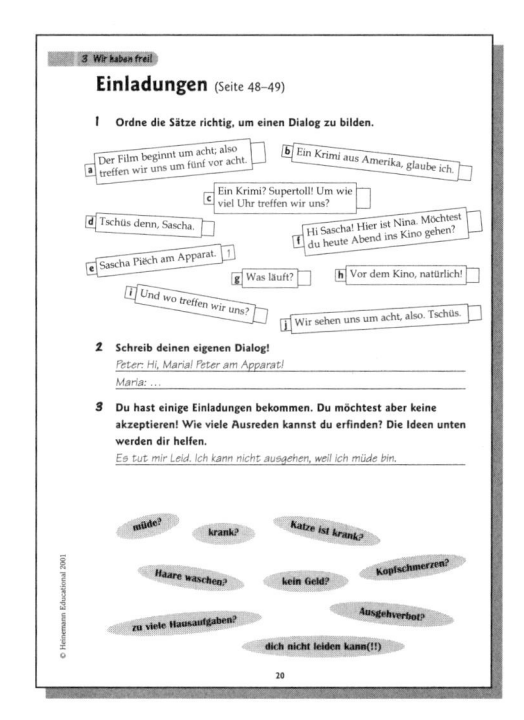

1 1 – ja, 2 – ja, 3 – nein, 4 – nein
2 open-ended
3 open-ended

p. 20

1 1e, 2f, 3g, 4b, 5c, 6a, 7i, 8h, 9j, 10d
2 open-ended
3 open-ended

p. 21

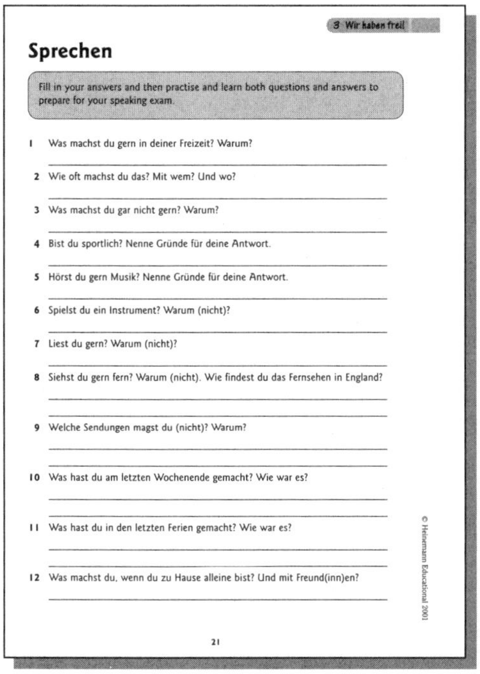

no answers – *Sprechen*

p. 22

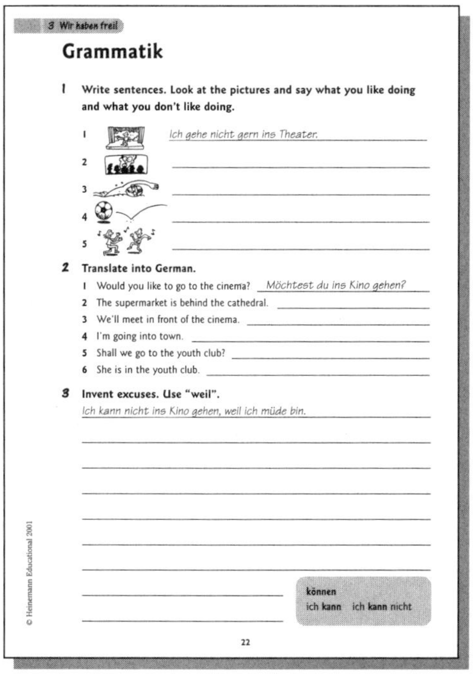

1 open-ended
2 1 Möchtest du ins Kino gehen? 2 Der Supermarkt ist hinter dem Dom. 3 Wir treffen uns vor dem Kino.
4 Ich gehe in die Stadt. 5 Wollen wir in den Jugendklub gehen? 6 Sie ist im Jugendklub.
3 open-ended

61

4 Urlaub (Student's Book pp. 56–73)

Topic area	Key language	Grammar	Skills
4.1 Woher kommst du? (pp. 56–57) Countries and nationalities Weather	in (Großbritannien) / in den (USA) / in der (Schweiz) Warschau ist in Polen. Ich bin / Er / Sie ist Amerikaner(in), Deutsche(r), Engländer(in) usw. Es ist kalt / neblig / stürmisch / sonnig / windig / wolkig / warm / kühl / nass / heiter. Es regnet / donnert und blitzt / friert / schneit / hagelt. Es gibt Frost / Gewitter / Nebel / Regen / Schauer / Sonne / Schnee / Sturm / Wind.	Nationalities (masculine and feminine)	Gist listening Coping with unknown vocabulary in reading passages
4.2 Wohin fahren wir? (pp. 58–59) Plan a holiday	Ich / Er / Sie möchte / will … Man kann … Wir möchten / Wir wollen … ans Meer / aufs Land / ins Ausland / nach Amerika / in die Berge fahren / am Strand liegen / im Meer schwimmen / zu einem Ferienpark fahren / einen Städtetour / Flugreise machen. Da kann man … gut schwimmen / in der Sonne liegen / faulenzen / wandern / Mountainbike fahren / in die Disco gehen. Können Sie mir bitte Informationen / eine Broschüre / einen Prospekt / einen Plan / eine Landkarte schicken?	Man kann …	Speaking in the future tense Writing a formal letter
4.3 Unterkunft (pp. 60–61) Find and book accommodation	Haben Sie ein Einzelzimmer / Doppelzimmer? Ich möchte / Wir möchten zwei Nächte / eine Woche bleiben. Halbpension / Vollpension Ist das Zimmer mit Dusche / Bad / Fernsehen / inklusive Frühstück? Gibt es ein Restaurant? Um wie viel Uhr ist das Frühstück / Abendessen? Kann ich bitte meinen Schlüssel haben / die Rechnung haben?		
4.4 Probleme mit der Unterkunft (pp. 62–63) Cope with accommodation problems	Wie viel kostet … ? Um wie viel Uhr gibt es … ? Ich möchte … Einzel- / Doppelzimmer reservieren. Der Aufzug / Das Bett / Die Dusche war kaputt. Das Frühstück war kalt. Die Zimmer waren schmutzig / klein / teuer. Ich möchte mit dem Direktor sprechen.		Dealing with the unpredictable in role-plays Writing to book a hotel room Useful transferable phrases
4.5 Die letzten Ferien (pp. 64–65) Describe a holiday in the past	Ich war / Wir waren in (Spanien). Ich bin / Wir sind mit meiner Familie / Freunden dorthin gefahren / eine Woche geblieben / mit dem Auto / Zug dorthin gefahren / mit dem Flugzeug usw. geflogen. Ich habe in einem Hotel / Wohnwagen usw. übernachtet. Wir haben auf einem Campingplatz gewohnt. Das Wetter war sonnig / kalt / heiß usw. Es hat (viel) geregnet.	Question words Revision of perfect tense *war / waren*	Use *wir* when describing holidays

4.6 **Urlaubsspaß** (pp. 66–67) Say what you did on holiday	*Ich habe / Wir haben / Er / Sie hat / Sie haben in Paris eingekauft / auf Urlaub gemangelt / am Abend getanzt / am ersten Tag Fotos gemacht / am zweiten Tag eine Rundfahrt gemacht / am nächsten Tag Freunde getroffen / Tennis gespielt / mich / uns / sich / gesonnt. Ich bin / Wir sind / Er / Sie ist / Sie sind in die Disco / ins Kino / Restaurant / Schwimmbad / Museum / Sportzentrum / zum Strand gegangen / geschwommen / gewandert / spazieren gegangen / Ski gefahren / ausgegangen.*	Perfect tense Auxiliary verb comes second after time phrase Learn answers about holidays for exam
4.7 **Todtnauer Ferienland** (pp. 68–69) Understand information about a holiday area	*Man kann ein Buch ausleihen / übernachten / kegeln / zelten / Ski laufen / Tischtennis spielen / Kaffee trinken / Minigolf spielen / eine Massage haben.*	Extracting information from an authentic text Advice on making a brochure

- The vocabulary and structures taught in Chapter 4 are summarised on the *Wörter* pages of the Student's Book, 70–71.
- Further speaking practice on the language of this chapter is provided on p. 73.
- Coursework pages relating to this chapter can be found on pp. 178–179.
- Further reading and writing practice on the language of this chapter is provided on pp. 192–193.
- For a selection of assessment tasks for Chapters 3 and 4, please refer to the separate Assessment Pack for your chosen examination board: AQA, OCR or Edexcel.

1 Woher kommst du?

(pp. 56–57)

Students will learn how to:
- talk about nationalities and countries
- talk about the weather

Key language
in Afrika / Amerika / Belgien / Dänemark / Frankreich / Griechenland / Großbritannien / Holland / Irland / Italien / Norwegen / Österreich / Polen / Rumänien / Russland / Schottland / Schweden / Spanien / Ungarn / Wales
in den Alpen / USA / in der Schweiz / Slowakei / Tschechischen Republik / Türkei
Warschau ist in Polen.
Ich bin / Er / Sie ist Amerikaner(in), Deutsche(r), Engländer(in) usw.
Est ist kalt / neblig / stürmisch / sonnig / windig / wolkig / warm / kühl / nass / heiter.
Es regnet / donnert und blitzt / friert / schneit / hagelt.

Grammar focus
- nationalities (masculine and feminine)

Skill focus
- gist listening
- coping with unknown vocabulary in reading passages

Resources
- Cassette B, Side A
- Workbook p. 23

Before starting this spread, revise by brainstorming names of European countries and cities in German. Do students remember any towns which are not the same in German and English? (e.g. *Rom, Köln, Genf*). Remind them that, even if the spelling is the same, the pronunciation might not be (London, Paris).

1 Hör zu! Was ist richtig? Was ist falsch? (Listening / Reading)

Students listen to the tape of a geography lesson as often as necessary in order to decide whether the statements are true or false. It is possible that they know the answers anyway, but the tape will help them with pronunciation.

More able students should be encouraged to provide the correct answers as well: *Falsch. München ist nicht in England, München ist in Deutschland.*

Answers
1 Falsch. 2 Falsch. 3 Richtig. 4 Falsch. 5 Richtig.
6 Richtig. 7 Falsch. 8 Richtig.

Lehrer: So, Leute, heute geht's um Städte und Länder. In welchem Land ist Köln?
Schülerin 1: Ich glaube, Köln ist in Deutschland, Herr Wolf.
Lehrer: Ja, das stimmt. Aber ist München auch in Deutschland?
Schülerin 2: Ja, natürlich! Klar ist München in Deutschland, im Süden.
Lehrer: Gut! Und in welchem Land ist Marseille?
Schülerin: 3: Marseille liegt in Frankreich, Herr Wolf. Das weiß ich, weil wir letztes Jahr in Frankreich waren.
Lehrer: So, so. Und ist Berlin in Frankreich?
Schüler 1: Nein, natürlich nicht! Berlin liegt in Deutschland, das weiß doch jeder!
Lehrer: Gut! Und in welchem Land ist Avila?
Schüler 2: Äh ... Avila ... Ist Avila in Italien?
Lehrer: Nein!
Schülerin 4: Ich weiß es, Herr Wolf. Avila ist in Spanien. Und Madrid ist auch in Spanien.
Lehrer: Richtig! Und wo ist Arhus?
Schüler 3: Äääh ... Ist Arhus in Dänemark?
Schüler 4: Ja. Und Kopenhagen ist die Hauptstadt von Dänemark.

2 Partnerarbeit. (Speaking)

Working in pairs, students ask and answer simple questions about towns and countries in Europe. They can continue this activity by making up lots of extra questions of their own.

Grammatik: Nationalitäten (nationalities)

A list showing the masculine and feminine versions of nationalities. Students can refer to this list when doing exercise 3.

3 Schreib einen Satz für jede Person. (Writing)

Students write sentences giving the nationality of the people in the pictures.

Answers
1 Thomas ist Deutscher. 2 Mary ist Irin. 3 Johan ist Holländer. 4 Susie ist Engländerin. 5 Paco ist Spanier.
6 Giovanni ist Italiener.

Tip box

Students don't need to understand every word to comprehend the sense of a listening passage. This point is made several times in *Logo! 4*. Students must be reminded to concentrate on capitalising on what they do understand, rather than being intimidated by what they don't.

4 Hör zu! Wo sind die Personen? (Listening / Writing)

Students listen to people describing the weather where they are. With the help of the weather map provided, they must work out where each person is and write it down.

Logo! 4 4 Urlaub

After completing this exercise, students can do some oral pair-work based on the same weather map:
A: Wie ist das Wetter?
B: Es regnet.
A: Du bist in Großbritannien.
B: Richtig!

Answers

1 in der Schweiz, 2 in Spanien, 3 in England, 4 in Frankreich, 5 in Belgien, 6 in Norwegen, 7 in Italien, 8 in Holland

Further practice of the language and vocabulary of this unit is given on the following page.
Workbook: p. 23

1 – Hallo, Mutti! Hier spricht Angela!
  – Hallo, Angela! Wo bist du denn?
  – Ich bin in [bleep] und es ist sehr kalt!
2 – Hallo, Olli! Wir sitzen jeden Tag am Strand, weil es hier in [bleep] so warm ist.
3 – Na, Klaus, wie ist das Wetter in [bleep]?
  – Was denkst du? Ich bin doch in [bleep]. Es regnet, natürlich!
4 – Hier in [bleep] ist es sehr windig! Aber das finden wir eigentlich ganz gut, weil wir segeln.
5 – Wie ist das Wetter in [bleep]?
  – Nicht besonders gut. Es ist neblig. Es ist gefährlich, wenn wir Autobahn fahren.
6 – Ist es schön in [bleep]?
  – Nein, es ist stürmisch! Es donnert und blitzt hier. Schrecklich!
7 – Ist es kalt in [bleep]?
  – Nein, Gott sei Dank, hier in Venedig ist es ganz sonnig!
8 – Wo bist du, Silke?
  – Gestern waren wir in Belgien, aber heute sind wir in [bleep]. Hier ist es leider wolkig.

5 Lies die Wettervorhersage rechts und beantworte die Fragen auf Englisch. (Reading)
Students read a typical German newspaper weather report and answer some questions in English.

Answers

1 in the south and south-east, 2 highest temperature in south and south-east, 3 cloudy with some showers, 4 frost, 5 wind from the north, 6 continuing cool on Saturday, frost on Sunday.

Tip box
The compound word *Tageshöchtemperaturen* is used as an example to show how to work out the meaning of the whole word by looking at the separate parts. If time permits, students might like to look for more examples of compound words for others to work out.

6 Schreib eine Postkarte aus dem Urlaub. Schreib, wo du bist, wie das Wetter ist und auch andere Informationen. (Writing)
Following the example given, students write a holiday postcard, making up the weather conditions.

2 Wohin fahren wir? (pp. 58–59)

Students will learn how to:
- plan a holiday

Key language
Ich / Er / Sie möchte / will ...
Man kann / Da kann man ...
Wir möchten / Wir wollen ...
  in die Berge fahren.
  am Strand liegen.
  im Meer schwimmen.
  zu einem Ferienpark fahren.
Können Sie mir bitte Informationen / eine Broschüre schicken?

Grammar focus
- *man kann ...*

Skill focus
- speaking in the future tense
- writing a formal letter

Resources
- Cassette B, Side A
- Workbook p. 24
- Sprechen p. 73, Gespräch 1

Before starting this spread, discuss in English what considerations are important when planning a holiday. Find out where students prefer to go. How much of this can they already say in German?

1 Hör zu! Verbinde die Namen mit den Bildern. (Listening)
Students listen to a family discussing holiday plans and write letters to indicate which pictures show what the individual people want to do. This may well need to be heard several times. Make sure students realise that they are giving two answers for each person.

Answers
1 Hans: a, h, 2 Helga: b, g, 3 Jessica: c, e, 4 Frank: d, f

> **Vater (Hans):** Also, was machen wir in den Sommerferien? Bleiben wir zu Hause oder fahren wir weg? Was meinst du, Helga?
> **Mutter (Helga):** Also, Hans, du weißt, was ich mag. Ich möchte ans Meer fahren, vielleicht nach Frankreich oder Spanien. Ich möchte schwimmen, am Strand liegen, lesen und faulenzen. Ist das nicht eine tolle Idee, Jessica?
> **Jessica:** Ach nee, dazu habe ich keine Lust! Das ist doch langweilig. Ich möchte zu einem Ferienpark. Da wird es es mehr für junge Leute geben, Discos zum Beispiel. Nicht wahr, Frank?
> **Frank:** Discos? Um Gottes Willen, das ist nichts für mich. Ich möchte lieber in die Berge fahren. Da werden wir schön wandern und Mountainbike fahren können. Du auch, Vati?
> **Vater:** Mountainbike fahren ... dafür bin ich zu alt. Ich möchte lieber eine Städtetour machen und etwas Kultur genießen, ein paar Schlösser und Museen ansehen ...

Tip box
In German, as in English, you can use the present to express future intent. However, to gain a high mark in a Writing or Speaking Test, students need to use the 'proper' future tense. Recognising the future in Reading and Listening Tests is important too. Check that students also remember how to use *ich will* and *ich möchte* to express what they *want* to do.

Wiederholung: können (to be able to)
Man kann is used with the infinitive at the end of the sentence. Tell students that they are being reminded about this because it's such a common and useful expression for talking about hobbies, holidays, towns, etc.

2 Partnerarbeit. (Speaking)
Working in pairs, students ask and answer questions about holidays and what one can do. Students should take it in turns to ask and answer questions and they are welcome to think up further prompts of their own.

3 Lies den Brief und beantworte die Fragen auf Deutsch (ganze Sätze, bitte!). (Reading / Writing)
As a result of the family disagreement in exercise 1, Hans Golinski has written this letter asking for advice. Students read the letter and write sentences describing what sort of holiday each family member has in mind. Marking can be flexible.

Answers
1 Er möchte einen kulturellen Urlaub machen. 2 Sie möchte am Strand liegen und im Meer schwimmen. 3 Sie möchte zu einem Ferienpark fahren. 4 Er möchte in die Berge fahren.

4 Schreib einen Brief an einen Verkehrsverein. (Writing)
Encourage students to write in as much detail as they can. This work should be collected and marked.

Tip box
Instructions on how to start and finish a formal letter and a reminder to use the *Sie* form. Emphasise to students that they are very likely, at Higher Level (and in real life) to have to write a formal letter asking for information.

Die Lösung!
Students read the final solution to the problem of a holiday destination to suit all the members of the Golinski family. Ask them to explain it orally in English.

Further practice of the language and vocabulary of this unit is given on the following pages.
Speaking: p. 73, Gespräch 1
Workbook: p. 24

# 3 Unterkunft (pp. 60–61)

Students will learn how to:
- find and book accommodation

Key language	Gibt es ein Restaurant / einen Aufzug?
Haben Sie ein Einzelzimmer / Doppelzimmer?	Um wie viel Uhr ist das Frühstück / Abendessen?
Ich möchte / Wir möchten …	Kann ich bitte meinen Schlüssel haben / die Rechnung haben?
zwei Nächte / eine Woche bleiben.	
Halbpension / Vollpension.	**Resources**
Ist das Zimmer mit Dusche / Bad / Fernsehen / inklusive Frühstück?	• Cassette B, Side A • Workbook p. 25 • Sprechen p. 73, Rollenspiel 1

Start this spread by asking students what vocabulary they recall for describing facilities in a hotel.

1 Hör zu! Welches Zimmer nimmt Herr Franz? (Listening)

Students listen to a conversation and choose one picture which describes which room Herr Franz takes.

Answer

room c

> Herr Franz: Guten Abend!
> Empfangsperson: Guten Abend. Was kann ich für Sie tun?
> Herr Franz: Haben Sie ein Zimmer frei?
> Empfangsperson: Für wie viele Personen?
> Herr Franz: Für zwei Personen.
> Empfangsperson: Also ein Doppelzimmer … Moment mal … Ja, wir haben ein Doppelzimmer frei im ersten Stock.
> Herr Franz: Ist das Zimmer mit Bad?
> Empfangsperson: Nein, nicht mit Bad, mit Dusche. Natürlich hat das Zimmer Fernsehen, Radio und Telefon.
> Herr Franz: Hat das Zimmer zwei Einzelbetten?
> Empfangsperson: Nein, ein Doppelbett.

2 Partnerarbeit. Partner(in) A (▲) stellt die Fragen. Partner(in) B (●) erfindet Antworten. (Speaking)

Working in pairs, students construct a lengthy conversation using lots of vocabulary and structures connected with accommodation. Advise them to look at all the pictures and symbols carefully before they start and make sure that students do the activity, taking it in turns to ask and answer questions.

3a Hör zu, lies das Gespräch und beantworte die Fragen auf Deutsch (ganze Sätze, bitte!). (Listening / Reading)

The conversation continues. This time, it is printed on the page. Students answer questions using full sentences in German, so they need to tread carefully.

Answers

1 Es kostet €60,00 pro Person. 2 Es kostet €120,00 pro Nacht. 3 Ja, der Preis ist inklusive Frühstück. 4 Nein, er bezahlt mit Visakarte (Kreditkarte). 5 Es ist im ersten Stock. 6 Frühstück ist von acht Uhr bis neun Uhr dreißig.

3b Partnerarbeit. Lest das Gespräch aus Übung 3a und ändert es. (Speaking)

Working in pairs, students change elements of the conversation in exercise 3a and read out the changed version.

4 Schau die Hotelwerbung an. Richtig, falsch oder nicht im Text? (Reading)

Students look at the hotel information and say whether the statements are true, false or not in the text.

Answers

1 Falsch. 2 Richtig. 3 Falsch. 4 Richtig. 5 Richtig. 6 Falsch. 7 Richtig. 8 Nicht im Text.

5 Schreib eine Anzeige für ein Hotel, wenn möglich auf Computer. (Writing)

Using the advertisement in exercise 4 as a prompt, invite students to invent a hotel and construct an advert for it. Alternatively, they can take a real hotel in their area and devise an advert for it in German. This activity can be done on a computer using a drawing programme.

Further practice of the language and vocabulary of this unit is given on the following pages.
Speaking: p. 73, Rollenspiel 1
Workbook: p. 25

Logo! 4 4 Urlaub

4 Probleme mit der Unterkunft (pp. 62–63)

Students will learn how to:
- cope with accommodation problems

Key language	Skill focus
Gibt es ein Restaurant / einen Aufzug? Wie viel kostet …? Um wie viel Uhr gibt es …? Ich möchte … Einzel- / Doppelzimmer reservieren. Der Aufzug / Das Bett / Die Dusche war kaputt. Das Frühstück war kalt. Die Zimmer waren schmutzig / klein / teuer. Ich möchte mit dem Direktor sprechen.	• dealing with the unpredictable in role-plays • writing to book a hotel room • useful transferable phrases **Resources** • Cassette B, Side A • Workbook p. 26 • Sprechen p. 73, Rollenspiel 2

Start this spread by asking students what kind of problems might cause them to complain about accommodation. How much of this would they be able to do in German?

1 Lies das Telefax und beantworte die Fragen auf Deutsch (ganze Sätze, bitte!). (Reading / Writing)

Students read a fax sent to a hotel in Lübeck and answer questions about it in full German sentences. This is best done as an individual exercise, either in class or for homework.

Answers

1 Sie möchte zwei Zimmer reservieren. 2 Sie möchte ein Doppelzimmer mit zwei Einzelbetten reservieren. 3 Sie will im Juli nach Lübeck fahren. 4 Sie möchte zwei Nächte bleiben. 5 Ja, sie möchte Frühstück und Abendbrot (Halbpension). 6 Weil ihr Mann sein Bein gebrochen hat.

Tip box
Advice on how to cope with the unpredictable in role-plays. Emphasise to students that this really is a fundamental difference between Foundation and Higher role-play. They must keep their wits about them and be ready to act upon unpredicted responses. They should use all the role-play exercises in *Logo! 4* as flexible tools which they can adapt as they wish, making the conversations as natural as possible and testing the alertness of their partners. These tasks are not as 'wooden' as Foundation Level role-plays.

2 Partnerarbeit. Partner(in) A (▲) stellt Fragen. Partner(in) B (●) erfindet Antworten. (Speaking)

Working in pairs, students create short hotel dialogues based on the prompts provided.

Tip box
Help with phrases to book a hotel room. Point out how much can be achieved with a relatively limited range of phrases. Those listed here will probably cover any eventuality likely to crop up in GCSE (or in real life) in the area of accommodation.

3 Schreib einen Brief an ein Hotel. Reserviere diese Zimmer. (Writing)

Based on these prompts, students write a letter to reserve two hotel rooms.

4 Hör zu. Richtig, falsch oder nicht im Text? (Listening)

Students listen to a conversation in which Frau Haas complains about the hotel and decide whether the statements are true, false or not mentioned. If they are false, students can correct them: *Nein, der Aufzug war nicht in Ordnung, er war kaputt.*

Answers

1 Nicht im Text. 2 Falsch. 3 Falsch. 4 Falsch. 5 Nicht im Text. 6 Falsch.

Frau Haas und ihre Familie sind im Hotel Prinzmeier, aber Frau Haas ist unzufrieden.

Frau Haas: Also, wir sind mit diesem Hotel nicht zufrieden! Wir haben ein Zimmer mit zwei Einzelbetten für die Kinder reserviert, aber das Zimmer hat ein Doppelbett. In unserem Zimmer ist die Dusche kalt und der Fernseher ist kaputt! Die Zimmer sind auch schmutzig und in meinem Frühstück habe ich eine Fliege gefunden! Es gibt einen Aufzug, aber der ist auch kaputt. Die Zimmer sind klein und viel zu teuer. Was sagen Sie dazu?
Empfangsperson: Es tut mir Leid, Frau Haas.
Frau Haas: Ich möchte mit dem Direktor sprechen.
Empfangsperson: Selbstverständlich, Frau Haas.

5 Partnerarbeit. (Speaking)

Working in pairs, students use the prompts to make a conversation about accommodation problems. They should also make up other similar conversations of their own.

6 Schreib einen Brief an ein schreckliches Hotel. Was war nicht in Ordnung? (Writing)

Students use the prompts to help them to write a letter complaining about a hotel. Encourage them to add even more horrors if they wish. This sort of letter may well crop up in the Higher Writing exam (and possibly in real life!).

> Further practice of the language and vocabulary of this unit is given on the following pages.
> Speaking: p. 73, Rollenspiel 2
> Workbook: p. 26

Logo! 4 4 Urlaub

5 Die letzten Ferien (pp. 64–65)

Students will learn how to:
- describe a holiday in the past

Key language
Ich war / Wir waren in (Spanien).
Ich bin / Wir sind …
   mit meiner Familie / Freunden dorthin gefahren.
   eine Woche / zwei Wochen geblieben.
   mit dem Auto / Zug / Bus / Rad dorthin gefahren.
   mit dem Flugzeug geflogen.
Ich habe in einem Hotel / Gasthaus / Wohnwagen übernachtet.
Wir haben auf einem Campingplatz gewohnt.
Das Wetter war sonnig / stürmisch / regnerisch / windig / neblig / warm / kalt / heiß / super / okay / schlecht / gut / nicht gut.
Es hat (viel) geregnet.

Grammar focus
- question words
- revision of perfect tense
- *war / waren*

Skill focus
- use *wir* when describing holidays

Resources
- Cassette B, Side A
- Workbook p. 27
- Sprechen p. 73, Gespräch 2

Before starting this spread, conduct a brief revision session to check that students are still confident about using the perfect tense.

1a Hör zu und lies die Texte. Welche vier Buchstaben passen zu Jasmin, zu Benjamin und zu Samira? (Listening / Reading)

Students listen to three young people describing their holidays and choose letters to identify who did what. Make sure students realise that they need to write four letters for each person. This can be done as a 'pure' listening with the text covered up if you wish.

Answers
Jasmin: c, f, h, j. **Benjamin:** b, d, i, l. **Samira:** a, e, g, k

> **Jasmin:** Also, ich bin mit meinen Freunden und Freundinnen nach Spanien gefahren. Wir waren in einem Wohnwagen in der Nähe von Tarragona. Wir sind mit dem Zug dorthin gefahren. Wir sind zwei Wochen geblieben. Das Wetter war super! Nur Sonne!
>
> **Benjamin:** Hier spricht der Benjamin! Also, ich war mit meiner Familie in Polen. Wir waren drei Wochen dort. Wir sind mit dem Auto nach Polen gefahren.
> Wir haben auf einem Campingplatz übernachtet. Es war okay, aber das Wetter war schlecht. Nur Regen! Auf dem Campingplatz! Furchtbar!
>
> **Samira:** Ich war eine Woche mit meiner Freundin in Amerika, in Kalifornien.
> Wir sind natürlich mit dem Flugzeug geflogen. Fliegen ist sehr schnell. Wir haben in einem Hotel gewohnt. Glücklicherweise war das Wetter schön warm.

1b Lies die Texte aus Übung 1a nochmal und beantworte die Fragen (ganze Sätze, bitte!). (Reading / Writing)

Now students reread the texts from exercise 1a and answer the same questions about all three of the people. They must write in German, in full sentences.

Answers
Jasmin: 1 Sie ist nach Spanien gefahren. 2 Sie ist zwei Wochen geblieben. 3 Sie ist mit dem Zug dorthin gefahren. 4 Sie hat in einem Wohnwagen gewohnt. 5 Sie ist mit ihren Freunden und Freundinnen gefahren. 6 Das Wetter war super.
Benjamin: 1 Er ist nach Polen gefahren. 2 Er ist drei Wochen geblieben. 3 Er ist mit dem Auto dorthin gefahren. 4 Er hat auf einem Campingplatz gewohnt. 5 Er ist mit seiner Familie gefahren. 6 Das Wetter war schlecht.
Samira: 1 Sie ist nach Amerika gefahren. 2 Sie ist eine Woche geblieben. 3 Sie ist mit dem Flugzeug geflogen. 4 Sie hat in einem Hotel gewohnt. 5 Sie ist mit ihrer Freundin gefahren. 6 Das Wetter war schön warm.

1c Partnerarbeit. Hier sind Jasmins Antworten. Du bist Benjamin oder Samira. Beantworte die Fragen. Dann erfinde Antworten für *dich*. (Speaking)

Again based on the same information, students conduct detailed interviews with the three people. Jasmin's answers are provided, so having read that version out, they must do the activity again with Benjamin and Samira. Finally, they answer for themselves, either telling the truth or inventing the answers.

Tip box
Explanation as to why German e-mail writers may add an -e after the vowel rather than use a character with an umlaut (computers may not reproduce characters with umlauts). The same applies to ß – writers replace with *ss*.
Indicate to students that they may need to do the same when writing e-mails in German.

2a Lies die E-Mail und beantworte die Fragen auf Deutsch (ganze Sätze, bitte!). (Reading / Writing)

Students read an e-mail about a holiday and answer questions in full German sentences.

Answers
1 Nein, er ist nach Irland gefahren. 2 Er ist zwei Wochen geblieben. 3 Er ist mit dem Auto dorthin gefahren. 4 Das Wetter war neblig und es hat geregnet. 5 Er ist mit seiner Familie dorthin gefahren. 6 Sie haben in einem Hotel übernachtet.

Wiederholung: Das Perfekt (perfect)
A revision of the perfect tense.

Grammatik: war / waren (was)
An explanation of the way to say 'was': *war / waren*.

These two grammar items can't be re-emphasised often enough! Remind students that they need to use both past tense forms in order to gain a high grade in the exam.

Tip box
Use *wir* when talking about holidays taken with other people. This will help to avoid the *ich* syndrome and will help make students sound more natural.

2b Du bist Lars. Schreib eine E-Mail an Uli mit den Informationen unten rechts. (Writing)
Students write a similar e-mail themselves, based on the information provided.

2c Erfinde jetzt eine E-Mail für dich. (Writing)
Finally, students invent their own e-mail about a past holiday. Remind them that this is a very common topic for Speaking and Writing Tests and needs to be well prepared.

Further practice of the language and vocabulary of this unit is given on the following pages.
Speaking: p. 73, Gespräch 2
Workbook: p. 27

Logo! 4 4 Urlaub

6 Urlaubsspaß (pp. 66–67)

Students will learn how to:
- say what they did on holiday

Key language
Ich habe / Wir haben / Er / Sie hat / Sie haben …
  in Paris eingekauft / auf Urlaub geangelt / am Abend getanzt / am ersten Tag Fotos gemacht / am zweiten Tag eine Rundfahrt gemacht / am nächsten Tag Freunde getroffen / Tennis gespielt / mich / uns / sich gesonnt.
Ich bin / Wir sind / Er / Sie ist / Sie sind …
  in die Disco / ins Kino / Restaurant / Schwimmbad / Museum / Sportzentrum / zum Strand gegangen / geschwommen / gewandert / spazieren gegangen / Ski gefahren / ausgegangen.

Grammar focus
- perfect tense

Skill focus
- auxiliary verb comes after time phrase
- learn answers about holidays for exam

Resources
- Cassette B, Side A
- Workbook p. 28
- Lesen / Schreiben A p. 192
- Kursarbeit pp. 178–179

Start the unit by finding out what students would say in answer to the question *Was hast du auf Urlaub gemacht?*

1a Hör zu! Wer hat was gemacht? (Listening)
The same three youngsters as in the previous spread tell a radio phone-in what they did on holiday. Students choose letters to show which illustrations apply to which person. There are two for each.

Answers
1 Jasmin; d, e, 2 Benjamin: a, f, 3 Samira: b, c

> Discjockey: Also, Jasmin, du warst in Spanien. Was hast du da gemacht?
> Jasmin: Na ja, am ersten Tag sind wir ins Museum gegangen. Das war unheimlich langweilig! Aber am zweiten Tag sind wir ins Freibad gegangen. Das war toll!
> Discjockey: Und du, Benjamin? Was hast du in Polen gemacht?
> Benjamin: Wir haben eine Rundfahrt gemacht. Das war nicht sehr interessant! Aber dann sind wir in die Diskothek gegangen. Das war super!
> Discjockey: Und du, Samira? Wie war es in Kalifornien?
> Samira: Es war herrlich! Ich bin ins Fitnesszentrum gegangen und natürlich habe ich viele Fotos gemacht.

1b Schreib die Sätze aus Übung 1a auf. (Writing)
Having identified which pictures apply to which person, students write out the answers in full sentences.

Answers
1 Jasmin ist ins Museum und ins Freibad gegangen. 2 Benjamin hat eine Rundfahrt gemacht und ist in die Disco gegangen. 3 Samira ist ins Fitnesszentrum gegangen und hat auch viele Fotos gemacht.

2 Lies die Broschüre und beantworte die Fragen auf Deutsch (ganze Sätze, bitte!). (Reading / Writing)
Students read a magazine article and answer twelve questions in full German sentences. This activity is suitable for quiet classwork or homework.

Answers
1 Sie war auf Mallorca. 2 Sie hat einen Ausflug nach Palma gemacht. 3 Sie hat die Stadt angesehen. 4 Sie ist ins Restaurant gegangen. 5 Sie hat Fisch (Paella) gegessen. 6 Sie ist im Meer geschwommen. 7 Sie hat Tischtennis gespielt. 8 Sie ist ins Konzert gegangen. 9 Die Musik war schlecht. 10 Sie hat sich jeden Tag am Strand gesonnt. 11 Sie ist in eine Disco gegangen. 12 Sie ist um drei Uhr nach Hause gegangen.

3 Partnerarbeit. (Speaking)
Students construct an interview about a past holiday. Encourage them to make up several more interviews, using their own prompts.

Tip box
When starting a sentence with a time phrase, the auxiliary verb comes second and the past participle goes to the end of the sentence. There is no room for extensive demonstration of this in the book. However, you can practise swopping round the order of all the expressions in the Key language box: *In Paris habe ich gegessen. Auf Urlaub haben wir geangelt*, etc.

4a Schreib einen Brief aus Frankreich. Füll die Lücken aus. (Writing)
Students copy out this letter, filling in the information as illustrated.

Answers
1 Frankreich, 2 toll / super, 3 La Rochelle, 4 Kino, 5 Disco, 6 Schwimmbad, 7 super / toll, 8 Theater, 9 langweilig, 10 Strand

4b Schreib jetzt deinen eigenen Brief wie der Brief in Übung 4a. (Writing)
Now students write a similar letter, based on information made up by themselves.

73

5 Partnerarbeit. Partner(in) A stellt die Fragen. Partner(in) B erfindet Antworten. (Speaking)
By conducting this interview, students are replicating part of the conversation section of the Speaking Test. Answers should be as detailed and informative as they can manage.

Tip box
Advice to students to learn their corrected answers for use in the Speaking or Writing Test.

Further practice of the language and vocabulary of this unit is given on the following pages.
Reading and Writing A: p. 192
Workbook: p. 28

Kursarbeit
The activities in this unit form an ideal introduction to coursework preparation. Specific coursework practice on this topic is provided on pp. 178–179.

Logo! 4 · 4 Urlaub

7 Todtnauer Ferienland
(pp. 68–69)

Students will learn how to:
- understand information about a holiday area

Key language
Man kann …
ein Buch ausleihen / übernachten / kegeln / zelten / Ski laufen / Tischtennis spielen / Kaffee trinken / Minigolf spielen / eine Massage haben.

Skill focus
- understanding information from an authentic text

- advice on making a brochure

Resources
- Cassette B, Side A
- Lesen / Schreiben B p. 193

Start this spread by explaining that it is largely for self-study. In real life, students will have to extract information from written sources which contain much that they don't understand and the same is true for the reading section of the GCSE exam.

Make sure that students realise that this is a text from a fully authentic source, so it will not be easy. However, the questions will help them to home in on the required information.

Tip box
Advice to students to pick out the information they need and not to worry about understanding every word. Encourage them not to panic if they don't understand everything. Tell them to look for words they *do* understand (for example, cognates) and to try and get a general idea of what the text is about.

1a Beantworte die Fragen mit „Ja, das kann man" oder „Nein, das kann man nicht". (Reading)
The information needs to be extracted from the text, so give students plenty of time. They can refer to the glossary and use dictionaries as well.

Answers
1 Ja, das kann man. 2 Ja, das kann man. 3 Ja, das kann man. 4 Nein, das kann man nicht. 5 Ja, das kann man. 6 Ja, das kann man. 7 Nein, das kann man nicht. 8 Ja, das kann man. 9 Nein, das kann man nicht. 10 Ja, das kann man.

1b Partnerarbeit. Partner(in) A (▲) stellt die Fragen aus Übung 1a. Partner(in) B (●) antwortet. (Speaking)
Students repeat exercise 1a, this time in the form of a question and answer dialogue.

1c Schreib Informationen über die Ferienorte auf. (Writing)
Again based on the answers to exercise 1a, students write down information about the various holiday villages.

2 Mach mit Hilfe eines Computers eine Broschüre für eine Region, die du kennst (z. B. Peak District, Pennines, New Forest). Was kann man da machen? (Writing)
Based on a provided example, students make a brochure advertising an area they know. This activity offers good ICT possibilities and the result could be used to illustrate a presentation in the Speaking Test.

Tip box
Advice about making a brochure about an area students know.

Further practice of the language and vocabulary of this unit is given on the following page.
Reading and Writing B: p. 193

All the vocabulary and structures from this chapter are listed on the *Wörter* pages at the end (pp. 70–71). These can be used for revision by covering up either the English or the German. Students can check here to see how much they remember from the chapter.

For more speaking practice to do with this chapter, use p. 73.

Further grammar and speaking practice of the language of this chapter is provided on pp. 30–31 of the Workbook.

Assessment material for Chapters 3 and 4 are available after Chapter 4.

Kursarbeit

4 Die Ferien (pp. 178–179)

The coursework spreads in *Logo! 4* give regular, guided practice in preparing for the coursework element of the GCSE exam.

The spreads always start with a model text on each theme (at a higher level than that expected by the student) which acts as a stimulus to give students ideas of what they might include in their own piece of work. Students are encouraged to look at the detail of the text through the guided reading activities. They are gradually guided to produce good German sentences in the tasks through to the final task, which is to produce an extended piece of writing. The *Hilfe* column is a feature on all the spreads. It reminds students of language they might include and particular structures that will raise the level of their writing. Remind students who are capable of achieving a Higher grade that they should always include examples of two or three tenses in their writing.

This spread guides students to produce an extended piece of writing on the topic of holidays.

1 Lies den Bericht. Schreib die braunen Wörter auf Deutsch und Englisch auf.
Students read the report and write out the brown words in both German and English.

Answers

es gab = there was; vom Anfang an = from the beginning; angenehm = pleasant / nice; Imbiss = snack; Eltern = parents; Berge = mountains; glücklicherweise = luckily / fortunately; nie = never; immer = always; Urlaub = holiday

2 Schreib diese Ausdrücke auf Deutsch auf.
Students write out the expressions listed in German.

Answers

1 Es war wirklich fantastisch! 2 Es gab so viel zu tun. 3 Wir sind sehr früh von zu Hause losgefahren. 4 Ich hatte mein eigenes Zimmer. 5 Das Essen war auch spitze. 6 Fast jeden Tag. 7 Das Wetter war meistens gut. 8 Ich habe oft mit ihnen Englisch gesprochen. 9 Dieser Urlaub hat mir sehr gut gefallen. 10 Hoffentlich fahren wir auch nächstes Jahr wieder nach Österreich.

3 Verbinde die deutschen und die englischen Sätze und Satzteile.
Students match up the German expressions with their English equivalents.

Answers

1 c, 2 f, 3 h, 4 d, 5 a, 6 e, 7 b, 8 g

4 Du bist Udo. Beantworte diese Fragen.
Students answer the questions as if they were Udo.

Answers

1 Mein Urlaub in Österreich war wirklich fantastisch. 2 Ich habe vierzehn Tage in Kitzbühel verbracht. 3 Kitzbühel liegt in Tirol. 4 Ich bin mit dem Auto dahingefahren. 5 Ich habe einen Imbiss gegessen und Orangensaft und Cola getrunken. 6 Das Hotel war echt super. 7 Ich bin im Freibad geschwommen; habe Radtouren gemacht; bin mit der Seilbahn bis zum Gipfel des Kitzbühler Horns gefahren und habe ein Picknick gemacht. 8 Das Wetter war meistens gut. 9 Ich habe immer Shorts und T-Shirts getragen. 10 Ich möchte wieder nach Österreich fahren.

5 Schreib jetzt deinen eigenen Bericht über einen Urlaub.
Students should now write their own report about a holiday using the *Hilfe* column as support.

Hilfe
Tips for writing about holidays:
- writing in a logical order
- using some time phrases with the verb coming in second position
- including some opinions and giving reasons for opinions

Workbook (pp. 23–31)

p. 23

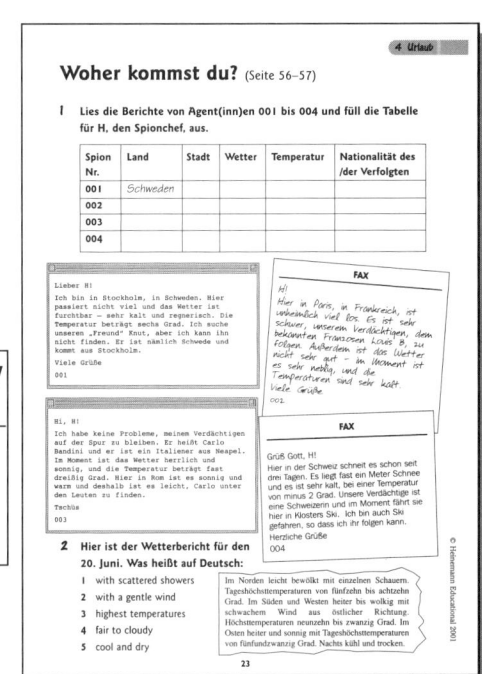

1

Spion Nr.	Land	Stadt	Wetter	Temperatur	Nationalität des / der Verfolgten
001	Schweden	Stockholm	regnerisch	kalt (6 Grad)	Schwede
002	Frankreich	Paris	neblig	kalt	Franzose
003	Italien	Rom	sonnig	heiß (30 Grad)	Italiener
004	die Schweiz	Klosters	Schnee	kalt (–2 Grad)	Schweizerin

2 **1** mit einzelnen Schauern, **2** mit schwachem Wind, **3** Höchsttemperaturen, **4** heiter bis wolkig, **5** kühl und trocken

p. 24

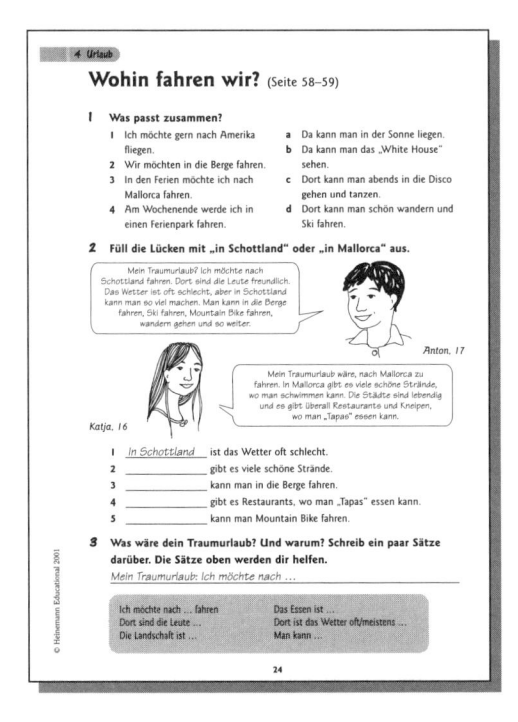

1 **1** b, **2** d, **3** a, **4** c

2 **1** In Schottland ist das Wetter oft schlecht. **2** In Mallorca gibt es viele schöne Strände. **3** In Schottland kann man in die Berge fahren. **4** In Mallorca gibt es Restaurants, wo man „Tapas" essen kann. **5** In Schottland kann man Mountainbike fahren.

3 open-ended

pp. 25–26

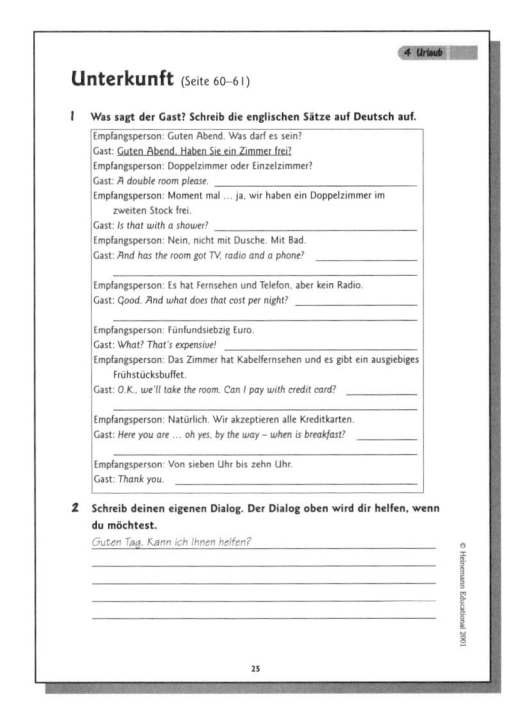

1 Empfangsperson: Guten Abend. Was darf es sein?
Gast: Guten Abend. Haben Sie ein Zimmer frei?
Empfangsperson: Doppelzimmer oder Einzelzimmer?
Gast: Ein Doppelzimmer, bitte.
Empfangsperson: Moment mal … ja, wir haben ein Doppelzimmer im zweiten Stock frei.
Gast: Ist das Zimmer mit Dusche?
Empfangsperson: Nein, nicht mit Dusche. Mit Bad.
Gast: Und hat das Zimmer Fernsehen, Radio und Telefon?

pp. 25–26

Empfangsperson: Es hat Fernsehen und Telefon, aber kein Radio.
Gast: Gut. Und was kostet das pro Nacht?
Empfangsperson: Fünfundsiebzig Euro.
Gast: Was? Das ist aber teuer!
Empfangsperson: Das Zimmer hat Kabelfernsehen und es gibt ein ausgiebiges Frühstücksbuffet.
Gast: Okay, wir nehmen das Zimmer. Kann ich mit Kreditkarte bezahlen?
Empfangsperson: Natürlich. Wir akzeptieren alle Kreditkarten.
Gast: Bitte schön … ach, übrigens – wann ist Frühstück?
Empfangsperson: Von sieben Uhr bis zehn Uhr.
Gast: Danke schön.

2 open-ended

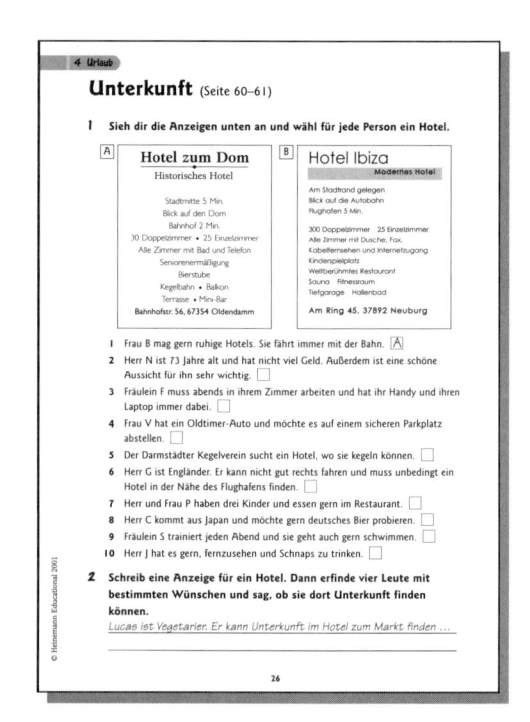

1 **1** Hotel zum Dom, **2** Hotel zum Dom, **3** Hotel Ibiza, **4** Hotel Ibiza, **5** Hotel zum Dom, **6** Hotel Ibiza, **7** Hotel Ibiza, **8** Hotel zum Dom, **9** Hotel Ibiza, **10** Hotel Ibiza
2 open-ended

p. 27

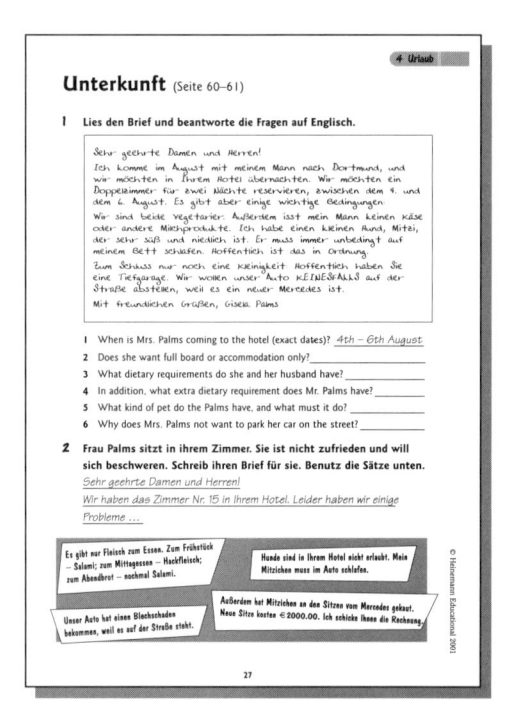

1 **1** 4th–6th August. **2** Full board. **3** They are both vegetarians. **4** He eats no dairy products. **5** They have a little dog. It must sleep on the bed. **6** Because it is a new Mercedes.
2 open-ended

p. 28

1 open-ended
2 Christa ist mit dem Auto nach Italien gefahren. Sie hat in einem Wohnwagen in der Nähe von Ravenna übernachtet. Die Reise hat zwölf Stunden gedauert. Sie ist drei Wochen geblieben und das Wetter war supertoll.

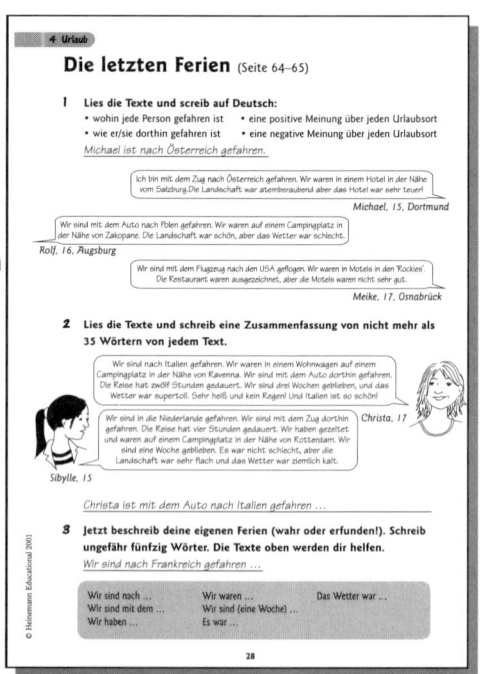

Sibylle ist mit dem Zug in die Niederlande gefahren. Die Reise hat vier Stunden gedauert. Sie war auf einem Campingplatz in der Nähe von Rotterdam. Sie ist eine Woche geblieben. Das Wetter war kalt.
(These are two possible summaries. Students may express the information given as they wish as long as it is linguistically correct.)
3 open-ended: overlook minor errors

Logo! 4   4 Urlaub

p. 29

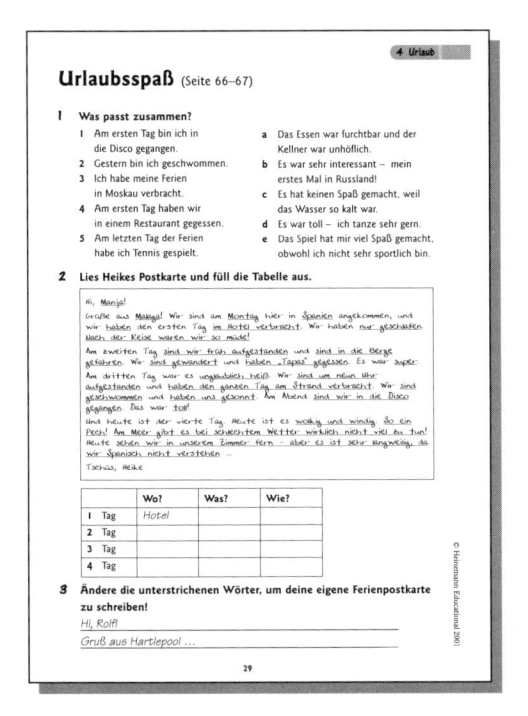

p. 30

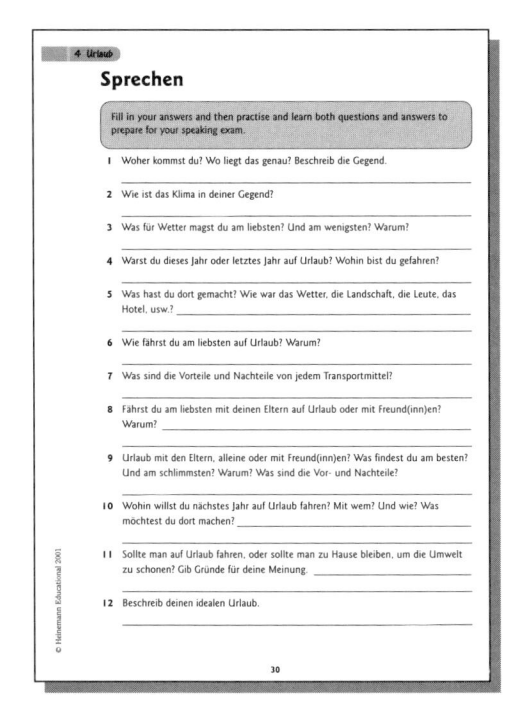

1 1 d, 2 c, 3 b, 4 a, 5 e

no answers – *Sprechen*

2

	Wo?	Was?	Wie?
1. Tag	Hotel	geschlafen	müde
2. Tag	Berge	gewandert, Tapas gegessen	super
3. Tag	Strand, Disco	geschwommen, gesonnt	toll
4. Tag	Zimmer	fernsehen	langweilig

3 open-ended: overlook minor errors

p. 31

1 1 Sie kommt aus Italien. Sie ist Italienerin. 2 Er kommt aus Wales. Er ist Waliser. 3 Er kommt aus Irland. Er ist Ire. 4 Sie kommt aus der Schweiz. Sie ist Schweizerin. 5 Sie kommt aus Frankreich. Sie ist Französin.

2 open-ended

3 open-ended

79

5 Meine Stadt (Student's Book pp. 74–89)

Topic area	Key language	Grammar	Skills
5.1 Wo ich wohne (pp. 74–75) Talk about your home town	Ich wohne in … … ist eine Kleinstadt / Großstadt / Industriestadt / Hafenstadt / Touristenstadt / ein Dorf. … liegt in … / auf dem Land / an der Küste / am Meer / Nordengland usw. Es gibt … Wir haben … (k)einen Bahnhof / Dom / (k)eine Brücke / Kirche / (k)ein Krankenhaus / Museum. … hat ungefähr … Einwohner.	Use of *kein* in accusative: *keinen, keine, kein*	Using the topic for presentation or coursework
5.2 Was gibt es zu tun? (pp. 76–77) What there is to do in town	Was gibt es in deiner Stadt zu tun? Mann kann (nicht) gut essen gehen / Sport treiben / einkaufen. Es gibt (nicht) viele Geschäfte. … ist (nicht) gut für junge Leute. Wir haben (k)ein Kino / (k)ein Jugendzentrum usw.	*man kann* + infinitive	Writing a description of your home town
5.3 Wie komme ich …? (pp. 78–79) Find the way	Gibt es hier in der Nähe …? Wo ist (die) nächste …? Wie komme ich am besten …? Geh / Gehen Sie … geradeaus / links / rechts / über den Marktplatz / die Brücke. bis zur Ampel / zum Marktplatz / am Kino / an der Kirche vorbei / um die Ecke. Nehmen Sie / Nimm die erste / zweite Straße links / rechts. Er / Sie / Es ist auf der rechten / linken Seite.	Revision: for 'it' use *er / sie / es* Asking for and giving directions Imperative: *du* and *Sie* forms	Listening skills: listening for key words
5.4 Transportmöglichkeiten (pp. 80–81) Get around by public transport	Wie fahre / komme ich am besten zum Flughafen / zur Stadtmitte / nach Berlin? Fahren Sie mit der Straßenbahn / mit dem Bus. Haben Sie einen Stadtplan von Berlin / eine Broschüre über Berlin / einen Fahrplan für …? usw.	*mit* used with modes of transport	Use *nach* with a named town, *zum / zur* with other places
5.5 Die Bundesbahn (pp. 82–83) Ask for information at a train station	Wann fährt der nächste Zug nach (Bromberg)? Von welchem Gleis? Einfach oder hin und zurück? einmal / zweimal / dreimal Was kostet die Karte? Wann kommt der Zug in (Bromberg) an? Muss ich umsteigen? Muss ich einen Zuschlag zahlen? erste / zweite Klasse signs in a station		Tips for role-plays
5.6 Meine Traumstadt (pp. 84–85) Advantages and disadvantages of where you live	Ich wohne / lebe (nicht) gern / lieber / am liebsten … in der Großstadt / in der Kleinstadt / in einem Dorf / auf dem Land, weil sie / es lebendig / laut / schön / ruhig / schmutzig / langweilig ist. Er würde lieber / am liebsten (in den Alpen) wohnen. Wenn ich Zeit / viel Geld hätte … würde ich reisen / in Amerika leben / ein Haus kaufen usw.	*Weil* sends verb to the end of the sentence Conditional: *Wenn ich … hätte, würde ich …*	

80

5.7 Deutsche Städte, englische Städte (pp. 86–87) Compare English and German towns	… ist älter / kleiner / größer / moderner / ruhiger / teuerer / billiger / besser / schlechter / abwechslungsreicher als … … ist die größte / kleinste / älteste / modernste / ruhigste / abwechslungsreichste Stadt.	Comparative, superlative

- The vocabulary and structures taught in Chapter 5 are summarised on the *Wörter* pages of the Student's Book. 88–89.
- Further speaking practice on the language of this chapter is provided on p.106.
- Coursework pages relating to this chapter can be found on pp. 180–181.
- Further reading and writing practice on the language of this chapter is provided on pp. 194–195.
- For a selection of assessment tasks for Chapters 5 and 6, please refer to the separate Assessment Pack for your chosen examination board: AQA, OCR or Edexcel.

1 Wo ich wohne (pp. 74–75)

Students will learn how to:
- talk about their home town

Key language
Ich wohne in ...
... ist eine Kleinstadt / Großstadt / Hafenstadt / Industriestadt / Touristenstadt / ein Dorf / die Hauptstadt von ... / ein Vorort von ...
... liegt in Nordengland / Ostschottland / Südwales / Westirland / Nordirland / auf dem Land / an der Küste / am Meer.
Es gibt ...
Wir haben ...
  (k)einen Bahnhof / Dom / Fluss / Marktplatz / Park / Zoo.
  (k)eine Brücke / Kirche / Tankstelle / Universität.
  (k)ein Krankenhaus / Museum / Rathaus / Schloss.
  viele Geschäfte / einige Schulen.
  ... hat ungefähr ... Einwohner.

Grammar focus
- not a: *keinen, keine, kein*

Skill focus
- using the topic for presentation or coursework

Resources
- Cassette B, Side A
- Workbook p. 32
- Sprechen p. 106, Gespräch 1

Before starting this spread, remind students that this is a common topic in GCSE exams and could be considered for an oral presentation. Ask them to contribute as much information as they can remember about their home town.

1a Lies den Text. Sind die Sätze richtig oder falsch? (Reading)

Students read the text about a fictional Austrian town and note down whether the ten sentences are true or false.

Answers
1 Falsch. 2 Falsch. 3 Falsch. 4 Falsch. 5 Falsch.
6 Richtig. 7 Falsch. 8 Richtig. 9 Richtig. 10 Richtig.

1b Schreib die richtigen Antworten aus Übung 1a auf. (Writing)

This exercise refers to the same text. Students take the sentences which they have decided are false and write down the correct versions.

Answers
1 Logo ist eine Kleinstadt. 2 Logostadt liegt in Südösterreich. 3 Es gibt ungefähr 6000 Einwohner in Logostadt. 4 Logostadt hat einen Bahnhof. 5 Logostadt hat kein Krankenhaus. 7 Es gibt ein Einkaufszentrum in Logostadt.

2 Hör zu! Wer lügt? Wer wohnt in Logostadt? Wer wohnt nicht in Logostadt? Mach Notizen und schreib „er / sie lügt" oder „er / sie lügt nicht" (lügen = to lie). (Listening)

Students note down which of the people live in Logostadt and which don't. Make sure students understand exactly what the task is here. Some of the people on the tape are saying things which aren't true (with reference to the illustration on the right of the exercise). This means that they can't live in Logostadt.

Suggested procedure: on the first hearing, students should make notes about what the people are saying about what there is and what there isn't in their town. On the second hearing, they should compare what the people are saying with the illustration and decide whether they are telling the truth. For example, Richard claims that there is no zoo In Logostadt, whereas in fact, there is. So he isn't telling the truth about where he lives.

Answers
1 Richard: Fluss ✔, Zoo ✘. Nein, er wohnt nicht in Logostadt. 2 Bettina: Rathaus ✔, Marktplatz ✔, Schloss ✔. Ja, sie wohnt in Logostadt. 3 Uli: Museum ✔, Bahnhof ✘. Nein, er wohnt nicht in Logostadt. 4 Margret: Park ✔, Fluss ✔. Ja, sie wohnt in Logostadt. 5 Mike: Dom ✔, Sportzentrum ✔. Nein, er wohnt nicht in Logostadt. 6 Gitti: Geschäfte ✔, Park ✔, Schloss ✘. Nein, sie wohnt nicht in Logostadt.

1 – Wohnst du in Logostadt, Richard?
  – Ja, klar! In Logostadt gibt es einen Fluss. Der heißt die Wimme. Was? Ob wir einen Zoo haben? Nein, wir haben keinen Zoo!
2 – Und du, Bettina?
  – Natürlich! Wir haben ein schönes Rathaus, einen tollen Marktplatz und auch ein sehr historisches Schloss.
3 – Wohnst du in Logostadt, Uli?
  – Jawohl! Das Heimatmuseum ist sehr interessant. Kann man mit dem Zug nach Logostadt fahren? Nein, das geht nicht, weil es keinen Bahnhof gibt.
4 – Und du, Margret?
  – Ja, Logostadt ist meine Stadt! Der Stadtpark ist schön. Da kann man joggen. Und der Fluss ist auch toll, weil man dort angeln und Boot fahren kann.
5 – Mike, bist du Logostädter?
  – Na klar! Wir haben einen alten Dom mit tollen Fenstern. Logostadt hat auch ein modernes Sportzentrum, wo man Squash spielen kann.
6 – Und wie ist es mit dir, Gitti?
  – Ja, ich wohne hier. Logostadt ist toll! Wir haben ganz viele Geschäfte und einen großen Park. Was? Ob es ein Schloss gibt? Nein, wir haben kein Schloss.

Grammatik: kein (no, not a)

Using *kein* to say there isn't something: *keinen, keine, kein*. For oral practice of this point, ask students questions on what there is in the nearest town. They reply, where appropriate, using *keinen / keine / kein*.

Make sure students realise that *nicht ein* is quite wrong.

3 Partnerarbeit. (Speaking)
Students construct a series of dialogues asking for and giving details about towns based on the prompts provided.

4 Beschreib *deine* Stadt. (Writing)
This writing exercise has been left as open as possible to allow students to go into as much detail as they can in writing about their home towns. Teacher input may well be helpful, because many towns have features which are unique to them. Tourist information offices often have brochures in German which can be very helpful. This is a task which will have to be collected in and marked.

Tip box
Use this topic for an illustrated presentation or for coursework (see pp. 180–181). Remind students that this is an ideal topic to learn by heart for an oral presentation or an extended piece of writing.

Further practice of the language and vocabulary of this unit is given on the following pages.
Speaking: p. 106, Gespräch 1
Workbook: p. 32

2 Was gibt es zu tun?

(pp. 76–77)

Students will learn how to:
- talk about what there is to do in town

Key language
Was gibt es in deiner Stadt zu tun?
Man kann (nicht) gut ...
　essen gehen.
　Sport treiben.
　einkaufen.
Es gibt (nicht) viele Geschäfte / Kneipen und Restaurants / (k)ein Sportzentrum.
... ist (nicht) gut für junge Leute.
Wir haben (k)ein Kino / (k)ein Jugendzentrum / (k)eine Disco.

Grammar focus
- *man kann ...* + infinitive

Skill focus
- writing a description of home town
- signs and directions around town

Resources
- Cassette B, Side A
- Workbook p. 33
- Sprechen p. 106, Gespräch 2

Start this spread by asking students for as many true responses as possible in answer to the question: *Was kann man in* (home town or nearest town or city) *machen?*

1 Lies den Text und wähle die richtige Antwort. Schreib Sätze. (Reading / Writing)

Students read an extract from an imaginary brochure about Logostadt and choose from possible answers. The correct answers should be written out in full sentences.

Answers

1 In Logostadt kann man gut tanzen gehen. 2 In Logostadt kann man gut essen gehen. 3 In Logostadt kann man einen Film sehen. 4 In Logostadt kann man ein Theaterstück sehen. 5 Logostadt ist gut für Sport. 6 Am Abend ist in Logostadt viel los.

2a Hör zu! Wer wohnt wo? (Listening)

Students listen to six people giving information about their towns and write down their names (correct spelling not crucial), plus the letter of the appropriate picture to show that they have understood.

Answers

1 Roland f, 2 Paula e, 3 Jochen a, 4 Margret d, 5 Manni c, 6 Angela b

> 1 **Roland:** Hier kann man gut essen gehen. Wir haben eine Pizzeria, zwei China-Restaurants und viele Kneipen. Gestern war ich in der Pizzeria.
> 2 **Paula:** Hier kann man gut Sport treiben. Wir haben einen Golfplatz, viele Tennisplätze und ein Sportzentrum.
> 3 **Jochen:** Die Stadt ist sehr gut für junge Leute. Es gibt Discos, Klubs und eine Bowlingbahn.
> 4 **Margret:** Hier kann man gut einkaufen. Wir haben einen großen Supermarkt, eine Fußgängerzone und ein Einkaufszentrum. Morgen gehen wir in die Stadt und kaufen Weihnachtsgeschenke.
> 5 **Manni:** Meine Stadt ist nicht gut für junge Leute. Wir haben keine Disco und kein Kino.
> 6 **Angela:** Hier ist es toll für Touristen. Es gibt einen Dom und auch ein Schloss.

2b Was kann man in den Städten in Übung 2a machen? (Writing)

Students write sentences beginning *Man kann ...* to show they have understood the information in exercise 2a. They may need to hear the tape again. Various formulations are acceptable as answers.

Suggested answers

1 Man kann gut essen gehen. 2 Man kann gut Sport treiben. 3 Man kann in die Disco gehen. 4 Man kann gut einkaufen. 5 Man kann nicht viel machen. 6 Man kann den Dom und das Schloss besichtigen.

3 Partnerarbeit. Partner(in) A (▲) stellt die Fragen. Partner(in) B (●) antwortet. (Speaking)

Students make up conversations asking and answering questions about what there is to do in three imaginary towns. If they want, they can invent further locations of their own.

4 Beschreib deine eigene Stadt / dein eigenes Dorf (80–100 Wörter). (Writing / Reading)

Students now write about what there is to do in their own home town. Advice about how to go about this is contained in the accompanying Tip box.

Tip box

Advice to use the questions from exercise 3 as cues when writing. Use some opinions and a past tense and make up details if necessary. Get the text checked and learn it for a presentation.

5 Verbinde die Schilder mit den Anweisungen. (Reading)

Students match the sentences to signs. Tell them that, even at Higher Level, a favourite kind of task in the Reading Test is a sign or notice, as would be seen in a town.

Answers

1 e, 2 f, 3 j, 4 h, 5 a, 6 i, 7 b, 8 d, 9 g, 10 c

Further practice of the language and vocabulary of this unit is given on the following pages.
Speaking: p. 106, Gespräch 2
Workbook: p. 33

Logo! 4 5 Meine Stadt

3 Wie komme ich …?

(pp. 78–79)

Students will learn how to:
- find the way

Key language
Gibt es hier in der Nähe …? Wo ist (die) nächste …? Wie komme ich am besten …?
Geh / Gehen Sie …
   geradeaus / links / rechts.
   über den Marktplatz / die Brücke.
   bis zur Ampel / zum Marktplatz.
   am Kino / an der Kirche vorbei.
   um die Ecke.
Nehmen Sie / Nimm …
   die erste / zweite Straße links / rechts.
Er / Sie / Es ist auf der rechten / linken Seite.

Grammar focus
- use *er / sie / es* for 'it'
- asking for and giving directions
- imperative: *du* and *Sie* forms

Skill focus
- listening skills: listening for key words.

Resources
- Cassette B, Side A
- Workbook p. 34
- Sprechen p. 106, Rollenspiel 1

Start this spread by checking that students remember how to ask the way. The teacher can call out places in a town or show any available flashcards, inviting students to ask the way to these places. How many expressions can they remember for *giving* directions in reply to the questions?

Tip box
This reminds students to listen for key words in directions and ask the person to repeat directions if necessary.

1a Hör zu und finde die Gebäude. (Listening)
Students listen to ten people asking the way and being given directions. They use the map on p. 78 to identify the locations being asked for and write letters to show they have understood.

Answers
1 b, 2 a, 3 j, 4 f, 5 c, 6 e, 7 i, 8 g, 9 h, 10 d

1 – Entschuldigen Sie, bitte. Wo ist der Hauptbahnhof?
  – Okay, gehen Sie geradeaus und nehmen Sie die fünfte Straße links. Der Bahnhof ist am Ende der Straße.
2 – Gibt es hier in der Nähe ein Krankenhaus?
  – Ja, gehen Sie immer geradeaus. Das Krankenhaus ist am Ende dieser Straße.
3 – Wo ist die nächste Bushaltestelle?
  – Nehmen Sie die erste Straße rechts. Die Haltestelle ist auf der rechten Seite.
4 – Entschuldigen Sie, wie komme ich am besten zum Rathaus?
  – Moment … Das Rathaus … Gehen Sie geradeaus, über den Marktplatz, dann nehmen Sie die erste Straße rechts nach dem Marktplatz und das Rathaus ist auf der rechten Seite.
5 – Gibt es ein Informationsbüro in der Stadt?
  – Jawohl. Gehen Sie geradeaus, an der Kirche vorbei und über die Brücke. Nehmen Sie dann die erste Straße links. Das Informationsbüro ist auf der rechten Seite.
6 – Entschuldigen Sie, wo ist der nächste Supermarkt?
  – Nicht sehr weit. Gehen Sie über die Ampel und nehmen Sie die zweite Straße links.
7 – Ist das Museum weit von hier?
  – Nein, nehmen Sie die erste Straße links. Das Museum ist am Ende der Straße.
8 – Gibt es hier in der Nähe eine Tankstelle?
  – Ja. Fahren Sie geradeaus, über die Ampel. Nehmen Sie dann die erste Straße links.
9 – Entschuldigen Sie, wo ist die nächste Post?
  – Nehmen Sie die zweite Straße rechts und gehen Sie am Kino vorbei. Die Post ist am Ende der Straße.
10 – Wie komme ich zur Sparkasse, bitte?
  – Nehmen Sie die vierte Straße rechts. Die Sparkasse ist auf der linken Seite.

1b Lies die Anweisungen, finde das Gebäude und schreib die Frage auf. (Reading / Writing)
Students read five similar directions. Having worked out where the people want to go, they write down the question they would have asked, beginning *Wie komme ich …?*

Answers
1 der Bahnhof. Wie komme ich am besten zum Bahnhof? 2 die Bushaltestelle. Wie komme ich am besten zur Bushaltestelle? 3 das Rathaus. Wie komme ich am besten zum Rathaus? 4 der Supermarkt. Wie komme ich am besten zum Supermarkt? 5 die Sparkasse. Wie komme ich am besten zur Sparkasse?

Tip box
Reminds students of expressions to use when asking the way to various places.

Wiederholung: der / die / das, er / sie / es (the, it)
Use *er / sie / es* depending on the gender of the noun when saying 'it'. Students can practise this by asking and answering simple questions about where places are:
A: Wo ist die Post?
B: Sie ist in der Stadtmitte.

2 Partnerarbeit. (Speaking)
In this pair-work exercise, students can practise all three ways of asking the way as suggested. The directions are

to be given by the partners, using the symbols. As an extension exercise, the pairs can continue with further similar conversations of their own invention.

3 Schreib einen Zettel an deinen neuen Freund / deine neue Freundin. Wie kommt man am besten vom Bahnhof zu deinem Haus? (Writing)

Students use the diagram to write down directions from the station to a house (for a friend, therefore, using the *du* form). For further practice, they can use the *Sie* form, and also try actually describing how to get to their own houses from the nearest station. This can be quite good fun because it can get so complicated.

> Further practice of the language and vocabulary of this unit is given on the following pages.
> Speaking: p. 106, Rollenspiel 1
> Workbook: p. 34

4 Transportmöglichkeiten
(pp. 80–81)

Students will learn how to:
- get around by public transport

Key language
Wie fahre ich am besten
...
zum Hafen / Flughafen / zur Stadtmitte / nach Berlin / Leipzig / Frankfurt?
Fahren Sie mit der U-Bahn / S-Bahn / Straßenbahn / mit dem Bus, Linie ... Richtung ...
Gehen Sie zu Fuß.
Haben Sie ...
einen Fahrplan für die Bundesbahn / Straßenbahn / S-Bahn / U-Bahn / Busse?
einen Stadtplan von Berlin?
eine Broschüre / eine Hotelliste über Berlin?

Grammar focus
- *mit* used with modes of transport

Skill focus
- *nach* with a named town, *zum / zur* otherwise

Resources
- Cassette B, Side A
- Workbook p. 35
- Sprechen p. 106, Rollenspiel 2
- Lesen / Schreiben B p. 195

---

1 Hör zu! Welches Bild passt zu welchem Dialog? (Listening)

Students listen to dialogues in a tourist office and write down letters to show that they have understood which dialogue goes with which illustration. Make sure that they realise that the photo at the top is for information only and is not connected with the exercise.

As an extra activity, invite students to listen again and note down, in English, all further details they can understand from each dialogue.

Answers
1 c, 2 e, 3 a, 4 f, 5 b, 6 d

1 – Guten Tag! Kann ich Ihnen helfen?
  – Ja. Wie komme ich am besten zum Hauptbahnhof?
  – Am besten nehmen Sie die Straßenbahn, Linie 5, Richtung Hauptbahnhof.
  – Ach so. Und wo ist die Straßenbahnhaltestelle?
  – Hier gleich um die Ecke.
2 – Guten Morgen! Ich brauche eine Toilette!
  – Okay, die nächste Toilette ist am Rathausplatz.
  – Ist das weit von hier?
  – Nein, nein. Sie können zu Fuß gehen.
3 – Wie komme ich zum Park-Hotel?
  – Am besten nehmen Sie den Bus, Linie 12, Richtung Stadtzentrum.
4 – Guten Tag. Ich möchte zum Schloss. Wie fahre ich am besten dahin?

  – Fahren Sie mit der U-Bahn, Linie 2, Richtung Zoo.
  – Haben Sie einen Fahrplan?
  – Ja, hier.
  – Was kostet er?
  – Nichts, der ist kostenlos.
5 – Ich möchte nach Dresden fahren.
  – Oha, dann müssen Sie mit dem Zug fahren.
  – Ja? Kann ich hier eine Fahrkarte kaufen?
  – Nein, der Fahrkartenschalter ist am Bahnhof.
6 – Guten Tag. Haben Sie eine Broschüre über die Sehenswürdigkeiten von Köln?
  – Selbstverständlich. € 1,00, bitte.

Tip box
This reminds pupils to use *nach* with a named town and *zum / zur* for other places.

Grammatik: mit + ... (travelling by ...)
This reminds students to use *mit* and the appropriate article to show modes of transport.

2 Partnerarbeit. (Speaking)
With the help of the Key language box provided on p. 80, students construct a dialogue in a tourist office based on the illustrations. Invite them also to make up further similar dialogues of their own.

3 Lies den Text. Was ist der Preis? (Reading / Writing)
Students read an extract from a tourist brochure and work out prices for the various items illustrated. The answers are to be written in full sentences.

Answers
1 Eine Broschüre über Berlin kostet € 1,00. 2 Ein Stadtplan von Frankfurt kostet € 1,50. 3 Ein Busfahrplan kostet € 0,50. 4 Ein Bahnfahrplan kostet € 2,50. 5 Eine Hotelliste ist kostenlos.

Further practice of the language and vocabulary of this unit is given on the following pages.
Speaking: p. 106, Rollenspiel 2
Reading and Writing B: p. 195
Workbook: p. 35

5 Die Bundesbahn (pp. 82–83)

Students will learn how to:
- ask for information at a train station

Key language	Skill focus
Wann fährt der nächste Zug nach (Bromberg)? Von welchem Gleis? Einfach oder hin und zurück? einmal / zweimal / dreimal Was kostet die Karte? Wann kommt der Zug in (Bromberg) an? Muss ich umsteigen? erste / zweite Klasse Muss ich einen Zuschlag zahlen? *signs at a station*	• tips for role-plays **Resources** • Cassette B, Side A • Workbook p. 36 • Sprechen p. 106, Rollenspiel 3

Before starting this spread, remind students that the topic of purchasing tickets for public transport often crops up at GCSE level. Ask them to contribute as many useful expressions as they can remember for use at a train station.

1 Hör zu! Wähle die richtige Antwort. (Listening)

Students listen to a conversation at a train station and choose from possible answers to the questions provided. More able students should write out the answers in full sentences.

Answers

1 Bornholm, 2 14 Uhr 30, 3 4, 4 hin und zurück, 5 €11,00, 6 16 Uhr 45, 7 in Strande

Kunde: Guten Tag! Wann fährt der nächste Zug nach Bornholm?
Beamtin: Um 14.30 Uhr.
Kunde: Von welchem Gleis?
Beamtin: Gleis 4.
Kunde: Eine Fahrkarte, bitte.
Beamtin: Einfach oder hin und zurück?
Kunde: Hin und zurück. Was kostet die Karte?
Beamtin: €11,00.
Kunde: Muss ich einen Zuschlag zahlen?
Beamtin: Nein, das ist ein D-Zug.
Kunde: Wann kommt der Zug in Bornholm an?
Beamtin: Um 16.45 Uhr.
Kunde: Muss ich umsteigen?
Beamtin: Ja, in Strande.

2 Hör zu, lies den Dialog und beantworte die Fragen (ganze Sätze, bitte!). (Listening / Reading / Writing)

This is a similar conversation. Students can read at the same time as listening, then answer German questions in full sentences.

Answers

1 Er fährt nach Bromberg. 2 Der Zug fährt um 14.40 Uhr ab. 3 Er fährt von Gleis 14. 4 Der Herr will eine einfache Karte. 5 Die Fahrkarte kostet sechs Euro. 6 Nein, er muss keinen Zuschlag zahlen. 7 Der Zug kommt um 14.54 an. 8 Nein.

Kunde: Guten Tag! Wann fährt der nächste Zug nach Bromberg?
Beamtin: Um 14.40 Uhr.
Kunde: Von welchem Gleis?
Beamtin: Gleis 14.
Kunde: Einmal, bitte.
Beamtin: Einfach oder hin und zurück?
Kunde: Einfach. Was kostet die Karte?
Beamtin: Sechs Euro.
Kunde: Muss ich einen Zuschlag zahlen?
Beamtin: Nein, das ist nicht nötig.
Kunde: Wann kommt der Zug in Bromberg an?
Beamtin: Um 14.54 Uhr.
Kunde: Muss ich umsteigen?
Beamtin: Nein.

3 Partnerarbeit. (Speaking)

Working in pairs, students construct dialogues for six destinations, based on the timetable provided.

4 Partnerarbeit. Lest den Dialog und macht Gespräche. (Reading / Speaking)

Students first read the conversation given and then construct six more train station conversations based on the cues provided.

Tip box

This provides advice to students to check role-play instructions carefully and to be prepared for unexpected responses from the examiner.

Tell them that not including everything you are asked to include can immediately mean unnecessary loss of marks. They must also be alert to what the examiner is saying, and not just plough on regardless. For example, the item they ask for may not be available, the train they want to catch may have been cancelled, etc. It is often possible to predict what the 'unexpected' bit is likely to be.

Logo! 4 5 Meine Stadt

5 Beschreib drei Fahrten mit dem Zug. (Writing)

Students look at the cues and, following the example provided, describe the journeys in the perfect tense. Various permutations of answer may be acceptable.

Answers

1 Roland: Ich bin nach Mainz gefahren. Ich habe eine einfache Karte gekauft, zweite Klasse. Die Karte hat fünfzehn Euro gekostet und ich bin in Wiesbaden umgestiegen. **2 Ilse:** Ich bin nach Graz gefahren. Ich habe eine Hin- und Rückfahrkarte gekauft, zweite Klasse. Die Karte hat 66 Schillinge gekostet. Ich bin nicht umgestiegen. **3 Jens:** Ich bin nach Bern gefahren. Ich habe eine einfache Karte gekauft, erste Klasse. Die Karte hat 62 Franken gekostet und ich bin in Luzern umgestiegen.

6 Welche Schilder haben welche Bedeutung? (Reading)

Remind students that signs from railway stations are commonly used in Reading Tests. These ones provide some practice in this, as they match signs to English words and write down the appropriate letters.

Answers

1 j, 2 d, 3 a, 4 b, 5 f, 6 g, 7 h, 8 i, 9 c, 10 e

Further practice of the language and vocabulary of this unit is given on the following pages.
Speaking: p. 106, Rollenspiel 3
Workbook: p. 36

6 Meine Traumstadt (pp. 84–85)

Students will learn how to:
- talk about the advantages and disadvantages of where you live

> **Key language**
> Ich wohne / lebe (nicht) gern / lieber / am liebsten ...
>   in einer Großstadt / in einer Kleinstadt / in einem Dorf / auf dem Land,
>   weil sie / es lebendig / laut / schön / ruhig / schmutzig / langweilig ist.
> Er würde lieber / am liebsten (in den Alpen) wohnen.
> Wenn ich Zeit / viel Geld hätte, würde ich ...
> Wenn ich im Lotto gewinnen würde, würde ich ...
>   reisen / in Amerika leben / ein Haus / Sportwagen kaufen.
>
> **Grammar focus**
> - *weil* sends verb to end of the sentence
> - conditional: *wenn ich ... hätte, würde ich ...*
>
> **Resources**
> - Cassette B, Side A

Start the unit by brainstorming, in English or German, the advantages and disadvantages of living in towns, cities or villages.

1a Hör zu! Wer wohnt wo? Wohnt er / sie gern oder nicht gern da? Schreib die Tabelle ab und füll sie aus. (Listening)

Students listen to some people being interviewed about where they live. The box must be copied out and two ticks inserted for each person, one to show where he / she lives and another to show whether he / she likes it. A photocopiable grid to accompany this exercise is available on p. 190 of this book.

Answers

1 Matthias: in der Großstadt, gern, 2 Irena: in einer Kleinstadt, gern, 3 Ricky: in einem Dorf, nicht gern, 4 Viktoria: auf dem Land, gern

> Journalist: Herzlich willkommen bei Jugend heute. Hier spricht Jürgen Meyer. Ich bin auf der Straße in Hamburg und mache Interviews mit jungen Leuten. Hallo!
> Matthias: Guten Tag, Jürgen. Also, ich bin der Matthias. Ich wohne sehr gern hier in Hamburg.
> Journalist: Warum denn?
> Matthias: Also, weil es in der Großstadt so viel zu erleben gibt: Konzerte, Kinos, Cafés usw.
> Journalist: Danke, Matthias. Und du? Wie heißt du?
> Irena: Ich bin die Irena. Ich wohne nicht in der Großstadt. Ich wohne in Neumünster. Ich wohne gern in der Kleinstadt, weil es ruhig ist, nicht so hektisch wie in Hamburg.
> Journalist: Danke. Und du, Ricky, wohnst du auch in Neumünster?
> Ricky: Nein, ich wohne in einem Dorf namens Heidkrug. Ich wohne nicht sehr gern da, weil es extrem langweilig ist. Da ist nichts los!
> Journalist: Schade, Ricky! Und zum Schluss noch Viktoria. Was meinst du?
> Viktoria: Ich wohne auf dem Land. Das ist perfekt für mich, weil die Landschaft so schön ist. Die Großstadt ist nichts für mich!

1b Schreib die Sätze aus Übung 1a auf. (Writing)

Students write the answers to exercise 1a out in full sentences.

Answers

1 Matthias wohnt gern in der Großstadt. 2 Irena wohnt gern in einer Kleinstadt. 3 Ricky wohnt nicht gern in einem Dorf. 4 Viktoria wohnt gern auf dem Land.

Wiederholung: weil (because)

Weil sends the verb to the end of the sentence. Remind students that this item is reiterated a number of times in *Logo! 4* because they need to use it correctly in order to gain points for giving reasons, explanations and opinions.

2 Partnerarbeit. (Speaking)

Following the cues provided, students make short questions and answers, giving reasons. Encourage them to make up some more of their own.

3 Lies den Artikel und beantworte die Fragen (ganze Sätze, bitte!). (Reading / Writing)

Before embarking on this text, students should be taken through the Grammar box below, which shows them how to manipulate the 'would if I could' construction.

They then read the extract from a magazine and answer the German questions in full sentences. Point out also that people often use *leben* as an equivalent of *wohnen*.

Answers

1 Frank wohnt in München. 2 Er würde lieber in den Alpen wohnen. 3 Er würde am liebsten in der Karibik wohnen. 4 Sie wohnt in Österreich. 5 Sie würde lieber in Spanien oder Italien wohnen. 6 Sie würde am liebsten in New York wohnen. 7 Er wohnt in Dortmund. 8 Nein, er wohnt nicht gern da. 9 Er würde lieber am Meer wohnen. 10 Er würde am liebsten in Paris wohnen.

Grammatik: wenn ich ..., würde ich ... (if I ..., I would ...)

The conditional. How to say what you would do if something happened. Get students to prepare answers to the questions: *Was würdest du machen, wenn du viel Geld hättest / Zeit hättest?*

4 Und du? Was würdest du machen, wenn du im Lotto gewinnen würdest? Wo würdest du leben? Was würdest du kaufen? (Writing)
Remind students that this is a favourite question in Speaking and Writing Tests at GCSE Higher Level, so they need to be prepared with a couple of answers. Other beginnings can be: *Wenn ich viel Geld hätte, … / Wenn ich Zeit hätte, …*

7 Deutsche Städte, englische Städte (pp. 86–87)

Students will learn how to:
- compare English and German towns

Key language	Grammar focus
… ist älter / kleiner / größer / moderner / ruhiger / teurer / billiger / besser / schlechter / abwechslungsreicher als …	• comparative, superlative
… ist die größte / kleinste / älteste / modernste / ruhigste / abwechslungsreichste Stadt.	**Resources** • Cassette B, Side A • Sprechen p. 106 • Lesen / Schreiben A p. 194 • Kursarbeit pp. 180–181

This is a reading and writing unit to conclude this chapter on where people live. Introduce it by asking students to come up with as many differences as they know between German and English towns.

1 Lies die Texte über die drei Städte und beantworte die Fragen auf Deutsch (ganze Sätze, bitte!). (Reading / Writing)

Students read the three extracts from brochures and answer the German questions in full sentences. If they are unsure about the superlative, direct them to the Grammar box below.

Answers

1 Delmenhorst ist die beste Stadt für junge Leute. 2 Bridport ist die ruhigste Stadt. 3 Delmenhorst ist die größte Stadt. 4 Bridport ist die kleinste Stadt. 5 Bridport ist die älteste Stadt. 6 Delmenhorst ist die abwechslungsreichste Stadt. 7 Delmenhorst ist die modernste Stadt. 8 Engelberg ist die beste Stadt für Kinder.

Grammatik: Der Komparativ (the comparative); der Superlativ (the superlative)

How to form the comparative and the superlative. Practise this informally by using classroom items and asking students to contribute comparative and superlative forms: *Das blaue Buch ist größer als das grüne Buch, aber das rote Buch ist das größte. / Oliver ist älter als Elizabeth, aber Tina ist die älteste.*

2 Vergleiche die drei Städte. (Writing)

Using the statistics provided in the grid, students write sentences using the comparative and superlative forms to compare the three towns.

Answers

1 Engelberg ist größer als Bridport, aber Delmenhorst ist die größte Stadt. 2 Engelberg ist kleiner als Delmenhorst, aber Bridport ist die kleinste Stadt. 3 Engelberg ist älter als Bridport, aber Delmenhorst ist die älteste Stadt. 4 Engelberg ist moderner als Bridport, aber Delmenhorst ist die modernste Stadt. 5 Engelberg ist ruhiger als Delmenhorst, aber Bridport ist die ruhigste Stadt. 6 Engelberg ist abwechslungsreicher als Bridport, aber Delmenhorst ist die abwechslungsreichste Stadt.

3 Jetzt vergleiche diese Restaurants. (Writing)

In a similar exercise, students now write sentences comparing three restaurants.

Answers

1 „Bei Heino" ist größer als „Pizza Palast", aber „Lukullus" ist das größte Restaurant. 2 „Bei Heino" ist kleiner als „Lukullus", aber „Pizza Palast" ist das kleinste Restaurant. 3 „Bei Heino" ist teurer als „Pizza Palast", aber „Lukullus" ist das teuerste Restaurant. 4 „Bei Heino" ist billiger als „Lukullus", aber „Pizza Palast" ist das billigste Restaurant. 5 „Bei Heino" ist ruhiger als „Pizza Palast", aber „Lukullus" ist das ruhigste Restaurant. 6 „Bei Heino" ist lebendiger als „Lukullus", aber „Pizza Palast" ist das lebendigste Restaurant.

4a Lies den Artikel und beantworte die Fragen. Schreib entweder „in England" oder „in Deutschland". (Reading)

Students read a magazine interview with an imaginary German actor. They answer the questions with *In England* or *In Deutschland*. Invite the more able to use full sentences and the inverted form: *In England gibt es …*

Answers

1 In England. 2 In England. 3 In England. 4 In Deutschland. 5 In Deutschland. 6 In Deutschland. 7 In Deutschland. 8 In Deutschland.

4b Vergleiche die Länder. Schreib Sätze. (Writing / Reading)

Based on some cues and the same article, students write sentences using the comparative to compare the things Freddi says about England and Germany. Make sure students realise that these are Freddi's subjective opinions and aren't necessarily factual comparisons!

Answers

1 England ist teurer als Deutschland. 2 Deutschland ist billiger als England. 3 In England ist das Frühstück größer als in Deutschland. 4 In Deutschland ist das Frühstück kleiner als in England. 5 In England ist das Wetter schlechter als in Deutschland. 6 In Deutschland

ist das Wetter besser als in England. **7** Deutschland ist kälter als England. **8** England ist wärmer als Deutschland. **9** England ist schmutziger als Deutschland. **10** Deutschland ist sauberer als England. **11** Die Menschen sind freundlicher in England als in Deutschland. **12** Die Menschen sind steifer in Deutschland als in England.

Further practice of the language and vocabulary of this unit is given on the following page.
Reading and Writing A: p. 194

Kursarbeit
The activities in this unit form an ideal introduction to coursework preparation. Specific coursework practice on this topic is provided on pp. 180–181.

All the vocabulary and structures from this chapter are listed on the *Wörter* pages at the end (pp. 88–89). These can be used for revision by covering up either the English or the German. Students can check here to see how much they remember from the chapter.

For more speaking practice to do with this chapter, use p. 106.

Further grammar and speaking practice on the language of this chapter is provided on pp. 37–38 of the Workbook.

Assessment materials for Chapters 5 and 6 are available after Chapter 6.

Kursarbeit

5 Marburg wartet auf Sie!

(pp. 180–181)

The coursework spreads in *Logo! 4* give regular, guided practice in preparing for the coursework element of the GCSE exam.

The spreads always start with a model text on each theme (at a higher level than that expected by the student) which acts as a stimulus to give students ideas of what they might include in their own piece of work. Students are encouraged to look at the detail of the text through the guided reading activities. They are gradually guided to produce good German sentences in the tasks through to the final task, which is to produce an extended piece of writing. The *Hilfe* column is a feature on all the spreads. It reminds students of language they might include and particular structures that will raise the level of their writing. Remind students who are capable of achieving a Higher grade that they should always include examples of two or three tenses in their writing.

This spread guides students to produce an extended piece of writing on the topic of a town.

1 Lies den Artikel und verbinde die deutschen und englischen Ausdrücke.
Students read the article and match up the English expressions with their German equivalents.

Answers
1 d, 2 g, 3 b, 4 f, 5 a, 6 h, 7 c, 8 e

2 Beantworte die folgenden Fragen auf Deutsch. Wähle a, b oder c.
Students choose the correct answers from the three options provided.

Answers
1 b, 2 c, 3 a, 4 c, 5 a, 6 b, 7 c, 8 b

3 Wähle jetzt eine andere Stadt oder Gegend und schreib eine ähnliche Broschüre (siehe Hilfe). Vergiss nicht, Folgendes zu erwähnen.
Students now write their own brochure about a town using the tips in the *Hilfe* column as support.

Hilfe
Tips for writing about a town or area:
- adapting language from similar texts
- including questions and quotations
- using lots of adjectives

# Workbook (pp. 32–38)

Logo! 4 5 Meine Stadt

p. 32

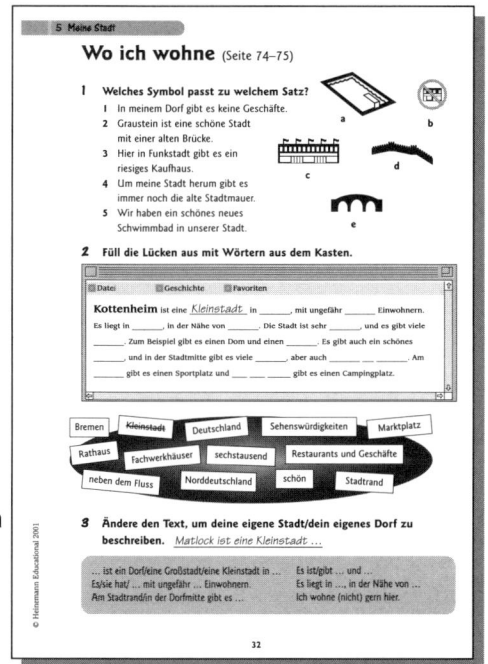

1 1 b, 2 e, 3 c, 4 d, 5 a
2 Kottenheim ist eine Kleinstadt in Deutschland, mit ungefähr sechstausend Einwohnern. Es liegt in Norddeutschland, in der Nähe von Bremen. Die Stadt ist sehr schön, und es gibt viele Sehenswürdigkeiten. Zum Beispiel gibt es einen Dom und einen Marktplatz. Es gibt auch ein schönes Rathaus, und in der Stadtmitte gibt es viele Fachwerkhäuser, aber auch Restaurants und Geschäfte. Am Stadtrand gibt es einen Sportplatz und neben dem Fluss gibt es einen Campingplatz.
3 open-ended

p. 33

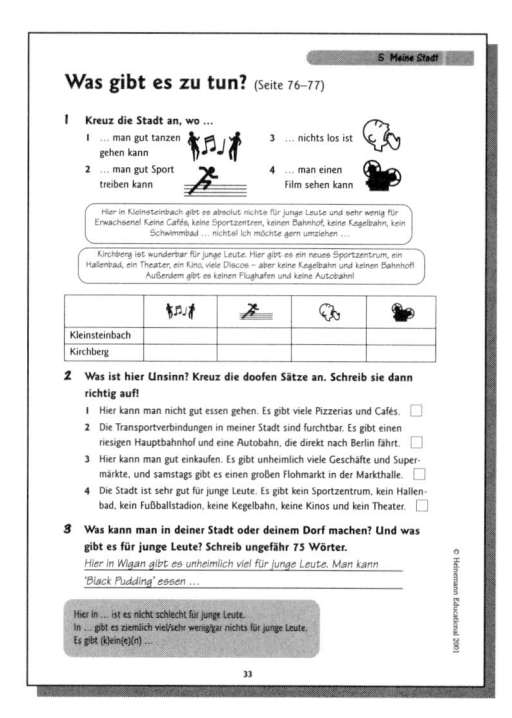

1

	🕺♪	🏃	🐑	🎥
Kleinsteinbach			✔	
Kirchberg	✔	✔		✔

2 sentences 1, 2 and 4 should be crossed off: corrected sentences open-ended, as long as they make sense
3 open-ended: overlook minor errors

p. 34

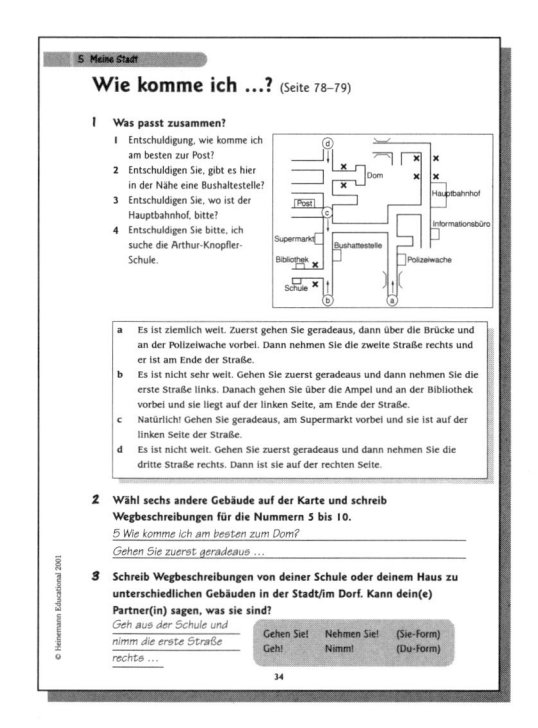

1 1 d, 2 c, 3 a, 4 b
2 open-ended
3 open-ended

95

p. 35

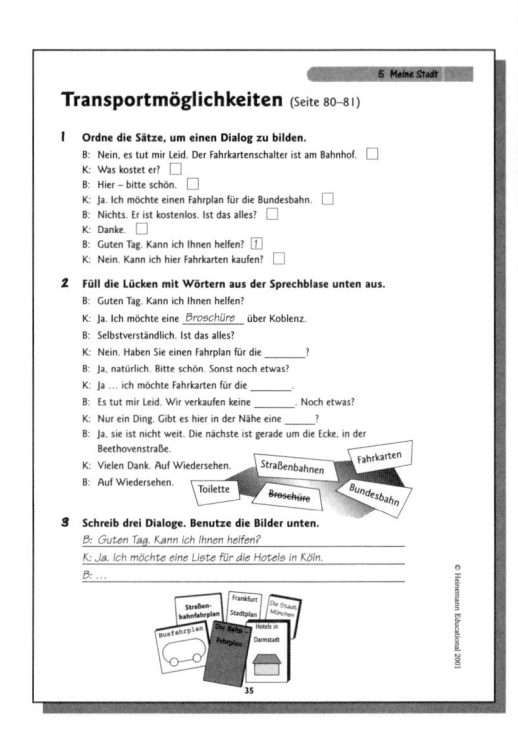

1 B: Guten Tag. Kann ich Ihnen helfen?
K: Ja. Ich möchte einen Fahrplan für die Bundesbahn.
B: Hier – bitte schön.
K: Was kostet er?
B: Nichts. Er ist kostenlos. Ist das alles?
K: Nein. Kann ich hier Fahrkarten kaufen?
B: Nein, es tut mir Leid. Der Fahrkartenschalter ist am Bahnhof.
K: Danke.

2 B: Guten Tag. Kann ich Ihnen helfen?
K: Ja. Ich möchte eine <u>Broschüre</u> über Koblenz.
B: Selbstverständlich. Ist das alles?
K: Nein. Haben Sie einen Fahrplan für die <u>Straßenbahnen</u>?
B: Ja, natürlich. Bitte schön. Sonst noch etwas?
K: Ja … ich möchte Fahrkarten für die <u>Bundesbahn</u>.
B: Es tut mir Leid. Wir verkaufen keine <u>Fahrkarten</u>. Noch etwas?
K: Nur ein Ding. Gibt es hier in der Nähe eine <u>Toilette</u>?
B: Ja, sie ist nicht weit. Die nächste ist gerade um die Ecke, in der Beethovenstraße.
K: Vielen Dank. Auf Wiedersehen.
B: Auf Wiedersehen.

3 open-ended

p. 36

1 1, 3
2 1 Um 11.39. 2 Um 09.47. 3 Nein. 4 Ja. 5 Gleis 2.
3 open-ended
4 open-ended

p. 37

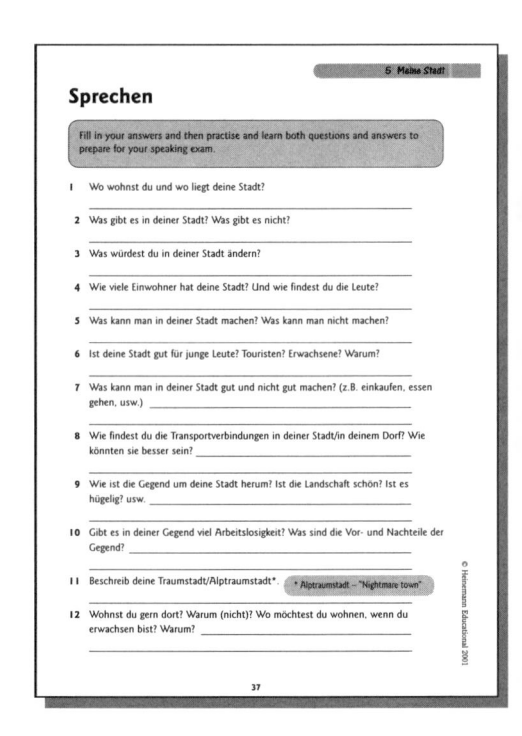

no answers – *Sprechen*

p. 38

1 **1** In meiner Stadt / Hier gibt es ein Schloss. **2** In meiner Stadt / Hier gibt es ein Sportzentrum. **3** In meiner Stadt / Hier gibt es keine Tankstelle. **4** In meiner Stadt / Hier gibt es keine Brücke. **5** In meiner Stadt / Hier gibt es ein Krankenhaus. **6** In meiner Stadt / Hier gibt es einen Bahnhof.

2 **1** Wie komme ich am besten zum Dom? **2** Wie komme ich am besten zum Informationsbüro? **3** Wie komme ich am besten zur Bushaltestelle? **4** Wie fahre ich nach Berlin? **5** Wie komme ich am besten zur Schule? **6** Wie fährt man am besten nach Frankfurt?

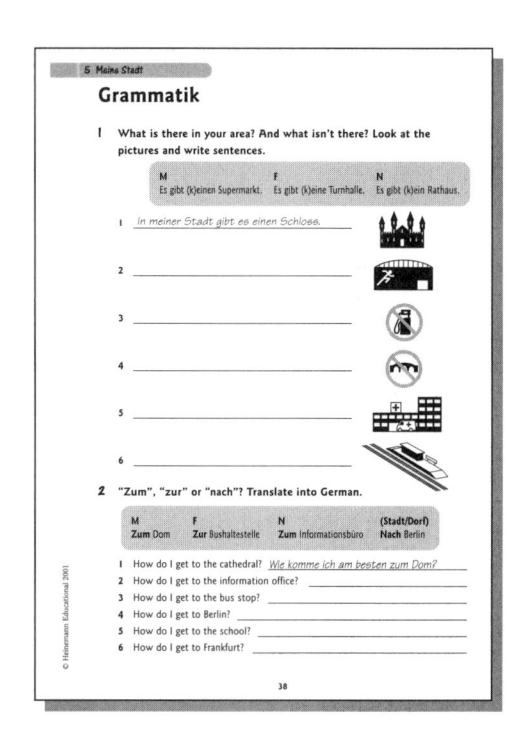

6 Einkaufen (Student's Book pp. 90–107)

Topic area	Key language	Grammar	Skills
6.1 Geschäfte und Öffnungszeiten (pp. 90–91) Shops and opening times	der Supermarkt, die Apotheke, die Bäckerei, die Buchhandlung, die Drogerie, die Konditorei, die Metzgerei, das Kaufhaus, das Schreibwarengeschäft Das Geschäft macht um … auf und um … zu. Wann macht … auf / zu? halb sieben / Viertel vor / nach elf / fünf nach / vor halb fünf Wo ist die nächste Apotheke?		Listening skills: preparation before listening and tips Giving detailed information on towns: include tenses and opinions
6.2 Preise usw. (pp. 92–93) Numbers, prices and food	Ich möchte bitte 500 Gramm … / ein Kilo Birnen. Bitte schön. Sonst noch etwas? Geben Sie mir bitte … Scheiben Käse / eine Packung Kekse / eine Dose Cola / eine Flasche Rotwein / eine Tüte Milch + other items. Ist das alles? Ja. Was macht das insgesamt? Zwei Packungen Chips kosten €1,00.	Quantities	Saying prices in euros
6.3 Im Kleidungsgeschäft (pp. 94–95) Shopping for clothes	Ich möchte / suche / brauche … + clothes items einen langen Mantel / eine neue Jacke / ein neues Hemd / neue Schuhe. Kann ich diesen Rock / diese Hose / dieses Kleid anprobieren? Haben Sie ihn / sie / es in Blau? Er / Sie / Es ist mir zu klein / groß / teuer. Was kostet er / sie / es? Kann ich mit Bargeld / Kreditkarte / per Scheck zahlen? Dieser / Diese / Dieses ist kleiner / größer / billiger / breiter.	Adjective endings (accusative after indefinite article) *dieser / diese / dieses*	Singular / plural items of clothing
6.4 Taschengeld (pp. 96–97) Spending pocket money	Wie viel Taschengeld bekommst / kriegst du? Ich bekomme € … pro Monat / Woche Was kaufst du damit? Ich kaufe CDs / Bonbons / Kleidung usw. Ich spare für die Ferien / einen Computer.		*kriegen* Advice for using this topic for the Speaking Test
6.5 Einkaufsbummel (pp. 98–99) Shopping in a department store	Wo ist …? Ich suche / brauche / will / möchte … die Herrenabteilung, Damenabteilung, Lebensmittelabteilung, Kinderabteilung, Haushaltsabteilung, Süßwarenabteilung, Schreibwarenabteilung, Schuhabteilung, Sportabteilung. Im Erdgeschoss / In der ersten, zweiten, dritten, vierten Etage. Der Ring ist alt / schmutzig / kaputt / zu eng / zu groß. Kann ich bitte eine neue Uhr haben / mein Geld zurückhaben?	Adjective endings (accusative after indefinite article)	Expressions to use when complaining in a shop
6.6 Auf der Post (pp. 100–101) At the post office	Was kostet ein Brief / eine Postkarte / eine Ansichtskarte / dieses Päckchen / dieses Paket nach …? Es wiegt … Es kostet … Eine Briefmarke zu fünfzig Cent. Zwei Briefmarken zu fünfundsiebzig Cent. Kann man hier telefonieren? Wo kann man einen Brief einwerfen / eine E-Mail schicken? Ich möchte ein Fax schicken.	*Kann ich …? Kann man …?*	Post office vocabulary Adapting dialogues

6.7 Verloren! (pp. 102–103) Reporting lost property	Ich habe meinen neuen Pass / meine kleine Uhr / mein blaues Handy verloren. Hast du / Haben Sie meinen alten Schlüssel gefunden? Ich habe ihn / sie / es im Bus / in der Stadt verloren. auf, unter, neben, in, hinter time expressions: heute Morgen, gestern Nachmittag, vorgestern, letzte Woche	Adjective endings in the accusative Prepositions: *auf, in, hinter, neben, unter*

- The vocabulary and structures taught in Chapter 6 are summarised on the *Wörter* pages of the Student's Book, 104–105.
- Further speaking practice on the language of this chapter is provided on p. 107.
- futher reading and writing practice on the language of this chapter is provided on pp. 196–197.
- For a selection of assessment tasks for Chapters 5 and 6, please refer to the separate Assessment Pack for your chosen examination board: AQA, OCR or Edexcel.

1 Geschäfte und Öffnungszeiten (pp. 90–91)

Students will learn how to:
- talk about shops and opening times

Key language
der Supermarkt, die Apotheke, die Bäckerei, die Buchhandlung, die Drogerie, die Konditorei, die Metzgerei, das Kaufhaus, das Schreibwarengeschäft
Das Geschäft macht um … auf und um … zu.
halb sieben
Viertel vor / nach elf
fünf nach / vor halb fünf
Wann macht … auf / zu?
Wo ist (die) nächste (Apotheke)?

Skill focus
- listening skills: preparing before listening
- tips for describing shops

Resources
- Cassette B, Side B
- Workbook p. 39
- Sprechen p. 107, Rollenspiel 1

Remind students that shopping is a frequent topic for GCSE tasks. Start the spread by seeing how many German words for types of shop they can remember without looking at the page.

1 Welches Geschäft ist das? (Reading)
Students read sentences about shops and work out which is which, noting down the name of the shop being described.

Answers

1 die Apotheke, 2 die Buchhandlung, 3 das Schreibwarengeschäft, 4 die Bäckerei, 5 die Metzgerei, 6 die Konditorei, 7 die Drogerie, 8 der Supermarkt / das Kaufhaus

2 Hör zu und lies. Richtig oder falsch? (Listening / Reading)
Students listen to a shopping conversation and answer true or false questions. They can do this with or without referring to the text on the page. This text lends itself to being read aloud and then, if wished, adapted by students.

Answers

1 Richtig. 2 Richtig. 3 Falsch. 4 Falsch. 5 Falsch. 6 Falsch.

Katharina: Also, was brauchen wir für unser Picknick?
Jasmin: Auf jeden Fall Brot. Wo ist die nächste Bäckerei?
Katharina: Weiß ich nicht. Aber hier ist die Metzgerei. Hier können wir Schinken kaufen.
Jasmin: Ja, aber … Moment, die Metzgerei ist geschlossen.
Katharina: Hmm … Aber ich möchte Kuchen kaufen. Gibt es hier in der Nähe eine Konditorei?
Jasmin: Nein, die nächste Konditorei ist sehr weit. Da können wir nicht zu Fuß gehen.
Katharina: Mensch! … Also, was brauchen wir noch? Tomaten, Äpfel, Apfelsinen … Wo ist der nächste Obst- und Gemüseladen?
Jasmin: Hier vorne, aber der ist auch geschlossen.
Katharina: Was? Weißt du was, Jasmin? Wir gehen zum Supermarkt!

3 Lies die Sätze und schau die Geschäfte in Übung 1 an. Welches Geschäft ist das? (Reading)
Students read the sentences about opening times and refer back to the illustration at the top of p. 90 in order to identify which shops are being referred to.

If necessary, do a quick revision of times with students. Write some digital times on the board or OHT for them to write down. Do some oral practice too, getting students to give you the correct time as quickly as possible.

Point out to students how vital it is to get the *halb* thing right. Recently, some German visitors to England missed their plane home as a result of inadvertently ordering their taxi an hour late.

Answers

1 die Metzgerei, 2 die Konditorei, 3 die Drogerie, 4 das Kaufhaus, 5 der Supermarkt

Tip box
This provides advice about looking carefully at the listening task and listening out only for what is needed to answer the questions.

4 Hör zu, schreib die Tabelle ab und füll sie aus (1–5). (Listening)
Students copy the table, then listen to some commercials for shops and fill in the details.

Answers

1 Buchhandlung, 9 Uhr, 18 Uhr, 2 Apotheke, 8 Uhr, 19 Uhr, 3 Kaufhaus, 8.30, 18.30, 4 Schreibwarengeschäft, 8.30, 18 Uhr, 5 Metzgerei, 8 Uhr, 18.15 Uhr

---

1 – Sind Sie eine Leseratte? Suchen Sie ein Buch als Weihnachtsgeschenk? Dann kommen Sie zu uns! Unsere Öffnungszeiten sind von 9 bis 18 Uhr.
2 – Wenn Sie Kopfschmerzen oder Halsschmerzen haben, finden sie bei uns die besten Medikamente. Wir machen um 8 Uhr schon auf und erst um 19 Uhr zu.

3 – Wollen Sie in der Stadt einkaufen? Kein Problem! Bei uns finden Sie auf fünf Etagen einfach alles: Kleider, Lebensmittel, Haushaltswaren, alles! Und wir haben lange Öffnungszeiten: 8.30 bis 18.30.

4 – In zwei Wochen wird das neue Schuljahr beginnen. Dann braucht ihr bestimmt neue Hefte und Kulis. Wir haben alle Schreibwaren. Wir machen schon um 8.30 auf und um 18 Uhr zu. Kommt zu uns nach der Schule.

5 – Bald ist Weihnachten! Haben Sie letztes Jahr bei uns Ihr Fleisch gekauft? Dann werden Sie dieses Jahr bestimmt wieder bei uns Ihr Fleisch kaufen! Unsere Öffnungszeiten für die Festtage: 8 Uhr bis 18.15.

5 Partnerarbeit. (Speaking)
Students, working in pairs, make up short conversations using the visual prompts provided and the structures practised on this spread.

6 Beantworte diese Frage: Kann man in deiner Stadt gut einkaufen? (Writing)
In writing their answer to this question, students should give as many details as they can about the shops in their own town. Encourage them to add opinions. This work will need to be collected in and marked.

Tip box
This provides help with describing shops in the students' own town in exercise 6.

Further practice of the language and vocabulary of this unit is given on the following pages.
Speaking: p. 107, Rollenspiel 1
Workbook: p. 39

2 Preise usw. (pp. 92–93)

Students will learn how to:
- talk about prices and quantities of food

Key language
Ich möchte / Wir möchten bitte …
   250 Gramm Äpfel /
   zwei Kilo Erdbeeren /
   500 Gramm Bananen /
   ein Kilo Birnen /
   Kirschen / Kartoffeln.
Bitte schön. Sonst noch etwas?
Geben Sie mir bitte …
   Pfirsiche / Tomaten /
   Butter / Zucker.
   … Scheiben Käse /
   Schinken / Salami.
   eine Packung Kekse /
   Chips.
   eine Dose Cola /
   Limonade / Sprudel /
   eine Flasche Rotwein /
   Weißwein / Bier /
   Mineralwasser / eine
   Tüte Milch / Apfelsaft /
   Orangensaft.
   sechs Eier / Brötchen /
   Apfelsinen.
Ist das alles?
Ja. Was macht das insgesamt?
Zwei Packungen Chips kosten € 1,00.

Skill focus
- how to say prices in euros

Resources
- Cassette B, Side B
- Workbook p. 40
- Sprechen p. 107, Rollenspiel 2

Before starting this unit, ask students to imagine they are about to go shopping at a market. How many items can they come up with that they could already buy in German? What do they remember about amounts and packaging?

1 Hör zu! Was kaufen Jasmin und Katharina? (Listening / Writing)
Students listen to a brief shopping conversation and write a sentence to say what items Jasmin and Katharina buy.

Answers
Jasmin und Katharina kaufen ein Kilo Erdbeeren, vier Apfelsinen, 500 Gramm Käse und ein Kilo Tomaten.

> Jasmin: So, endlich sind wir am Marktplatz gelandet. Guten Tag.
> Verkäufer: Guten Tag! Was kann ich für Sie tun?
> Jasmin: Ich hätte gern ein Kilo Erdbeeren.
> Verkäufer: Gern. Bitte schön. Sonst noch etwas?
> Katharina: Brauchen wir Äpfel?
> Jasmin: Nee, Äpfel mag ich nicht. Aber Apfelsinen … Wir möchten vier Apfelsinen, bitte.
> Verkäufer: Sonst noch einen Wunsch?
> Jasmin: Ja, ich nehme 500 Gramm Käse und ein Kilo Tomaten.
> Verkäufer: Alles?
> Katharina: Ja, was macht das, bitte?

2 Partnerarbeit. (Speaking)
Students make up short dialogues based on the picture cues provided and using the dialogue on the page as a model.

3 Schreib an deinen Bruder. (Writing)
Students exploit their imaginary sibling by writing a list of things for him to buy based on the picture prompts provided. They are welcome to extend the list with other items of their own choosing.

4 Was hast du heute Morgen im Supermarkt gekauft? Erfinde die Sachen. (Writing)
Students write down (in the perfect tense) an imaginary list of things they might have bought. There are no cues.

5a Hör zu! Was kosten die Picknicksachen? (Listening)
Students listen to some supermarket announcements about special offers and note down the details (including the amounts) in German.

Answers
1 zwei Päckungen Chips, € 1,00, 2 500 Gramm Käse, € 3,30, 3 10 Brötchen, € 1,75, 4 6 Scheiben Salami, € 1,50, 5 6 Bananen, € 1,60 oder ein Kilo Birnen, € 2,20, 6 4 Dosen Limonade, € 0,75 oder eine Flasche Mineralwasser, 50 Cent

> 1 – Meine Damen und Herren, wollen Sie heute ein Picknick machen? Dann haben wir ein Top-Angebot für Sie: zwei Packungen Knüsti Kartoffelchips für nur € 1,00.
> 2 – Greifen Sie zu! Super-Käse aus der Schweiz. 500 Gramm für nur € 3,30. Perfekt für Ihr Picknick!
> 3 – Noch ein Angebot, meine Damen und Herren. In unserer Bäckerei bekommen Sie zehn Brötchen für nur € 1,75.
> 4 – Brauchen Sie Wurst für Ihre Brötchen? Wir haben die Lösung! Sechs Scheiben Salami für nur € 1,50.
> 5 – Vergessen Sie das Obst nicht! In der Obst- und Gemüseabteilung haben wir sechs Bananen für € 1,60 oder ein Kilo Birnen für € 2,20. Mmm!
> 6 – Natürlich brauchen Sie etwas zu trinken: vier Dosen Limonade für nur € 0,75 oder eine Flasche Mineralwasser für 50 Cent!

5b Schreib die Sätze aus Übung 5a auf. (Writing)
Students write out the answers from exercise 5a in full sentences.

Answers
1 Zwei Päckungen Chips kosten € 1,00. 2 500 Gramm Käse kostet € 3,30. 3 Zehn Brötchen kosten € 1,75. 4 Sechs Scheiben Salami kosten € 1,50. 5 Sechs Bananen kosten € 1,60 oder ein Kilo Birnen kosten € 2,20. 6 Vier Dosen Limonade kosten € 0,75 oder eine Flasche Mineralwasser kostet 50 Cent.

6 Welches Schild passt zu welchem Satz? (Reading)

Remind students that, even at Higher Level, signs and notices from shops can feature as Reading Test items. Here, they must match sentences to words and write down the appropriate letters.

Answers

1 f, 2 g, 3 e, 4 d, 5 a, 6 b, 7 h, 8 c, 9 j, 10 i

Further practice of the language and vocabulary of this unit is given on the following pages.
Speaking: p. 107, Rollenspiel 2
Workbook: p. 40

3 Im Kleidungsgeschäft

(pp. 94–95)

Students will learn how to:
- shop for clothes

Key language
Ich möchte / suche / brauche ...
  einen langen Mantel / roten Pullover / grünen Schal / eine neue Jacke / graue Bluse / schwarze Jeans / blaue Krawatte / ein neues Hemd / neue Schuhe/ Socken / Handschuhe.
Kann ich diesen Rock / diese Hose / dieses Kleid anprobieren?
Haben Sie ihn / sie / es in Blau?
Er / Sie / Es ist mir zu klein / groß / teuer.
Was kostet er / sie / es?
Kann ich mit Bargeld / Kreditkarte / per Scheck zahlen?

Dieser / Diese / Dieses hier ist kleiner / größer / billiger / breiter.
Ach, ja er / sie / es ist besser.

Grammar focus
- adjective endings (accusative after indefinite article)
- dieser / diese / dieses

Skill focus
- singular / plural items of clothing

Resources
- Cassette B, Side B
- Workbook p. 41
- Sprechen p. 107, Rollenspiel 3

---

1 Hör zu! Was kaufen die Kunden? (Listening)

Students listen to five clothes shopping conversations, choose the appropriate answers from the illustrations provided and note down the correct letters. Tell them to be alert, as some traps are built in to this activity.

Answers
1 f, 2 b, 3 h, 4 e, 5 g

1 Kunde: Ich suche ein neues Hemd.
  Verkäuferin: Für Sie?
  Kunde: Ja, für mich.
  Verkäuferin: Welche Größe, bitte?
  Kunde: Größe 42.
  Verkäuferin: Und welche Farbe hätten Sie gern?
  Kunde: Weiß, glaube ich.
  Verkäuferin: Dieses hier kostet € 20,00.
2 Kunde: Guten Tag. Ich brauche eine neue Hose. Alle meine Hosen sind kaputt.
  Verkäuferin: Selbstverständlich. Welche Farbe, bitte?
  Kunde: Grau.
  Verkäuferin: Und welche Größe?
  Kunde: 36, glaube ich.
  Verkäuferin: Wie wär's mit dieser Hose? Sie kostet € 35,00.
3 Verkäuferin: Guten Tag.
  Kundin: Guten Tag. Ich suche einen langen Rock für eine Party.
  Verkäuferin: Kein Problem. Welche Farbe suchen Sie?
  Kundin: Ich glaube, rot.
  Verkäuferin: Hmm, einen roten Rock ... Hier, was meinen Sie dazu?
  Kundin: Haben Sie diesen Rock in meiner Größe?
  Verkäuferin: Welche Größe haben Sie?
  Kundin: 40.
  Verkäuferin: Jawohl ... und der Preis ist auch gut, nur 50,00.
4 Kundin: Guten Tag. Ich suche auch einen Rock.
  Verkäuferin: Auch in Rot?
  Kundin: Ja, warum nicht? Ich gehe am Wochenende zum Faschingsball, also brauche ich etwas Modisches.
  Verkäuferin: Wie wär's mit diesem kurzen Rock hier?
  Kundin: Hmm, nicht schlecht, aber bestimmt teuer. Was kostet er denn?
  Verkäuferin: Ah, da haben Sie Glück. Dieser ist im Sonderangebot, stark reduziert. Der kostet nur € 20,00.
  Kundin: Wirklich? Haben Sie ihn in Größe 42?
  Verkäuferin: Moment ... Ja, hier.
5 Verkäuferin: Bitte schön?
  Kunde: Guten Tag. Ich war letzte Woche hier und habe eine Hose anprobiert, aber leider hatten Sie sie nicht in meiner Größe.
  Verkäuferin: Was für eine Hose war das denn?
  Kunde: Also, das war eine leichte Hose in Weiß, für die Ferien.
  Verkäuferin: Ach ja, ich weiß Bescheid. Ich glaube .. ja, die hier, für € 48,00. Ist sie das?
  Kunde: Jawohl. Haben Sie sie jetzt in Größe 36?
  Verkäuferin: Ja. Wollen Sie sie anprobieren?

Tip box
Items of clothing which are counted as a single garment in German. This is seemingly a small point, but emphasise it, because few things sound odder in German than classic anglicisms such as *ein Paar Hosen!* (Students are also advised to just learn the plural of socks, gloves and shoes.)

Grammatik: Adjektive (Akkusativ) (adjectives – accusative)
This gives examples of accusative endings after the indefinite article. Practice of this point is given in exercise 2.

2 Was hast du gekauft? Schreib Sätze im Perfekt. (Writing)
Students practise using the perfect tense to write down descriptions of items they have bought. They are welcome to make up a few more of their own as well.

Answers
1 Ich habe eine schwarze Hose gekauft. Sie hat € 32,50 gekostet. 2 Ich habe einen langen grauen Mantel gekauft. Er hat € 125,00 gekostet. 3 Ich habe eine lange gelbe Hose gekauft. Sie hat € 17,50 gekostet.

> **4** Ich habe ein kurzes grünes Kleid gekauft. Es hat € 95,00 gekostet. **5** Ich habe eine blaue Jeans gekauft. Sie hat € 47,50 gekostet. **6** Ich habe rote Socken gekauft. Sie haben € 5,00 gekostet. **7** Ich habe schwarze Schuhe gekauft. Sie haben € 60,00 gekostet. **8** Ich habe ein weißes Hemd gekauft. Es hat € 25,00 gekostet.

3 Lies den Artikel und schau die Bilder an. Wer ist wer? (Reading)

Students study this magazine article about an awards ceremony, work out who is who on the basis of the descriptions and the illustrations and write down their names.

Answers
> **1** Vera Nowotna, **2** Richard Kolinski, **3** Rita Kolinski, **4** Sylvia Schiller, **5** Rudi Ratlos

4a Hör zu, lies den Text für das erste Gespräch und schreib die Informationen auf Englisch auf. (Listening / Reading)

Students listen to dialogues in a clothes shop and choose from alternative answers. Only the first of the three conversations is printed in the book, so in conversations 2 and 3 they will need to concentrate particularly hard.

Answers
> **1** too small, € 75,00, by credit card, **2** too big, € 45,00, by cheque, **3** too expensive, € 100,00, by credit card

> Konversation 1
> Kundin: Ich interessiere mich für dieses Kleid hier. Haben Sie es in Blau?
> Verkäuferin: Nein, leider nicht. Aber wir haben es in Schwarz.
> Kundin: Hmm … Kann ich es anprobieren?
> Verkäuferin: Natürlich.
> Kundin: Ach nein, es ist mir zu klein.
> Verkäuferin: Dieses hier ist größer.
> Kundin: Ach ja, es ist besser. Was kostet es?
> Verkäuferin: € 75,00.
> Kundin: Okay. Kann ich mit Kreditkarte zahlen?
>
> Konversation 2
> Kunde: Kann ich diesen Pullover anprobieren?
> Verkäuferin: Gern.
> Kunde: Ach nein, er ist mir zu groß.
> Verkäuferin: Dieser hier ist kleiner.
> Kunde: Ach ja, er ist besser. Was kostet er?
> Verkäuferin: € 45,00.
> Kunde: Okay. Kann ich per Scheck zahlen?
>
> Konversation 3
> Kundin: Kann ich diesen Rock anprobieren?
> Verkäuferin: Selbstverständlich.
> Kundin: Ja, er ist perfekt. Was kostet er?
> Verkäuferin: € 250,00.

> Kundin: Was? Er ist mir zu teuer!
> Verkäuferin: Dieser hier ist billiger, nur € 100,00.
> Kundin: Okay. Nehmen Sie Kreditkarten?
> Verkäuferin: Natürlich.

4b Partnerarbeit. Ändert die braunen Wörter aus Übung 4a. (Speaking)

Working in pairs, students use the printed conversation 1 from exercise 4a to carry out three substitution exercises.

Further practice of the language and vocabulary of this unit is given on the following pages.
Speaking: p. 107, Rollenspiel 3
Workbook: p. 41

4 Taschengeld (pp. 96–97)

Students will learn how to:
- talk about spending pocket money

Key language
Wie viel Taschengeld bekommst / kriegst du?
Ich bekomme € ... pro Monat / Woche.
Was kaufst du damit?
Ich kaufe CDs / Bonbons / Kleidung usw.
Ich spare für die Ferien / einen Computer.
Was hast du letzten Monat gekauft?
Ich habe ... gekauft.

Skill focus
- *kriegen*
- using this subject for the Speaking Test

Resources
- Cassette B, Side B
- Workbook p. 42
- Sprechen p. 107, Gespräch

If it's not too invidious, invite students to start the unit by saying (or making up) how much pocket money they get. Ask them to think of as many German words as they can in order to say what they spend their money on.

1a Hör zu! Wer bekommt was? Schreib die Tabelle ab und füll sie aus. (Listening)

Students listen to a radio phone-in about pocket money and what the callers do with it. They copy the grid and note down the amount of pocket money and the items.

Answers

Ines: € 10,00 pro Woche, Bonbons. Roland: € 50,00 im Monat, CDs, Kassetten. Anni: € 40,00 im Monat, Kleidung. Sven: € 12,50 pro Woche, Mofa. Paul: € 100,00 im Monat, Computerspiele.

> Moderator: Herzlich willkommen bei Jugend-Talk. Heute geht's um Taschengeld. Wie viel bekommt ihr, was macht ihr damit? Und wer ist dran?
> Ines: Hi, Uli. Hier spricht die Ines aus Kiel.
> Moderator: Hallo, Ines. Also, wie viel bekommst du?
> Ines: Also, ich kriege € 10,00 pro Woche.
> Moderator: So, und was machst du damit?
> Ines: Ach, ich kaufe Bonbons und so.
> Moderator: Na, denk an deine Zähne! Und du, Roland?
> Roland: Also, ich bin großer Musikfan, Uli. Ich gebe mein Geld für CDs und Kassetten aus.
> Moderator: Und wie viel bekommst du?
> Roland: Ich kriege € 50,00 im Monat.
> Moderator: Gut, und wer kommt jetzt?
> Anni: Ich bin's, Anni aus Oldenburg. Also, ich kriege nur € 40,00 im Monat und ich gebe alles für Kleider aus! Letzte Woche habe ich ein teures Kleid gekauft.
> Moderator: So, Kleider ... Und du, Sven, was machst du mit deinem Taschengeld?
> Sven: Nichts. Ich bekomme € 12,50 in der Woche und ich spare es. Ich spare auf eine Mofa. Hoffentlich werde ich nächstes Jahr genug Geld haben, um eine Mofa zu kaufen.
> Moderator: Tolle Sache. Und zum Schluss noch Paul. Wie viel kriegst du und wofür gibst du es aus?
> Paul: Ich habe Glück. Ich bekomme € 100,00 Taschengeld im Monat von meinen Eltern. Ich gebe alles für meinen Computer aus. Ich interessiere mich für Informatik.

Tip box
An explanation of the use of *kriegen*. Tell students that it would be very natural and perfectly acceptable to use this word in the Speaking Test.

1b Schreib die Sätze aus Übung 1a auf. (Writing)

Students write out, in full sentences, the information noted down in exercise 1a.

Answers

1 Ines bekommt € 10,00 pro Woche. Sie kauft Bonbons. 2 Roland bekommt € 50,00 im Monat. Er kauft CDs und Kassetten. 3 Anni bekommt € 40,00 im Monat. Sie kauft Kleidung. 4 Sven bekommt € 12,50 pro Woche. Er spart auf eine Mofa. 5 Paul bekommt € 100,00 im Monat. Er kauft Computerspiele.

2 Partnerarbeit. (Speaking)

Based on the cues provided and the model dialogue, students construct brief dialogues on the subject of pocket money. Make sure students take it in turns to ask and answer questions.

3 Lies den Artikel und beantworte die Fragen auf Englisch. (Reading)

Students read this magazine article about young people and their pocket money and answer the English questions about it. Remind them that they are likely to have to answer English questions in the Reading Test, especially when, as in this case, the text is quite dense.

Answers

1 telephones / mobile phones, 2 sweets, magazines, cigarettes, 3 no, 4 saves for a computer; buys magazines, sweets, clothes, 5 she spends so much on telephoning, 6 replacing her lost mobile phone, 7 he doesn't want a mobile, 8 buys clothes and saves for holidays

4 Schreib eine E-Mail an einen deutschen Freund / eine deutsche Freundin. (Writing)

Students use the structures practised in this spread to write an e-mail to an imaginary penfriend. Encourage them to write as much as they can – e-mails are cheap!

Tip box
This provides advice about using this topic for the Speaking Test and reminds students to include plenty of information, opinions and tenses.

Further practice of the language and vocabulary of this unit is given on the following pages.
Speaking: p. 107, Gespräch
Workbook: p. 42

5 Einkaufsbummel (pp. 98–99)

Students will learn how to:
- shop in a department store

Key language
Wo ist …?
Ich suche / brauche / will / möchte …
   die Herrenabteilung, Damenabteilung, Lebensmittelabteilung, Kinderabteilung, Haushaltsabteilung, Süßwarenabteilung, Schreibwarenabteilung, Schuhabteilung, Sportabteilung.
Im Erdgeschoss / In der ersten, zweiten, dritten, vierten Etage.
(Der Ring) ist …
   alt / schmutzig / kaputt / zu eng / zu groß.
Kann ich bitte …
   eine neue Uhr haben?
   mein Geld zurückhaben?

Grammar focus
- adjective endings: accusative after indefinite article

Skill focus
- expressions to use when complaining in a shop

Resources
- Cassette B, Side B
- Workbook p. 43
- Sprechen p. 107, Rollenspiel 4
- Lesen / Schreiben A p. 196

Start this spread by asking students to suggest problems they might encounter when shopping in a department store. Tell them that department stores such as *Horten*, *Hertie* and *Karstadt*, selling virtually everything, are still a feature of all German cities and are more common than in the UK.

1 Lies den Zettel und vervollständige die Sätze. (Reading)
Students read this note from Wiebke, complete the sentences and write them out. Variations are possible.

Answers
1 Wiebke und Martin sind in der Schweiz. 2 Der letzte Tag ist morgen. 3 Dann gehen sie ins Kaufhaus. 4 Für ihre Eltern müssen sie Geschenke kaufen. 5 Sie wollen auch noch Geschenke für ihre Freunden. 6 Wiebke wird Martin um 8 Uhr wecken.

2 Hör zu und notiere die Informationen für Mutti, Vati, Kati und Wiebke. (Listening / Writing)
Students listen to Martin and Wiebke deciding what to buy and note down the information about what they get, in which department and on what floor it is.

Answers
1 **Mutti:** Portemonnaie, Geschenkabteilung, dritte Etage, 2 **Vati:** Schlips, Herrenabteilung, zweite Etage, 3 **Kati:** Bonbons, Süßwarenabteilung, erste Etage, 4 **Wiebke:** Kulis, Schreibwarenabteilung, Erdgeschoss

> Wiebke: So, Martin, heute ist unser letzter Tag hier in Zürich. Wollen wir Souvenirs kaufen?
> Martin: Ja, und Geschenke. Was kaufen wir für Mutti?
> Wiebke: Mutti hat ihr Portemonnaie verloren, also braucht sie ein neues Portemonnaie. In welcher Abteilung findet man so was?
> Martin: Ich weiß … Entschuldigen Sie, wo ist die Geschenkabteilung?
> Verkäufer: In der dritten Etage.
> Wiebke: Danke. Und was kaufen wir für Papa?
> Martin: Papa braucht einen neuen Schlips. Seine alten Krawatten sind doch so hässlich!
> Wiebke: Richtig! Entschuldigen Sie, wo ist die Herrenabteilung?
> Verkäufer: In der zweiten Etage.
> Wiebke: Danke schön. Also, was kaufen wir für Kati?
> Martin: Ganz einfach: Bonbons!
> Wiebke: Natürlich! Entschuldigen Sie, wo ist die Süßwarenabteilung?
> Verkäufer: Die Süßwarenabteilung ist in der ersten Etage.
> Martin: So, und was kaufst du für dich?
> Wiebke: Ich brauche Kulis für die Schule. Hallo, wo ist die Schreibwarenabteilung?
> Verkäufer: Die ist hier im Erdgeschoss.
> Martin: Also, Erdgeschoss, erste Etage, zweite Etage, dritte Etage … Lasst uns den Aufzug nehmen!

3 Partnerarbeit. (Speaking)
Students use the speech bubbles and the directory from the department store to make short dialogues. Students should take it in turns to ask and answer questions.

4 Hör zu! Was ist das Problem? Schreib Sätze. (Listening / Writing)
Students listen to a series of complaints and write sentences in German to explain what they are. Words are provided to assist them.

Answers
1 Das Hemd ist schmutzig. 2 Die Bluse ist zu groß. 3 Das Brot ist alt. 4 Der Ring ist zu eng. 5 Die Handschuhe sind kaputt.

> 1 – Guten Tag. Ich möchte mich beschweren. Ich habe gestern dieses Hemd gekauft und es ist schmutzig. Das finde ich nicht in Ordnung. Kann ich bitte ein neues Hemd haben?
> 2 – Ich habe letzte Woche diese Bluse gekauft, aber sie ist zu groß. Kann ich bitte eine neue Bluse haben?
> 3 – Ich habe heute Morgen dieses Brot gekauft, aber es ist alt. Das geht nicht! Kann ich bitte ein neues Brot haben? Wenn nicht, möchte ich mit dem Direktor sprechen.
> 4 – Ich habe neulich diesen Ring gekauft, aber er ist zu eng. Kann ich bitte einen neuen Ring haben? Nein? Dann kann ich bitte mein Geld zurückhaben?

5 – Ich möchte mich beschweren. Ich habe gestern diese Handschuhe gekauft, aber sie sind kaputt. Kann ich bitte neue Handschuhe haben?

Tip box
A list of expressions to use when complaining in a shop. Remind students that these would be useful expressions to learn by heart.

5 Partnerarbeit. (Speaking)
Using the sample dialogue as a model, students, working in pairs, create a series of similar dialogues based on the cues provided.

Grammatik: Adjektive + Akkusativ (adjectives with the accusative)
Adjective endings in the accusative after the indefinite article. Remind students that if they don't put the correct endings on, it will sound grammatically incorrect, which will hinder communication. Give them a few words to practise with orally.
Teacher: der Mantel, grün
Student: Ich habe einen grünen Mantel gekauft.

6 Schreib einen Brief an ein Kaufhaus. Du hast etwas gekauft, aber es gibt ein Problem. (Writing)
Students use the structures practised in this spread to write a letter of complaint, based on the model provided. Tell pupils that letters of this type often crop up in the Writing Test.

Further practice of the language and vocabulary of this unit is given on the following pages.
Speaking: p. 107, Rollenspiel 4
Reading and Writing A: p. 196
Workbook: p. 43

6 Auf der Post (pp. 100–101)

Students will learn how to:
- communicate at the post office

Key language
Was kostet ein Brief / eine Postkarte / eine Ansichtskarte / dieses Päckchen / dieses Paket nach ...?
Es wiegt ...
Es kostet ...
Eine Briefmarke zu fünfzig Cent.
Zwei Briefmarken zu fünfundsiebzig Cent.
Kann man hier telefonieren?
Wo kann man einen Brief einwerfen / eine E-Mail schicken?
Ich möchte ein Fax schicken.

Grammar focus
- kann ich / man ...?

Skill focus
- post office vocabulary
- adapting dialogues

Resources
- Cassette B, Side B
- Workbook p. 44

Start the spread by asking students what vocabulary they remember which would be useful in a German post office.

1 Hör zu, lies die Gespräche und beantworte die Fragen auf Deutsch (ganze Sätze, bitte!). (Listening / Reading / Writing)

Students listen to a dialogue at a post office (also provided on the page) and answer questions about it in full sentences. More able students can do this activity 'unseen'. The dialogue also lends itself to reading aloud and being used for a substitution exercise.

Answers

> 1 Die Touristin schickt einen Brief. 2 Eine Briefmarke für einen Brief kostet 75 Cent. 3 Sie schickt fünf Ansichtskarten. 4 Eine Briefmarke für eine Ansichtskarte kostet 65 Cent. 5 Das Päckchen wiegt 600 Gramm. 6 Das Päckchen nach England kostet € 6,00. 7 Die Touristin zahlt € 10,00 insgesamt.

Touristin: Entschuldigen Sie, wo ist die nächste Post?
Passant: Hier doch!
Touristin: Ach, natürlich!

Touristin: Guten Tag. Ich möchte einen Brief nach England schicken. Was kostet das?
Beamtin: Nach England? 75 Cent.
Touristin: Und eine Ansichtskarte?
Beamtin: 65 Cent.
Touristin: Also, ich nehme fünf Briefmarken zu 65 Cent und eine zu 75 Cent.
Beamtin: Bitte schön.
Touristin: Und wie viel kostet dieses Päckchen, auch nach England?

Beamtin: Moment, wie viel wiegt das Päckchen? 600 Gramm ... nach England ... Das macht € 6,00, bitte schön.
Touristin: So, was macht das insgesamt?
Beamtin: Also, ein Brief, fünf Ansichtskarten, ein Paket, das macht ...

2 Hör zu! Was fehlt? Schreib die Sätze zu Ende. (Listening / Writing)

Students listen to a further post office conversation and complete sentences with the correct information in German. This time, there is no support on the page, so they must listen carefully.

Answers

> 1 Das Paket geht nach Australien. 2 Es wiegt 2400 Gramm. 3 Es kostet € 12,50. 4 Die Briefe und Ansichtskarten gehen nach Dänemark. 5 Die Briefmarken für Briefe kosten 75 Cent. 6 Die Briefmarken für Ansichtskarten kosten 65 Cent. 7 Die Kundin kauft insgesamt fünf Briefmarken. 8 Der Gesamtpreis ist € 16,05.

Kundin: Guten Tag. Ich möchte dieses Paket nach Australien schicken. Was kostet das, bitte?
Beamter: Hmm ... stellen Sie bitte das Paket auf die Waage ... wie viel wiegt es? Zweitausend vierhundert Gramm ... nach Australien ... Das macht € 12,50, bitte.
Kundin: Ich habe auch ein paar Briefe für Dänemark ...
Beamter: Nach Dänemark? Innerhalb der Europäischen Union kosten alle Briefe 75 Cent.
Tourist: Und Ansichtskarten?
Beamter: 65 Cent.
Tourist: Also, ich nehme drei Briefmarken zu 75 Cent und zwei zu 65 Cent.
Beamter: Bitte schön.
Tourist: So, was macht das insgesamt?
Beamter: Also, drei Briefe, zwei Ansichtskarten, ein Paket, das macht insgesamt € 16,05.

Tip box
This provides useful post office vocabulary.

3 Partnerarbeit. (Speaking)

Using the model provided, students, working in pairs, make short conversations based on cues. Students should take it in turns to ask and answer questions.

Tip box
Advice about how to adapt dialogues. Remind students that there are a few key expressions which, if learnt by heart, will certainly be useful in the exam.

4 Hör zu! Wer will was machen (1–4)? (Listening)

Students listen and identify the illustration which matches each of the four short dialogues.

Answers
1 d, 2 b, 3 c, 4 a

1 **Kunde:** Kann man von hier aus telefonieren?
  Angestellter: Natürlich. Die Telefonzelle ist dort drüben.
2 **Kundin:** Ich möchte ein Fax schicken. Geht das?
  Angestellter: Klar, das kostet € 1,00.
3 **Kunde:** Wo kann ich hier einen Brief einwerfen?
  Angestellter: Der Briefkasten ist da vorne links.
4 **Kundin:** Kann ich hier eine E-Mail schicken?
  Angestellter: Nein, aber in der Stadt gibt's ein Internet-Café.

5 Partnerarbeit. A (▲) stellt Fragen und B (●) erfindet Antworten. (Speaking)

Students ask and answer questions about what one can do in the post office. Students must take it in turns to ask and answer questions.

Further practice of the language and vocabulary of this unit is given on the following page.
Workbook: p. 44

7 Verloren! (pp. 102–103)

Students will learn how to:
- report lost property

Key language
Ich habe meinen neuen Pass / teuren Ring / alten Rucksack / neuen Fotoapparat / meine kleine Uhr / braune Tasche / schöne Kette / Brille / mein blaues Handy / bestes Portemonnaie / ganzes Geld verloren.
Hast du / Haben Sie meinen alten Schlüssel gefunden?
Ich habe ihn / sie / es im Bus / in der Stadt verloren.
auf, unter, neben, in, hinter

time expressions: heute Morgen, gestern Nachmittag, vorgestern, letzte Woche

Grammar focus
- adjective endings: accusative after *ein / mein / dein*, etc.
- prepositions: *auf, in, hinter, neben, unter*

Resources
- Cassette B, Side B
- Sprechen p. 107, Rollenspiel 5
- Lesen / Schreiben B p. 197

Start this spread by asking students for useful vocabulary for items which they might lose. Can they remember how to say 'I've lost …' in German?

1 Lies den Text und beantworte die Fragen. Schreib Sätze. (Reading / Writing)
Students read a text about a forgetful teenager and write sentences in answer to questions about it. If wished, this can be done in the form of silent classwork or homework.

Answers
1 Anja hat eine kleine Uhr verloren. 2 Sie war auf dem Tisch. 3 Sie hat dann ihren Schlüssel verloren. 4 Er war in Anjas Tasche. 5 Sie hat auch ihre Tasche verloren. 6 Sie war unter dem Stuhl. 7 Sie hat ihr Handy verloren. 8 Es war neben dem Computer.

2 Am nächsten Tag hat Anja noch mehr Sachen verloren! Hör zu und wähle die richtige Antwort. (Listening / Reading)
Students listen to a conversation between Anja, who has lost yet more items, and her mother. They then select from three answers in each case. If wished, they can write out the correct sentences.

Answers
1 einen Pullover, 2 auf dem Tisch, 3 ihren Fotoapparat, 4 in dem Rucksack, 5 unter dem Stuhl, 6 ihre Brille, 7 auf dem Bett

---

Anja: Mutti, ich habe meinen blauen Pullover verloren. Weißt du, wo er ist?
Mutter: Ja, Anja, dein Pullover ist da, auf dem Tisch.
Anja: Oh ja, danke. Aber wo ist denn mein Fotoapparat? Jetzt habe ich meinen Fotoapparat verloren!
Mutter: Keine Sorge, Anja. Ich habe deinen Fotoapparat gefunden. Er ist in deinem Rucksack.
Anja: Aber wo ist denn der Rucksack? Jetzt habe ich meinen neuen Rucksack verloren!
Mutter: Kein Problem, Anja. Der neue Rucksack ist dort, unter dem Stuhl.
Anja: Gott sei Dank! … Aber … Moment … Wo ist meine Brille? Jetzt habe ich habe meine Brille verloren.
Mutter: Nein, Anja, es ist okay. Ich habe deine Brille gefunden. Sie ist da, auf dem Bett.

3 Partnerarbeit. (Speaking)
In pairs, students conduct lost property dialogues based on the prompts provided.

4 Lies den Brief und beantworte die Fragen auf Deutsch (ganze Sätze, bitte!). (Reading / Writing)
Students read a letter to a restaurant owner and answer questions about it in full sentences.

Answers
1 Er war am letzten Freitag im Restaurant. 2 Das Essen war ganz prima. 3 Er hat sein Portemonnaie verloren. 4 Es ist / war ein schwarzes Portemonnaie. 5 Kreditkarten und Geld waren darin.

5 Schreib einen ähnlichen Brief. (Writing)
Students write a similar letter to that in exercise 4. They are to make up the details themselves.

Grammatik: Präpositionen (prepositions)
auf, in, unter, hinter, neben take the dative when no movement is involved. Examples are shown with the definite and indefinite article and with a possessive.

6 Beschreib dieses Bild. Was liegt wo? (Writing)
Students practise using prepositions with the dative by writing German sentences describing where the things in the picture are. More details and practice are available in the Grammar section.

Answers
1 Ein Handy ist auf dem Tisch. 2 Die CD ist neben dem Telefon. 3 Die Hose ist unter dem Bett. 4 Der Walkman ist in dem Schrank. 5 Das Buch ist auf dem Fernseher. 6 Das Radio ist neben der Vase. 7 Der Hamster ist unter dem Sofa. 8 Die Katze ist hinter der Gardine.

Logo! 4　6 Einkaufen

Further practice of the language and vocabulary of this unit is given on the following pages.
Speaking: p. 107, Rollenspiel 5
Reading and Writing B: p. 197

All the vocabulary and structures from this chapter are listed on the *Wörter* pages at the end (pp. 104–105). These can be used for revision by covering up either the English or the German. Students can check here to see how much they remember from the chapter.

For more speaking practice to do with this chapter, use p. 107.

Further grammar and speaking practice on the language of this chapter is provided on pp. 45–46 of the Workbook.

Assessment materials for Chapters 5 and 6 are available after Chapter 6.

Workbook (pp. 39–46)

p. 39

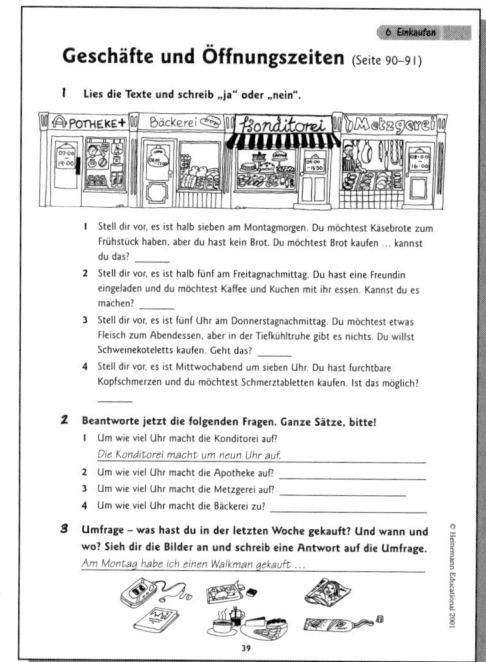

1 1 Ja.
2 Nein.
3 Nein. 4 Ja.
2 1 Die Konditorei macht um neun Uhr auf. 2 Die Apotheke macht um sieben Uhr auf. 3 Die Metzgerei macht um acht Uhr auf. 4 Die Bäckerei macht um fünf / siebzehn Uhr zu.
3 semi-open-ended: as long as they mention the items pictured, students can phrase their answers as they wish, and supply any times and any plausible shops

p. 40

1 1 c, 2 e, 3 f, 4 a, 5 d, 6 b
2 open-ended, as long as the items are plausible together
3 Verkäufer: Guten Tag. Was darf es sein?
Kundin: Guten Tag. Ich hätte gern eine Packung Kekse.
Verkäufer: Bitte schön. Sonst noch etwas?
Kundin: Ja, ich möchte auch 500 Gramm Bananen.
Verkäufer: Bitte schön. Ist das alles?
Kundin: Ja. Was macht das insgesamt?
Verkäufer: Drei Euro fünfzig … danke. Auf Wiedersehen.
Kundin: Auf Wiedersehen.
4 open-ended

p. 41

1

	Kleidungsstück	Farbe	Preis
Kundin 1	Rock	rot	€ 80,00
Kundin 2	Jacke	blau	€ 120,00

2 Die erste Kundin hat sich für einen gelben <u>Rock</u> interessiert. Dann hat sie denselben Rock in Rot <u>anprobiert</u> und er hat gut gepasst. Sie hat ihn <u>gekauft</u> und hat mit Kreditkarte <u>bezahlt</u>. Die zweite Kundin hat eine <u>blaue Jacke</u> anprobiert, aber sie war ihr zu <u>klein</u>. Danach hat sie eine andere Jacke <u>anprobiert</u> und sie hat gut gepasst. Die Jacke hat <u>hundertzwanzig</u> Euro gekostet und die Kundin hat bar bezahlt.
3 open-ended

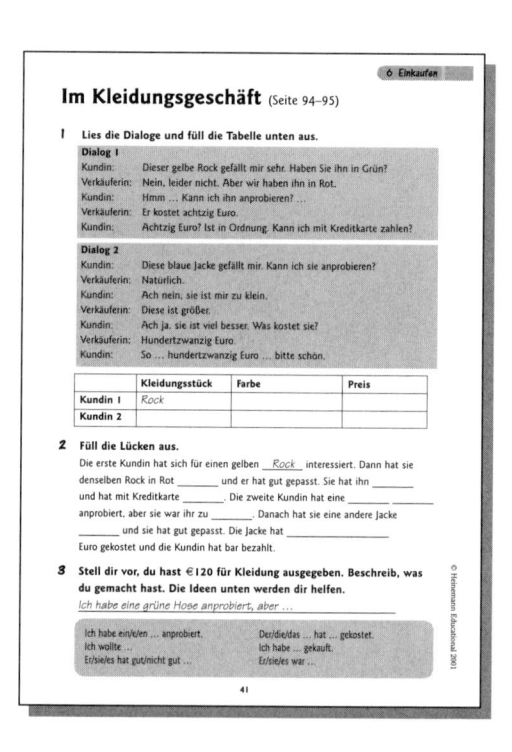

p. 42

1 **1** Hanno bekommt €12,50 pro Woche. Er gibt es für Zeitschriften, Zigaretten und CDs aus. **2** Nola bekommt €25,00 pro Monat. Sie gibt es für Telefonkarten, Hamburger und Schokolade aus. **3** Wiebke bekommt €30,00 pro Monat. Sie gibt es für Computerspiele, Kleider und Schreibwaren aus.

2

Name	Wie viel	Wie oft	Von wem	Gibt aus für …	Spart für …
Jasmin	€12,50	Woche	Vater, Mutter	Zeitschriften, Bonbons, Telefonkarten	Mofa
Erika	€62,50	Monat	Mutter, Großeltern	Zigaretten, Getränke, Zeitschriften	Computer
Torsten	€17,50	Woche	Eltern	Telefonkarten, Bonbons, Hamburger	Flugtickets

3 open-ended

p. 43

1 **1** c, **2** d, **3** e, **4** a, **5** f, **6** b

2a Brauchen Sie neue Sportschuhe? Sportschuhe haben wir in der <u>Süßwarenabteilung</u> in der zweiten Etage. Und wenn Sie Damenblusen dazu brauchen, die sind in der <u>Schreibwarenabteilung</u> in der dritten Etage. Suchen Sie zufällig Käse? Den gibt es in unserer ausgezeichneten <u>Sportabteilung</u> im Erdgeschoss. Und wenn Sie Bonbons zum Essen möchten, finden Sie sie in der <u>Herrenabteilung</u> in der ersten Etage.

2b Brauchen Sie neue Sportschuhe? Sportschuhe haben wir in der Sportabteilung in der zweiten Etage. Und wenn Sie Damenblusen dazu brauchen, die sind in der Damenabteilung in der dritten Etage. Suchen Sie zufällig Käse? Den gibt es in unserer ausgezeichneten Lebensmittelabteilung im Erdgeschoss. Und wenn Sie Bonbons zum Essen möchten, finden Sie sie in der Süßwarenabteilung in der ersten Etage.

3 Kunde: Guten Tag. Ich möchte mich beschweren.
Verkäuferin: Was ist das Problem?
Kunde: Ich habe diesen Pullover gekauft, aber er ist zu klein.
Verkäuferin: Es tut mir Leid. Wann haben Sie den Pullover gekauft?
Kunde: Gestern.
Verkäuferin: Möchten Sie ihr Geld zurückhaben oder einen neuen Pullover?
Kunde: Ich möchte bitte mein Geld zurück.
Verkäuferin: Natürlich.

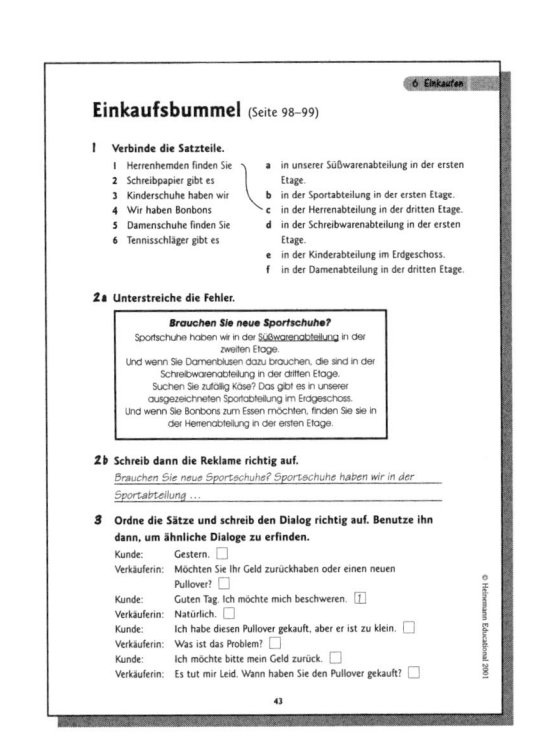

p. 44

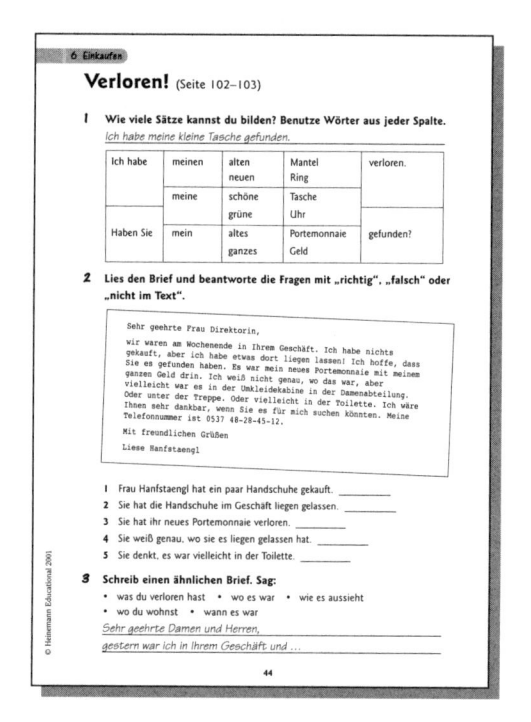

1 open-ended
2 1 Falsch. 2 Falsch. 3 Richtig. 4 Falsch. 5 Richtig.
3 open-ended

p. 45

no answers – *Sprechen*

p. 46

1 1 Ich möchte zweihundertfünfzig Gramm Butter. 2 Ich möchte ein Kilo Bananen. 3 Ich möchte zwei Scheiben Käse. 4 Ich möchte fünfhundert Gramm Äpfel. 5 Ich möchte drei Scheiben Salami. 6 Ich möchte zwei Kilo Kartoffeln.
2 1 Ich möchte einen roten Schal. 2 Ich möchte eine graue Krawatte. 3 Ich möchte braune Schuhe. 4 Ich möchte einen grünen Mantel. 5 Ich möchte ein blaues Kleid. 6 Ich möchte eine gelbe Hose.
3 open-ended – the following answers are possible:
1 Das Kleid ist grün. 2 Ich habe ein grünes Kleid. 3 Die Hose meines Bruders ist rot. 4 Mein Bruder hat eine rote Hose. 5 Ich habe einen schwarzen Mantel. 6 Mein Mantel ist schwarz.

7 Freizeit und Urlaub (Student's Book pp. 108–123)

Topic area	Key language	Grammar	Skills
7.1 Geld! (pp. 108–109) Managing money	*Kann ich bitte einen Reisescheck wechseln? Ich möchte englisches / amerikanisches Geld in Euro wechseln. Ich möchte einen Zehneuroschein / zwei Zwanzigeuroscheine / zwei Eurostücke. Bargeld oder Reisescheck? Kannst du mir zehn Euro leihen?*		Money vocabulary Places to exchange money
7.2 Imbiss und Café (pp. 110–111) Order a snack or a drink	*Ich möchte / nehme … eine Portion Pommes (frites) mit Ketchup / Mayonnaise / Senf / Kartoffelsalat / eine Brat- / Bockwurst / ein halbes Hähnchen / ein Wiener Schnitzel / einen Apfel- / Orangensaft / eine Cola / Limonade / ein Stück Apfelkuchen / Erdbeertorte / Kirschtorte mit / ohne Sahne / eine Tasse Kaffee / ein Kännchen Schokolade / ein Glas Tee mit / ohne Milch.*		*Imbiss* vocabulary Café vocabulary
7.3 Im Restaurant (pp. 112–113) Going out for a meal	*Ich möchte einen Tisch für vier Personen. Kann ich bitte … die Speisekarte sehen? eine Gabel haben? zahlen? Ich möchte / nehme Hühnersuppe / Fisch / Fleisch / Spaghetti / ein Glas Weißwein. Was für Suppen / Eis haben Sie? Als Vorspeise / Hauptspeise / Nachtisch möchten / nehmen wir … Ich bin satt. Das Essen ist kalt.*		Vocabulary for courses on a menu
7.4 Ausreden (pp. 114–115) Make explanations and excuses	*Möchtest du heute Abend ins Kino gehen? Ich kann / konnte nicht schwimmen gehen, weil ich … krank bin / war / kein Geld habe / hatte / müde bin / war / zu viele Hausaufgaben habe / hatte / mein Projekt schreiben musste / Schnupfen hatte. Ja, ich komme gern mit.*	*weil* sends verb to end of sentence Present tense *können (ich, du, er / sie, wir* forms) Imperfect tense of *sein, haben, können, müssen (ich, er / sie / es, wir, Sie, sie* forms)	*Hast du Lust …?*
7.5 Was läuft im Kino? (pp. 116–117) Find out what's on	*Was für ein Film ist das? Das ist ein Krimi / Liebesfilm / Horrorfilm / Western / Spionagefilm / Sciencefictionfilm / Zeichentrickfilm / Musical / Rockmusik / klassische Musik. Wann beginnt der Film / das Stück / das Konzert? Die Vorstellung beginnt um … Was kostet der Eintritt? Der letzte / beste Film, den ich gesehen habe, war … Das letzte / beste Theaterstück / Konzert, das ich gesehen habe, war …*	Using the perfect tense	
7.6 Was hast du gemacht? (pp. 118–119) Talk about activities in the past	*Ich habe / Wir haben … einen Film gesehen / Musik gehört / ferngesehen usw. Ich bin / Wir sind … um … Uhr in die Stadt / ins Kino gegangen Das Essen war schlecht. Die Musik war laut. Am Wochenende bin ich ins Restaurant gegangen usw.*	Perfect tense: formation, auxiliary verb second in sentence Imperfect: *sein, gehen, kommen, sehen, lesen (ich, er / sie, wir, sie* forms)	Extending sentences for writing at Higher Level

117

| 7.7 Feste (pp. 120–121) Festivals in Germany | *der Osterhase, die Ostereier, die Bescherung, Heiligabend der Erste / Zweite Weihnachtstag, Silvester Ich finde Weihnachten / Ostern / den Karneval toll / doof / wunderbar / furchtbar. Mein Lieblingsfest ist … Zu Weihnachten / Ostern / zum Karneval haben wir …* | - | *Ich freue mich auf …* Expressing opinions: *ich finde; Lieblings-* Using Christmas topic for presentation or coursework |

- The vocabulary and structures taught in Chapter 7 are summarised on the *Wörter* pages of the Student's Book, 122–123.
- Further speaking practice on the language of this chapter is provided on pp. 140–141.
- Coursework pages relating to this chapter can be found on pp. 182–183.
- Further reading and writing practice on the language of this chapter is provided on pp. 198–199
- For a selection of assessment tasks for Chapters 7 and 8, please refer to the separate Assessment Pack for your chosen examination board: AQA, OCR or Edexcel.

Logo! 4 7 Freizeit und Urlaub

1 Geld! (pp. 108–109)

Students will learn how to:
- manage money

Key language
Kann ich bitte einen Reisescheck wechseln?
Ich möchte englisches / amerikanisches Geld in Euro wechseln.
Ich möchte einen Fünfeuroschein / Zehneuroschein / zwei Zwanzigeuroscheine / zwei Eurostücke.
Bargeld oder Reisescheck?
Kannst du mir zehn Euro leihen?

Skill focus
- money vocabulary
- places to exchange money

Resources
- Cassette C, Side A
- Workbook p. 47
- Sprechen p. 140, Rollenspiel 1

Start this spread by reminding students that, despite the abolition of the German mark, they will still have to use banks in order to change sterling money and traveller's cheques into euros.

The *Sparkasse* chain can be found in most German towns and the word is often used instead of *Bank*.

1 Hör zu, lies das Gespräch und beantworte die Fragen (ganze Sätze, bitte!). (Listening / Reading / Writing)

Students read and listen to a dialogue at a bank and answer German questions in full sentences.

Answers

1 Andreas war in England. 2 Er hat englisches Geld. 3 Er geht zur Sparkasse. 4 Er hat fünfundzwanzig englische Pfund. 5 Er bekommt fünfunddreißig Euro. 6 Er bekommt vier Scheine (drei Zehneuroscheine und einen Fünfeuroschein). 7 Er bekommt sieben Münzen (drei Zweieurostücke und vier Eurostücke). 8 Er muss unterschreiben.

Andreas war in England, aber jetzt ist er wieder in Deutschland. Er hat englisches Geld. Weil er europäisches Geld braucht, geht er zur Sparkasse.

Bankangestellte: Guten Tag. Bitte schön?
Andreas: Ich möchte englisches Geld in Euro wechseln.
Bankangestellte: Selbstverständlich. Ist das Bargeld oder ein Reisescheck?
Andreas: Bargeld.
Bankangestellte: Wie viel Pfund haben Sie?
Andreas: Fünfundzwanzig englische Pfund.
Bankangestellte: So, das macht … Moment … fünfunddreißig Euro. So, bitte schön, drei Zehneuroscheine und ein Fünfeuroschein.
Andreas: Oh, kann ich für zehn Euro Kleingeld haben?
Bankangestellte: Natürlich. Hier …drei Zweieurostücke und vier Eurostücke. Wollen Sie bitte hier unterschreiben?

2 Hör zu und schau die Bilder an. Was für Geld brauchen diese Personen? (Listening / Reading)

Students listen to a variety of people talking about types of money, link the sentences to illustrations and write down the appropriate letters. You may wish to tell students that some answers are repeated, while other pictures are distractors.

Answers

1 j, 2 h, 3 i, 4 c, 5 b, 6 j, 7 g, 8 e, 9 i, 10 a

1 – Papa, kannst du mir bitte ein Zweieurostück leihen? Ich will Kaugummi kaufen.
2 – Gestern habe ich ein Fünfzigcentstück verloren und heute habe ich es in der Waschmaschine gefunden!
3 – Hast du einen Zehneuroschein in deiner Tasche?
4 – Können Sie diesen Zwanzigeuroschein wechseln? Danke!
5 – Ich musste mit einem Fünfzigeuroschein für eine Tüte Pommes frites bezahlen, weil ich kein Kleingeld hatte.
6 – Ein Zweieurostück ist ungefähr so viel wert wie ein US-Dollar.
7 – Immer wenn ich zum Supermarkt gehe, vergesse ich das Eurostück für den Einkaufswagen.
8 – Gestern habe ich einen Fünfeuroschein auf der Straße gefunden.
9 – Leihst du mir einen Zehneuroschein? Du kriegst ihn nächste Woche wieder.
10 – Mit einem Hunderteuroschein kann man ziemlich viel kaufen.

Tip box
This gives advice on where to change money in Germany.

3 Partnerarbeit. (Speaking)

Working in pairs, students construct dialogues in a bank based on the cues provided.

Tip box
This points out the difference between *Stück* and *Münze* plus the useful words: *Bargeld, Kleingeld*.

4 Lies den Text und bring die Bilder in die richtige Reihenfolge. (Reading)

Students read the conversation between Andreas and Carla and put the pictures into the correct order. Remind students that 'putting into order' is a common task type at GCSE.

Answers

1 d, 2 b, 3 a, 4 e, 5 c

> Further practice of the language and vocabulary of this unit is given on the following pages.
> Speaking: p. 140, Rollenspiel 1
> Workbook: p. 47

Logo! 4 7 Freizeit und Urlaub

2 Imbiss und Café (pp. 110–111)

Students will learn how to:
- order a snack and a drink

Key language
Ich möchte / nehme …
  eine Portion Pommes (frites) mit Ketchup / Mayonnaise / Senf / Kartoffelsalat / Salat.
  eine Brat- / Bockwurst / ein Wienerschnitzel.
  ein halbes Hähnchen.
  einen Apfel- / Orangensaft.
  eine Cola / Limonade.
  ein Stück Apfelkuchen / Erdbeertorte / Kirschtorte mit /
  ohne Sahne.
  eine Tasse Kaffee.
  ein Kännchen Schokolade.
  ein Glas Tee mit / ohne Milch.

Skill focus
- *Imbiss* vocabulary
- café vocabulary

Resources
- Cassette C, Side A
- Workbook p. 48

Start this spread by asking students to contribute as many types of German snack as they can remember.

1 Wie viel haben diese Personen bezahlt? Schreib Sätze. (Reading / Writing)

Students study the price list from a German *Imbiss* and also read the information in the speech bubbles. They then write sentences about how much the people pay. They should pay attention to replying in the same tense as in the speech bubble.

Answers
1 Sie haben €7,25 bezahlt. 2 Sie haben €6,05 bezahlt. 3 Sie bezahlen €3,00. 4 Sie muss €34,00 bezahlen.

Tip box
This provides an explanation of what is sold at an *Imbiss*.

2 Hör zu und lies den Text. Wer bestellt was? (Listening / Reading / Writing)

Students read and listen to a conversation between Andreas and Carla at *Ollis Imbiss*. They write sentences about what they eat and drink. More able students can do this as a 'pure' listening activity, i.e. without the text in front of them.
This script lends itself also to being read aloud and to being adapted in a substitution activity.

Answers
Carla isst eine Bratwurst mit Pommes frites und Ketchup und trinkt eine Cola. Andreas isst ein halbes Hähnchen mit Kartoffelsalat und Ketchup und Senf. Er trinkt eine Limonade.

Carla: Andreas, ich habe Hunger. Wollen wir zum Hamburger-Restaurant?
Andreas: Ach nee, ich bin auch hungrig, aber ich möchte lieber zum Imbiss. Da gibt's eine größere Auswahl.
Carla: Okay … Guck mal, Ollis Imbiss. Perfekt!

Andreas: So, was willst du denn essen?
Carla: Hmmm … Was gibt's? Würstchen, Bockwurst, Bratwurst. Ich glaube, ich nehme eine Bratwurst.
Besitzer: Mit Pommes frites?
Carla: Ja, bitte, und Ketchup.
Besitzer: Bitte schön. Und für Sie, junger Mann?
Andreas: Ich nehme ein halbes Hähnchen.
Besitzer: Ein halbes Hähnchen, jawohl. Und eine Portion Pommes für Sie auch?
Andreas: Nein, ich nehme Kartoffelsalat dazu.
Besitzer: Auch mit Ketchup? Oder mit Mayonnaise?
Andreas: Ja, Ketchup, und auch Senf, bitte.
Besitzer: Bitte schön. Und möchten Sie etwas dazu trinken?
Carla: Ja, bitte. Ich nehme eine Cola.
Andreas: Und für mich bitte eine Limonade.

3 Hör zu! Wähle a, b oder c. (Listening / Reading)

Explain to students that the scene is in a typical German café, ubiquitous but favoured more by the older generation than the younger! They have no support in print on the page, so they will need to listen closely to be sure of who is who. They choose from multiple-choice answers.

Answers
1 b, 2 c, 3 b, 4 a

Im Café
Frau Meyer: Guten Tag, Frau Schlüter.
Frau Schlüter: Guten Tag, Frau Meyer. Was nehmen Sie heute?
Frau Meyer: Also, Ich glaube, ich nehme wie immer eine Tasse Kaffee.
Frau Schlüter: Und für mich, wie immer, ein Glas Tee.
Frau Meyer: Möchten Sie auch Kuchen, Frau Schlüter?
Frau Schlüter: Ach ja, ich glaube, ich nehme wie immer ein Stück Apfelkuchen. Und Sie, Frau Meyer?
Frau Meyer: Ich nehme wie immer ein Stück Erdbeertorte mit Sahne. Fräulein!

Tip box
This provides information about how drinks are served in German cafés.

4 Partnerarbeit. Bestellt die folgenden Sachen. (Speaking)

Working in pairs, students create short *Imbiss* dialogues based on an example provided and picture cues. Make sure that both students get to play both roles.

**5 Gruppenarbeit. Schreibt mit drei oder vier anderen Schülern ein Gespräch (wie das Gespräch in Übung 2), in dem ein paar junge Leute zum Imbiss essen gehen.
(Writing / Reading)**
Students write a playscript for a conversation similar to that in exercise 2.

Further practice of the language and vocabulary of this unit is given on the following page.
Workbook: p. 48

Logo! 4 7 Freizeit und Urlaub

3 Im Restaurant (pp. 112–113)

Students will learn how to:
- order in a restaurant

Key language
Ich möchte einen Tisch für vier Personen.
Kann ich bitte …
   die Speisekarte sehen?
   eine Gabel haben?
   zahlen?
Ich möchte / nehme …
   Hühnersuppe / Fisch / Fleisch / Spaghetti.
Was für Suppen / Eis haben Sie?
Als Vorspeise / Hauptspeise / Nachtisch möchten / nehmen wir …
   Minestrone / Eiersalat / Steak / Omelett / Schokoladenpudding.
Zu trinken möchten wir Rotwein / Limonade / Mineralwasser.
Das Essen ist kalt.

Skill focus
- vocabulary for courses on a menu

Resources
- Cassette C, Side A
- Workbook p. 49
- Sprechen p. 140, Rollenspiel 2

Start this spread by finding out how much students know about eating out in Germany: common types of restaurant (Chinese, Greek, Turkish, Italian but fewer Indian restaurants). What typical German dishes do they know? Mention *Rouladen*, *Eisbein* (shock!), *Schnitzel*, *Eintopf*, etc.

1 Was passt zusammen? Schreib Sätze. (Reading)
Students link the illustrations to the speech bubbles and copy out the appropriate sentences.

Answers

1 Herr Ober! Was für Suppen haben Sie? 2 Herr Ober! Ich möchte ein Glas Weißwein. 3 Ich möchte bitte einen Tisch für vier Personen. 4 Herr Ober! Das Essen ist kalt! 5 Herr Ober! Kann ich zahlen? 6 Herr Ober! Was für Eis haben Sie? 7 Herr Ober! Kann ich bitte die Speisekarte sehen? 8 Herr Ober! Kann ich bitte eine Gabel haben?

2 Hör zu! Wer nimmt was? Schreib die Tabelle ab und füll sie aus. (Listening)
Students copy out the grid, then listen to the conversation as often as they need in order to fill in all the information about who orders what. There is no support on the page and some built-in traps, so they need to listen closely.

Answers
Vater: 3, 11, 5, 10.
Mutter: 6, 4, 7.
die Kinder: 1 (×2), 2 (×2), 8 (×2)

Vater: Hallo, ist das Restaurant „Julio"?
Besitzer: Ja.
Vater: Ich möchte einen Tisch für vier Personen reservieren.
Besitzer: Für vier Personen … Wann denn?
Vater: Heute Abend um acht.
Besitzer: Geht in Ordnung. Bis dann.

Vater: So, was wollen wir denn essen?
Mutter: Ich weiß nicht. Herr Ober! Kann ich bitte die Speisekarte sehen?
Kellner: Bitte schön.
Mutter: Also, ich fange an. Was für Suppen haben Sie?
Kellner: Minestrone, Hühnersuppe …
Mutter: Als Vorspeise nehme ich eine Hühnersuppe. Und du, Gert, nimmst du auch Hühnersuppe?
Vater: Nein, ich nehme Minestrone. Kinder, möchtet ihr auch eine Vorspeise?
Carla: Nein, danke. Wir essen lieber Nachtisch!
Vater: Also, als Hauptspeise möchte ich Lasagne. Du, Petra?
Mutter: Ich probiere den Fisch … Forelle mit Senfsoße und Reis. Andreas, was nimmst du?
Andreas: Für mich bitte Spaghetti mit Tomatensoße. Und du, Carla?
Carla: Für mich auch. Aber nicht so viel.
Kellner: Und zu trinken?
Vater: Ich nehme ein Glas Weißwein.
Mutter: Und ich nehme Mineralwasser. Ich muss fahren. Kinder?
Andreas: Wir möchten Cola.

Kellner: Möchten Sie einen Nachtisch?
Kinder: Oh ja, bitte!
Mutter: Was für Eis haben Sie?
Kellner: Erdbeer, Schokolade, Zitrone …
Carla: Ich nehme ein gemischtes Eis mit Sahne.
Andreas: Ich auch!
Vater: Und ich nehme einen Joghurt.
Mutter: Ich nehme nichts. Ich bin satt!

3 Partnerarbeit. Vervollständigt das Gespräch und erfindet zwei weitere Gespräche. (Speaking / Writing)
This is an open-ended pair-work exercise. Students make up the contents of the three conversations.

4 Hör zu und lies das Gespräch. Wer braucht was? Schreib vier Sätze. (Listening / Reading / Writing)
Students listen to and read a conversation in a less-than-satisfactory restaurant, then write German sentences to say what each of the people needs. This conversation can be read aloud in preparation for exercise 5.

Answers

1 Andreas braucht einen Löffel. 2 Carla braucht heißes / warmes Essen. 3 Petra braucht ein Messer und eine Gabel. 4 Der Vater braucht Salz und Pfeffer.

Andreas: Moment, … Ich habe keinen Löffel. Herr Ober, kann ich bitte einen Löffel haben?
Kellner: Oh, entschuldigen Sie. Bitte schön!
Carla: Igitt! Mein Essen ist kalt! Es schmeckt nicht!
Kellner: Oh, das tut mir Leid. Geben Sie mir das Essen zurück und ich lasse es wieder warm machen.
Petra: Das gibt's doch nicht! Ich habe kein Messer und keine Gabel!
Kellner: Oh, Verzeihung! Bitte schön.
Gert: Aber wo ist das Salz? Wo ist der Pfeffer? Herr Ober! Können wir bitte Salz und Pfeffer haben?
Kellner: Oh, entschuldigen Sie. Natürlich doch. Bitte schön.
Gert: So, das reicht mir. Lasst uns nach Hause gehen. Herr Ober, kann ich bitte zahlen?
Kellner: Gern. Bitte schön, hier ist die Rechnung.
Gert: Mein Gott! Das stimmt nicht! Sechshundert Euro!
Kellner: Oha … Es tut mir Leid. Ich meine sechzig Euro, nicht sechshundert Euro. Hat's geschmeckt?
Gert: Nein! Das ist ein schreckliches Restaurant!

5 Gruppenarbeit. Schreibt ein kurzes Theaterstück über vier Personen, die in einem schrecklichen Restaurant Probleme haben. Nehmt als Beispiel den Text aus Übung 4. (Speaking)

Now students, in small groups, make up a playscript for a similar catastrophic restaurant experience. They can make it as mad as they want.

6 Entwerfe eine Speisekarte! (Writing)

Students can use their ICT skills to make a menu in German. Much vocabulary is available on this spread, but the teacher may well need to provide more. Items should be grouped under *Vorspeisen, Hauptspeisen, Nachspeisen* and *Getränke*.

Tip box

This lists vocabulary for courses to be found on a menu.

Further practice of the language and vocabulary of this unit is given on the following pages.
Speaking: p. 140, Rollenspiel 2
Workbook: p. 49

Logo! 4 7 Freizeit und Urlaub

4 Ausreden (pp. 114–115)

Students will learn how to:
- make explanations and excuses

Key language	Grammar focus
Möchtest du heute Abend / am Wochenende / am Samstag ins Kino gehen? Ich kann / konnte nicht schwimmen gehen, weil ich … krank bin / war. kein Geld habe / hatte. müde bin / war. zu viele Hausaufgaben habe / hatte. mein Projekt schreiben musste. Schnupfen hatte. Ja, ich komme gern mit.	• *weil* (verb to end of sentence) • *können* (ich, du, er / sie, wir forms) • present tense • imperfect of *sein, haben, können, müssen* (ich, er / sie, wir, Sie, sie forms) **Skill focus** • *Hast du Lust …?* **Resources** • Cassette C, Side A • Workbook p. 50

Remind students that they gain points in exams for giving reasons and explanations for things. Start this spread by asking students to contribute, in German if possible, as many excuses as they can for not doing homework, missing school, being late for an appointment, etc.

1a Hör zu und schau die Bilder an. Was möchten sie machen? Warum geht es nicht? (Listening)

Students listen to some people declining invitations and giving reasons. For each answer, they must give a letter and a number.

Answers

1 e, 3, 2 d, 2, 3 b, 4, 4 c, 1, 5 a, 5

1 – Johannes, möchtest du am Sonntag schwimmen gehen?
   – Nein, ich kann nicht schwimmen gehen, weil ich müde bin.
2 – Etta, möchtest du ins Kino gehen?
   – Es tut mir Leid, ich kann nicht ins Kino gehen, weil ich kein Geld habe.
3 – Ayse, möchtest du morgen in die Stadt kommen?
   – Leider kann ich nicht in die Stadt kommen, weil ich zu viele Hausaufgaben habe.
4 – Richard, möchtest du am Sonnabend zum Fußballspiel gehen?
   – Est tut mir Leid. Ich möchte zum Fußballspiel gehen, aber ich kann es nicht, weil ich krank bin.
5 – Tim, möchtest du am Freitag in die Disco kommen?
   – Ja, ich komme gern mit!

Wiederholung: weil (because)

A reminder that *weil* sends the verb to the end of the sentence.

1b Schreib die Sätze aus Übung 1a auf. (Writing)

Students write out the answers to exercise 1a in the *ich* form. More able students should be asked to do the same exercise in the third person singular: *Johannes kann nicht schwimmen gehen, weil er müde ist.*

Answers

1 Ich kann nicht schwimmen gehen, weil ich müde bin. 2 Ich kann nicht ins Kino gehen, weil ich kein Geld habe. 3 Ich kann nicht in die Stadt kommen, weil ich zu viele Hausaufgaben habe. 4 Ich kann nicht zum Fußballspiel gehen, weil ich krank bin. 5 Ja, ich komme gern mit / in die Disco.

Grammatik: können (Präsens) (can – present tense)

The *ich, du, er / sie* and *wir* forms of *können* showing how the infinitive goes to the end of the sentence.

2 Partnerarbeit. (Speaking)

In pairs, students make a dialogue based on the picture cues provided. Students should take it in turns to ask and answer questions.

3a Lies die E-Mail und beantworte die Fragen (ganze Sätze, bitte!). (Reading / Writing)

Students read the e-mail and answer the questions in full sentences using *weil*. This is a fairly challenging task, which will require concentration. Variations are possible.

Answers

1 Anja kann am Samstag nicht in die Disco gehen, weil sie kein Geld hat. 2 Samira kann nicht ins Kino gehen, weil sie ihr Projekt schreiben muss. 3 Samira kann nicht zum Tennisklub gehen, weil sie Schnupfen hat. 4 Samira ist traurig, weil die Ferien bald vorbei sind. 5 Udo soll eine Text-Nachricht schicken, weil Samiras Mutter sauer ist, wenn Samira zu viel telefoniert.

3b Schreib eine Antwort auf Samiras E-Mail aus Übung 3a. (Writing)

Point out that, aside from answering Samira's questions, this task also offers the opportunity for some more extended and adventurous writing. It will need to be taken in and marked.

Tip box

An explanation of the meaning of *Hast du Lust …?* Tell pupils that this is an extremely common and useful expression. *Ich habe keine Lust* is the equivalent of the English 'I don't feel like it'.

4 Lies Samiras Tagebuch und beantworte die Fragen im Imperfekt. (Reading / Writing)
Students read a diary extract and answer questions about it using *weil* and the imperfect.

Answers

> 1 Samira konnte am Montag nicht ins Kino gehen, weil sie ein Projekt schreiben musste. 2 Samira konnte am Dienstag nicht zum Tennisklub gehen, weil sie Schnupfen hatte. 3 Samira konnte am Freitag ins Hallenbad gehen, weil sie wieder gesund war. 4 Anja konnte nicht in die Disco gehen, weil sie kein Geld hatte.

Grammatik: Das Imperfekt (the imperfect tense)
Students are given the *ich, er / sie, wir, Sie* and *sie* imperfect forms of the following verbs: *sein, haben, können, müssen*. A more detailed explanation of the imperfect and practice are to be found in the Grammar section.

5 Schreib dein Tagebuch für die letzte Ferienwoche. (Writing)
Ask students to write a diary of their own last week of the holidays. It doesn't have to be true, but remind them that, as the end of the book is approaching, they need to concentrate on interesting content, accuracy, a range of tenses and opinions and reasons: all the things that examiners will be looking for. This work will need to be taken in and marked.

> Further practice of the language and vocabulary of this unit is given on the following page.
> Workbook: p. 50

Logo! 4 7 Freizeit und Urlaub

5 Was läuft im Kino?
(pp. 116–117)

Students will learn how to:
- find out what's on
- describe a film / play / book

Key language
Das ist ein …
  Krimi / Liebesfilm / Horrorfilm / Western / Sciencefictionfilm / Zeichentrickfilm.
Wann beginnt der Film / das Stück / das Konzert?
Die Vorstellung beginnt um …
Was kostet der Eintritt?
Der letzte / beste Film, den ich gesehen habe, war …
Das letzte / beste Theaterstück / Konzert, das ich gesehen habe, war …

Grammar focus
- *der letzte Film, den ich gesehen habe …*
- perfect tense

Resources
- Cassette C, Side A
- Sprechen p. 140, Rollenspiel 3
- Lesen / Schreiben A p. 198

Start this spread by doing a class survey to establish what's on at the local cinema this week. Can students remember how to describe different types of film?

1 Lies die Werbung und beschreib die Filme. (Reading / Writing)
Students read newspaper adverts for a cinema programme and write down detailed information in German about what's on.

Answers
1 Im Regina 1 läuft „Das Biest". Das ist ein Horrorfilm. Die erste Vorstellung beginnt um 18 Uhr und die letzte Vorstellung beginnt um 23 Uhr. Der Eintritt kostet € 5,50. 2 Im Regina 2 läuft „Tony das Pony". Das ist ein Kinderfilm. Die erste Vorstellung beginnt um 15.30 und die letzte Vorstellung beginnt um 17.30 Uhr. Der Eintritt kostet € 6,00. 3 Im Regina 3 läuft „Sonnenuntergang in Rio". Das ist ein Liebesfilm. Die erste Vorstellung beginnt um 18.30 und die letzte Vorstellung beginnt um 21 Uhr. Der Eintritt kostet € 4,50. 4 Im Regina 4 läuft „Die Marsmenschen". Das ist ein Sciencefictionfilm. Die erste Vorstellung beginnt um 19 Uhr und die letzte Vorstellung beginnt um 22 Uhr. Der Eintritt kostet € 5,50.

2 Hör zu und beantworte die Fragen auf Deutsch. (Listening / Reading)
Students listen to three people enquiring about events and answer questions about the conversation. Make sure they realise that only dialogue 1 is printed on the page; the other two are 'pure' listening activities.

Answers
1 ein Liebesfilm, 2 um 20 Uhr, 3 € 4,00, 4 am Samstag, 5 nein, 6 nein, 7 „Romeo und Julia", 8 vier, 9 das Stück ist ausverkauft

1 – Hallo, hier das Appollo-Kino.
 – Guten Tag. Was läuft heute, bitte?
 – „Emma".
 – Was für ein Film ist das?
 – Das ist ein Liebesfilm.
 – Wann beginnt die Vorstellung?
 – Um 20 Uhr.
 – Und was kostet der Eintritt?
 – € 4,00.
2 – Guten Abend, Stadthalle Bremen. Kann ich Ihnen behilflich sein?
 – Guten Abend. Können Sie mir sagen, was für ein Konzert am Samstag stattfindet?
 – Jawohl, das sind die Oberneuländer Musikanten.
 – So? Ist das eine Rockband?
 – Nein, eigentlich nicht …
 – Klassische Musik?
 – Nein, das ist deutsche Volksmusik.
 – Hmmm … nein, ich glaube nicht. Auf Wiederhören.
3 – Hallo, hier spricht das Schiller-Theater.
 – Guten Tag. Welches Stück läuft nächste Woche?
 – „Romeo und Julia" von William Shakespeare.
 – Super! Ich möchte vier Plätze reservieren.
 – Es tut mir Leid, aber das Stück ist ausverkauft.
 – Wirklich? Wie schade!

3 Partnerarbeit. Partner(in) A (▲) stellt Fragen, B (●) erfindet die Antworten. Macht drei Gespräche. (Speaking)
Students, working in pairs, make open-ended conversations about what is on at the cinema. An example is provided and further conversations should be made up by the students themselves, so a few minutes' preparation will be useful. Encourage them to add in further questions and answers to make the conversations as natural-sounding as possible (e.g. asking for information to be repeated, when it finishes, how long it lasts, who the star is, etc.).

4 Du hast diese Filme gesehen. Beschreib sie! (Writing)
Students read details about three films and write about them in the past tense, providing as much detail as they can. Remind them that descriptions of favourite films / books / plays, or those they have most recently seen or read, are a common topic in Writing and Speaking tests. This is a challenging task, which should be approached carefully and will need to be marked in detail.

Students will see that, in the example, it says *Ich habe … gefunden*. You could explain that the imperfect form *Ich fand …* is also useful for expressing opinions.

5 Beschreib einen Film, ein Theaterstück oder ein Konzert, den / das du wirklich gesehen hast. (Writing)
Students now put what they have practised on this spread to good use by writing as detailed information as possible about entertainments they have experienced in the past.

Further practice of the vocabulary and language of this unit is given on the following pages.
Speaking: p. 140, Rollenspiel 3
Reading and Writing A: p. 198

Logo! 4 7 Freizeit und Urlaub

6 Was hast du gemacht?
(pp. 118–119)

Students will learn how to:
- talk about activities in the past

Key language
Was hast du / habt ihr gestern Abend gemacht?
Ich habe / Wir haben …
  Musik gehört.
  Hausaufgaben gemacht.
  einen Film gesehen.
  ferngesehen.
  gearbeitet.
  Tischtennis / Computer / Fußball gespielt.
Ich bin / Wir sind … um … Uhr …
  in die Stadt / ins Kino / Bett gegangen.
Das Essen war schlecht / toll.
Die Musik war laut.
Am Wochenende bin ich / sind wir ins Restaurant gegangen / nach Hause gekommen / abgefahren / angekommen / gewandert.

Gestern / Dann habe ich / haben wir gegessen / eingekauft.

Grammar focus
- perfect tense: formation, verb comes second in sentence
- Imperfect tense of *sein, gehen, kommen, sehen, lesen* (*ich, er / sie, wir, sie* forms)

Skill focus
- extending sentences for writing at Higher Level

Resources
- Cassette C, Side A
- Workbook p. 51
- Sprechen p. 140, Gespräch 1
- Kursarbeit pp. 182–183

Start this spread by reminding students of the three most common situations in which they will need to use the perfect tense: talking or writing about a past holiday, last weekend or yesterday. Elicit as many responses as possible, true or otherwise, to the question *Was hast du gestern gemacht?*

1 Wer ist wer? (Reading)
Students do a simple matching exercise in which they look at the text messages and match them to the pictures by writing letters.

Answers
1 e, 2 b, 3 d, 4 c, 5 a

Wiederholung: Das Perfekt (the perfect tense)
A reminder of the formation of the perfect tense and a reminder that the auxiliary verb must come second in a sentence.

2a Hör zu und beantworte die Fragen auf Deutsch (kurze Antworten). (Listening / Writing)
Students write German answers to questions about a taped conversation. Recommend them to make notes during the first hearing. Full sentences are not necessary.

Answers
1 zu einer Party, 2 getanzt, 3 Würstchen, 4 Bier, 5 um Mitternacht, 6 Hausaufgaben, 7 ferngesehen, 8 um halb elf

> Carla: Hallo, Julia. Na, wie geht's?
> Julia: Nicht so gut. Ich bin sehr spät ins Bett gegangen.
> Carla: Ja? Wieso?
> Julia: Na ja, ich bin zu einer Party gegangen. Das war nicht schlecht. Wir haben getanzt, Würstchen gegessen und ein bisschen zu viel Bier getrunken. Und die Musik war extrem laut.
> Carla: Oha. Um wie viel Uhr bist du ins Bett gegangen?
> Julia: Um Mitternacht. Und du, Carla? Was hast du gestern Abend gemacht?
> Carla: Ach, ganz langweilig. Ich habe meine Hausaufgaben gemacht und dann habe ich ferngesehen.
> Julia: So? Um wie viel Uhr bist du ins Bett gegangen?
> Carla: Nicht so spät wie du! Um halb elf.

2b Schreib die Antworten aus Übung 2a auf. (Writing)
Students now write down all the information from exercise 2a in full sentences, making a paragraph describing what Julia and Carla did last night.

Answers
Julia ist zu einer Party gegangen. Da hat sie getanzt. Sie hat Würstchen gegessen und Bier getrunken. Sie ist um Mitternacht ins Bett gegangen.
Carla hat ihre Hausaufgaben gemacht. Sie hat dann ferngesehen. Sie ist um halb elf ins Bett gegangen.

3 Partnerarbeit. (Speaking)
Working in pairs, students ask and answer questions about things they have recently done, based on picture prompts.

4 Lies den Artikel und wähle die richtigen Antworten. Schreib die Sätze auf. (Reading / Writing)
Students read a magazine article, choose from multiple-choice answers and write out the answers.

Answers
1 Carla und Andreas sind mit dem Zug gefahren. 2 Sie sind am Nachmittag abgefahren. 3 Sie sind am Abend angekommen. 4 Die Übernachtung in der Jugendherberge war schrecklich. 5 Es gab ein Problem mit anderen Kindern. 6 Am Sonnabend sind sie spazieren gegangen. 7 Beide sind ins Museum

gegangen. **8** Am Deutschen Eck kommen zwei Flüsse zusammen. **9** Die Pommes im Imbiss haben gut geschmeckt. **10** Sie haben den Film komisch gefunden.

Grammatik: Das Imperfekt (the imperfect)
The imperfect forms of *sein, gehen, kommen, sehen* and *lesen* are given (*ich, er / sie, wir, sie* forms). Feel free to give students extra practice with these forms by providing present tense sentences and asking students to put them into the imperfect:
Teacher: Heute gehe ich in die Stadt. Gestern ...
Student: Gestern ging ich in die Stadt.

5 Was hast du am Wochenende gemacht? Schreib einen Bericht. (Writing)
This being such a common theme at GCSE level, make sure students write as much as they possibly can, following the suggestions in the Tip box. Take their work in and mark it.

Tip box
Ideas for students to extend the sentences they write to meet the requirements of the Writing Test at Higher Level.

Further practice of the language and vocabulary of this unit is given on the following pages.
Speaking: p. 140, Gespräch 1
Workbook: p. 51

Kursarbeit
The activities in this unit form an ideal introduction to coursework preparation. Specific coursework practice on this topic is provided on pp. 182–183.

Logo! 4　7 Freizeit und Urlaub

7 Feste (pp. 120–121)

Students will learn how to:
- talk about festivals in Germany

Key language
der Osterhase,
die Ostereier
die Bescherung
Heiligabend
der Erste / Zweite
Weihnachtstag
Silvester
Ich finde Weihnachten /
Ostern / den Karneval …
 toll / doof / wunderbar /
 furchtbar.
Mein Lieblingsfest ist …
Zu Weihnachten / Ostern /
zum Karneval haben wir
…

Skill focus
- *Ich freue mich auf …*
- expressing opinions: *Ich finde …*; *Lieblings-*
- using Christmas topic for presentation or coursework

Resources
- Cassette C, Side A
- Sprechen p. 140, Gespräch 2
- Lesen / Schreiben B p. 199

Start this spread by finding out as much as possible about what students know about *Fasching* and German customs at Easter and Christmas. This can be done in English if required.

1 Lies den Artikel und beantworte die Fragen (ganze Sätze, bitte!). (Reading / Writing)

Students read an article about three festivals and answer questions in full German sentences.

Answers

1 Ostern ist ungesund. 2 Der Osterhase bringt die Ostereier. 3 Die Bescherung ist am 24. Dezember. 4 Sie gehen in die Kirche. 5 Der 24. Dezember heißt Heiligabend. 6 Man sagt „der Zweite Weihnachtstag". 7 Man trinkt Sekt zu Silvester. 8 Der Karneval beginnt im November. 9 Fasching ist ein anderes Wort für Karneval. 10 Man feiert Karneval in Süddeutschland.

2 Hör zu! Richtig, falsch oder nicht im Hörtext? (Listening)

Remind students that this format (true, false or not given) is sometimes used in GCSE exams. They may need to listen to the tape several times.

Answers

1 Richtig. 2 Nicht im Text. 3 Falsch. 4 Falsch. 5 Richtig. 6 Nicht im Text. 7 Nicht im Text. 8 Richtig. 9 Richtig.

> Moderatorin: Guten Abend und Herzlich willkommen bei „Jugend Heute". Heute ist unser Thema „Was ist dein Lieblingsfest"? Hallo! Na, wie heißt du?
> Alex: Alex.
> Moderatorin: Und was meinst du denn, Alex?

> Alex: Keine Frage, Anita! Mein Lieblingsfest ist der Karneval! Der Karneval beginnt im November. Ich komme aus Köln, da ist Karneval ganz groß. Viel essen, viel trinken und viel feiern! Karneval macht Spaß! Aber Ostern mag ich nicht, weil ich letztes Jahr zu viel Schokolade gegessen habe.
> Moderatorin: Danke. Und du? Wer bist du?
> Carolin: Ich bin Carolin.
> Moderatorin: Magst du auch Fasching?
> Carolin: Nein. Ich komme aus Norddeutschland. Da gibt's keinen Karneval. Mein Lieblingsfest ist Weihnachten! Da gibt's viele Geschenke. Ich gehe auch am 24. Dezember in die Kirche. Das ist auch wichtig. Ich freue mich schon auf Weihnachten.
> Moderatorin: Natürlich. Vielen Dank. So, wie heißt du und magst du auch Weihnachten?
> Torben: Ich bin der Torben. Selbstverständlich mag ich Weihnachten! Alle Leute mögen Weihnachten! Aber mein Lieblingsfest ist Ostern.
> Moderatorin: So? Warum denn?
> Torben: Weil ich gern Schokolade esse! Der Osterhase kommt im Frühling und bringt die Ostereier, sagen die Kinder. Ostern ist toll, finde ich.

Tip box
This shows how to say you are looking forward to something.

3 Lies den Text und beantworte die Fragen auf Deutsch (ganze Sätze, bitte!). (Reading / Writing)

Students read a past tense text and answer questions in German sentences, using the *wir* form.

Answers

1 Wir sind in die Stadt gegangen. 2 Da gab's ein Straßenfest. 3 Wir sind zu Freunden gegangen. 4 Wir haben geplaudert und viel Limonade getrunken. 5 Am Montag haben wir in der Schule gesungen und Spiele gespielt.

4 Partnerarbeit. Macht Dialoge. (Speaking)

Students, working in pairs, ask and answer questions about the three festivals covered here. Various choices are provided for three conversations, plus they can make up more of their own.

Tip box
This shows how to use *Ich finde / Ich habe … gefunden / Ich fand …* to express an opinion. Add *Lieblings-* to a noun to talk about your favourite thing. *Ich fand …* has cropped up a couple of times before and here it is presented officially.

5 Beschreib dein letztes Weihnachtsfest unter dem Titel „Weihnachten bei uns". (Writing)

Students write a detailed description of what they did last Christmas. As usual, encourage them to write as much as they can, including opinions. This work needs to be taken in and marked.

Tip box
Students can use the topic of festivals for a presentation or some coursework.

Further practice of the language and vocabulary of this unit is given on the following pages.
Speaking: p. 140, Gespräch 2
Reading and Writing B: p. 199

All the vocabulary and structures from this chapter are listed on the *Wörter* pages at the end (pp. 122–123). These can be used for revision by covering up either the English or the German. Students can check here to see how much they remember from the chapter.

For more speaking practice to do with this chapter, use p. 140.

Further grammar and speaking practice on the language of this chapter is provided on pp. 52–53 of the Workbook.

Assessment materials for Chapters 7 and 8 are available after Chapter 8.

Kursarbeit

7 Freizeit (pp. 182–183)

The coursework spreads in *Logo! 4* give regular, guided practice in preparing for the coursework element of the GCSE exam.

The spreads always start with a model text on each theme (at a higher level than that expected by the student) which acts as a stimulus to give students ideas of what they might include in their own piece of work. Students are encouraged to look at the detail of the text through the guided reading activities. They are gradually guided to produce good German sentences in the tasks through to the final task, which is to produce an extended piece of writing. The *Hilfe* column is a feature on all the spreads. It reminds students of language they might include and particular structures that will raise the level of their writing. Remind students who are capable of achieving a Higher grade that they should always include examples of two or three tenses in their writing.

This spread guides students to produce an extended piece of writing on the topic of hobbies

1 Schreib die braunen Ausdrücke auf Deutsch und Englisch hin.
Students write out all the brown words in German and English.

Answers

Es tut mir wirklich leid = I am really sorry; Ich muss dir alles erzählen = I must tell you everything; Ich bin auch besser geworden = I have improved; Er war nicht sehr froh darüber = He wasn't very happy about it; Ich bin auch oft ins Kino gegangen = I have also been to the cinema a lot; bin ich oft schwimmen gegangen = I have been swimming a lot; hat viel Spaß gemacht = was a lot of fun; ich muss jetzt Schluss machen = I must finish now

2 Du bist Karola. Beantworte die Fragen.
Students answer the questions as if they were Karola.

Answers

1 Ich wohne in Hamburg. 2 Meine Schulferien haben am 21. Juni begonnen. 3 Ich habe mit Freunden in der Sporthalle Tennis gespielt. 4 Ich habe am Sonntag das Tennisspiel gewonnen. 5 Das Wetter war recht warm. 6 Ich bin im neuen Freibad schwimmen gegangen. 7 Meine Eltern haben mir ein Fahrrad geschenkt. 8 Ich bin im Park Rad gefahren. 9 Ich habe in Lübeck Handball gespielt. 10 Das Handballturnier war fantastisch.

3 Du hast einen Brieffreund / eine Brieffreundin in Deutschland. Schreib einen Brief an ihn / sie und erzähle, was du in den letzten zwei Wochen in deiner Freizeit gemacht hast.
Students write a letter explaining what they have been doing over the past two weeks. A list is provided giving students an idea of what they might include, and support is also provided in the *Hilfe* column.

Hilfe
Tips for writing a letter to a friend:
- how to start and finish
- using the present, perfect and future tense
- remembering the order sequence: when, how, where (to)

Workbook (pp. 47–53)

p. 47

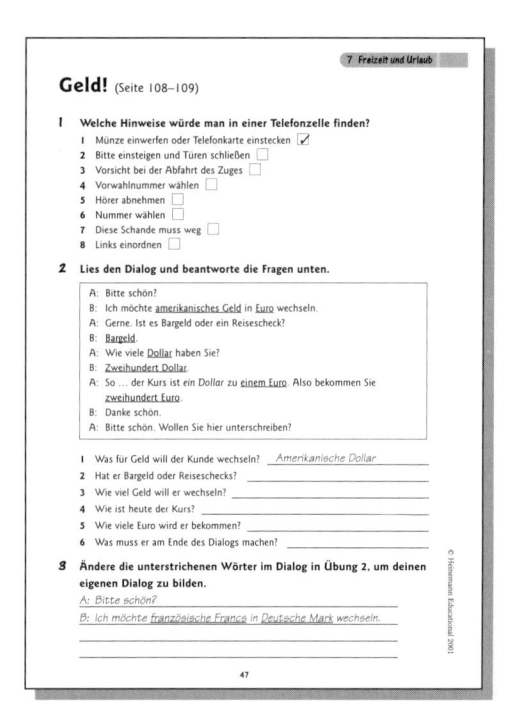

1 1, 4, 5, 6
2 **1** Amerikanische Dollar, **2** Bargeld, **3** Zweihundert Dollar, **4** Ein Dollar zu einem Euro, **5** Zweihundert Euro, **6** Unterschreiben
3 open-ended

p. 48

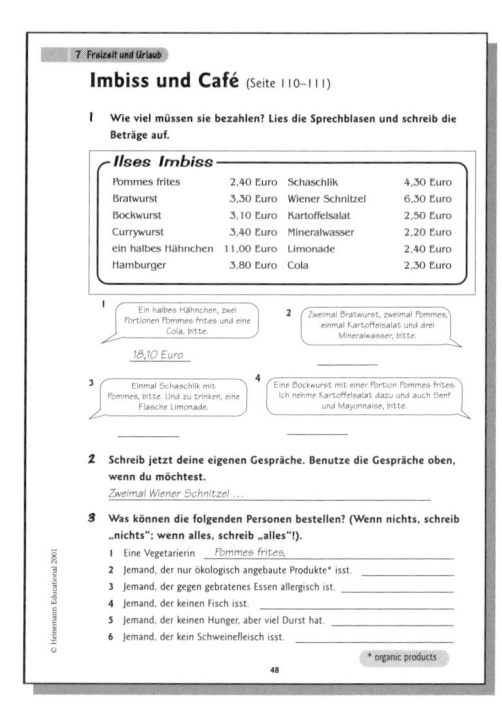

1 **1** €18,10, **2** €20,50, **3** €9,10, **4** €8,00
2 open-ended
3 **1** Pommes frites, Kartoffelsalat, Mineralwasser, Limonade, Cola. **2** Nichts! **3** Bockwurst, Kartoffelsalat, Mineralwasser, Limonade, Cola. **4** Alles! **5** Mineralwasser, Limonade, Cola. **6** Pommes frites, Hähnchen, Hamburger, Kartoffelsalat, Mineralwasser, Limonade, Cola.

p. 49

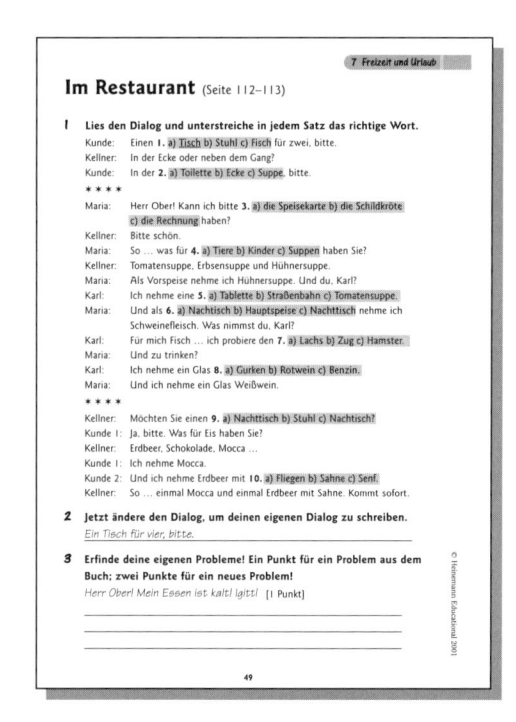

1 **1** a, **2** b, **3** a, **4** c, **5** c, **6** b, **7** a, **8** b, **9** c, **10** b
2 open-ended
3 open-ended

p. 50

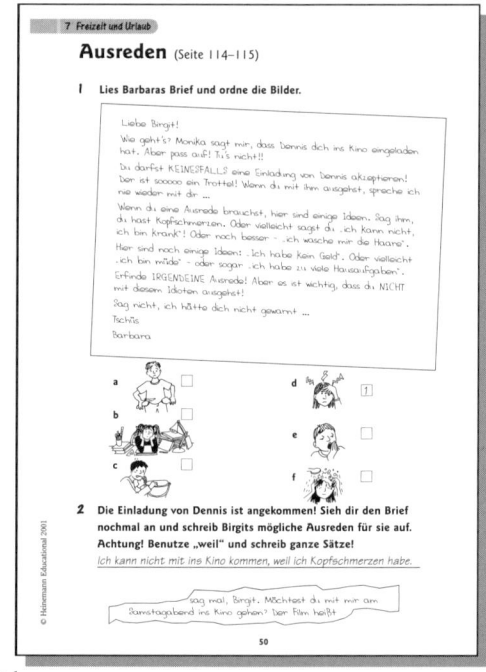

1 **1** d, **2** c, **3** f, **4** a, **5** e, **6** b
2 **1** Ich kann nicht mit ins Kino kommen, weil ich Kopfschmerzen habe. **2** Ich kann nicht mit ins Kino kommen, weil ich krank bin. **3** Ich kann nicht mit ins Kino kommen, weil ich mir die Haare wasche. **4** Ich kann nicht mit ins Kino kommen, weil ich kein Geld habe. **5** Ich kann nicht mit ins Kino kommen, weil ich müde bin. **6** Ich kann nicht mit ins Kino kommen, weil ich zu viele Hausaufgaben habe.

p. 51

1 Ahmed: b, d, h, k; Lotte: a, f, i, j; Markus: c, e, g, l

2 **1** Partizipien Perfekt (bold type), **2** Pronomina (underlined), **3** Meinungen (italics), **4** Zeitausdrücke (underlined twice)

Es war *nicht schlecht*. Wir haben **geredet**, Musik **gehört** und **getanzt**. Die Musik war aber *viel zu laut*. Und ehrlich **gesagt** habe ich zu viel Bier **getrunken**. Ich bin spät nach Hause **gegangen** und am folgenden Morgen war ich ein bisschen krank!

Ich hatte viel zu tun. Zuerst habe ich meine Hausaufgaben **gemacht** und danach habe ich mein Zimmer **aufgeräumt**. Erst dann habe ich ein bisschen **ferngesehen**, aber das Programm war *entsetzlich* und ich bin früh ins Bett **gegangen**.

Wir sind einkaufen **gegangen** und ich habe mir neue Sportschuhe **gekauft**. Dann sind wir ins Eiscafé **gegangen** und haben Spaghetti-Eis **gegessen** (*lecker!*). *Gegen Mittag* sind wir in die Bibliothek **gegangen** und danach sind wir ins Stadtmuseum **gegangen**. *Zum Einschlafen …*

3 open-ended

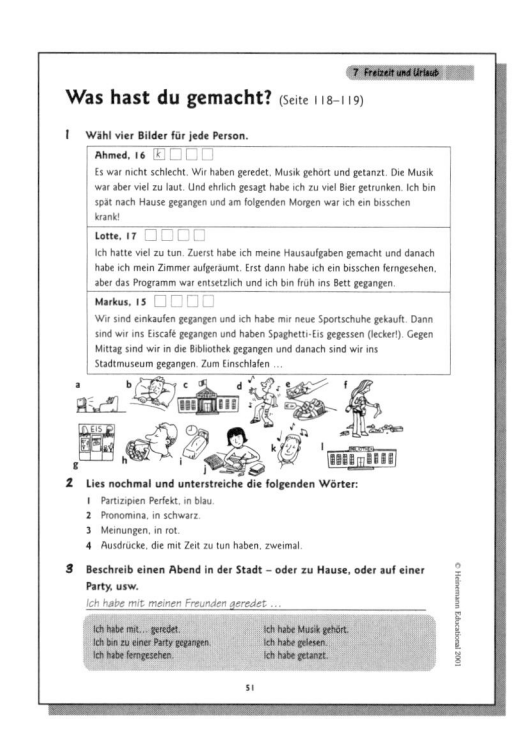

p. 52

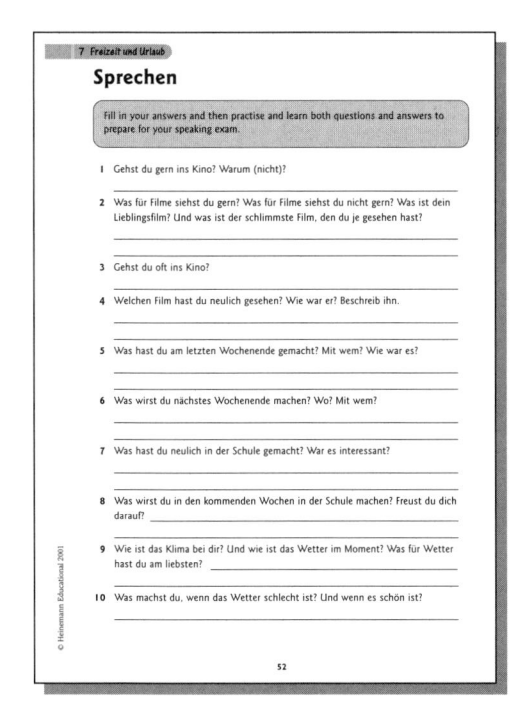

no answers – *Sprechen*

p. 53

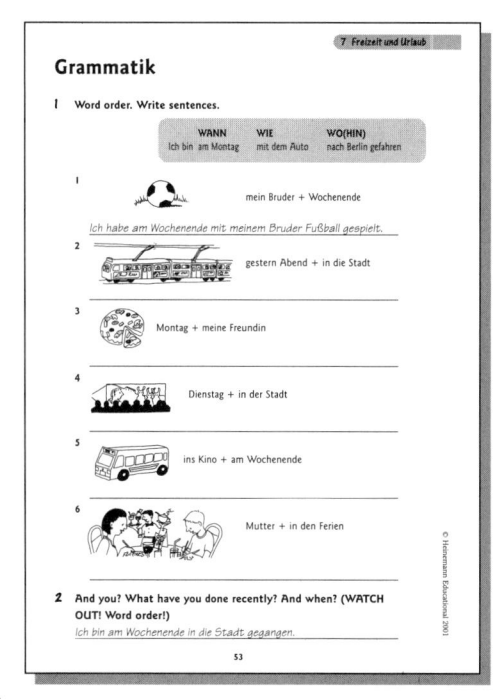

1 **1** Ich habe am Wochenende mit meinem Bruder Fußball gespielt. **2** Ich bin gestern Abend mit der Straßenbahn in die Stadt gefahren. **3** Ich habe am Montag mit meiner Freundin Pizza gegessen. **4** Ich habe am Dienstag in der Stadt einen Film gesehen. **5** Ich bin am Wochenende mit dem Bus ins Kino gegangen. **6** Ich habe in den Ferien mit meiner Mutter in einem Restaurant gegessen.

2 open-ended

8 Mein Leben zu Hause (Student's Book pp. 124–141)

Topic area	Key language	Grammar	Skills
8.1 Routine, Routine (pp. 124–125) Day-to-day activities	*Mein Wecker klingelt um … Uhr. Ich wache / stehe / rasiere mich / dusche / ziehe mich an / frühstücke / putze mir die Zähne / verlasse das Haus / esse Abendbrot / wasche mich / gehe schlafen um … Uhr. Ich bin um … Uhr aufgewacht / aufgestanden / nach Hause gekommen / schlafen gegangen. Ich habe um … Uhr gefrühstückt / das Haus verlassen.*	Reflexive verbs (*ich, er / sie* forms): present and perfect tense	Using time expressions
8.2 Essen (pp. 126–127) Talk about meals at home	*Ich esse gern / lieber / am liebsten Toast usw. Ich trinke gern / lieber / am liebsten Tee usw. Was isst / trinkst du zum Frühstück / Mittagessen / Abendessen? Zum Frühstück / Mittagessen / Abendessen esse / trinke ich … Ich habe gestern … gegessen / getrunken.*	*gern, lieber, am liebsten* Present and perfect tense of *essen* and *trinken*	
8.3 Gesundheit (pp. 128–129) Talk about a healthy lifestyle	*Um gesund zu bleiben, spiele ich Fußball / gehe ich schwimmen ins Fitnesszentrum / laufe ich Ski / rauche ich nicht / esse ich kein Fastfood / vegetarisch.*	*um … zu …*	
8.4 Aua! (pp. 130–131) Talk about illness and injury	*Ich habe (Ohren)schmerzen. Mein Bein tut weh. Ich habe mein Bein gebrochen. Ich habe meine Hand verletzt. Ich habe … Er / Sie hat … Durchfall / Fieber / Schnupfen / eine Grippe / einen Sonnenbrand. Ich bin müde. Er / Sie ist krank.*		*Es geht mir (nicht) gut / schlecht* Practising using *weil*
8.5 Beim Arzt (pp. 132–133) Visiting the doctor	*Ich habe Kopfschmerzen / Zahnschmerzen / Husten / Schnupfen / Grippe. Mein Kopf tut weh. Haben Sie etwas gegen Zahnschmerzen? Ich habe Tabletten / Hustensaft / eine Salbe. Sie muss im Bett bleiben / Tabletten nehmen.*	The imperative: *du* and *Sie* forms	Noticing imperfect forms in a text
8.6 Unfall! (pp. 134–135) Coping with a breakdown or accident	*Ich habe eine Panne. Der Motor / Die Batterie ist nicht in Ordnung. Wo ist die nächste Reparaturwerkstatt? Könnten Sie mir helfen / einen Mechaniker herschicken? Mein Auto steht auf der Bundesstraße … Ich habe einen Unfall gehabt. Ich habe mich verletzt. Können Sie einen Krankenwagen rufen?*	Imperfect forms used in reports and stories *Könnten Sie …?* *Könnten Sie …?*	Useful expressions when calling the emergency services
8.7 Problemseite (pp. 136–137) Dealing with teenage problems	*Ich bin zu schüchtern. Ich habe Pickel und trage eine Brille. Ich kann noch nicht sehr gut Deutsch sprechen. Meine Noten sind nicht sehr gut. Ich will mit meiner Clique nach … fahren. Meine Kleidung ist nicht modern und modisch. Ich war total betrunken.*	Imperatives	Reading strategies

- The vocabulary and structures taught in Chapter 8 are summarised on the *Wörter* pages of the Student's Book, 138–139.
- Further speaking practice on the language of this chapter is provided on p. 141.
- Further reading and writing practice on the language of this chapter is provided on pp. 200–201.
- For a selection of assessment tasks for Chapters 7 and 8, please refer to the separate Assessment Pack for your chosen examination board: AQA, OCR or Edexcel.

Logo! 4 8 Mein Leben zu Hause

1 Routine, Routine (pp. 124–125)

Students will learn how to:
- talk about day-to-day activities

Key language
Mein Wecker klingelt um ... Uhr.
Ich wache / stehe / rasiere mich / dusche / ziehe mich an / frühstücke / putze mir die Zähne / verlasse das Haus / esse Abendbrot / wasche mich / gehe schlafen um ... Uhr.
Ich bin um ... Uhr aufgewacht / aufgestanden / nach Hause gekommen / schlafen gegangen.
Ich habe um ... Uhr gefrühstückt / das Haus verlassen.

Grammar focus
- reflexive verbs (*ich, er / sie* forms): present and perfect tense

Skill focus
- using time expressions

Resources
- Cassette C, Side A
- Workbook p. 54
- Sprechen p. 141, Gespräch 1 + 2

Start the spread by revising how to tell the time in German. Then find out how much students remember about how to describe their daily routine.

1 Lies den Text. Was sagt Fatima? Schreib Sätze. (Reading)
Students look at pictures of Fatima's daily routine (on a school day) and write full sentences in German (identified and copied from the text) to describe each picture.

Answers
1 An einem Schultag klingelt mein Wecker um sechs Uhr dreißig. 2 Ich stehe um Viertel vor sieben auf. 3 Ich frühstücke um Viertel nach sieben. 4 Ich verlasse das Haus um ungefähr halb acht. 5 Ich mache um zwei Uhr meine Hausaufgaben. 6 Ich esse um sechs Uhr Abendbrot. 7 Um acht Uhr sehe ich meistens fern. 8 Ich gehe um halb elf schlafen.

2a Hör zu! Bring die Bilder in die richtige Reihenfolge und schreib die Uhrzeit auf. (Listening)
Make sure students understand precisely what they have to do here. Fatima describes her routine at the weekend (Saturday here). Students write down the letters in the order in which they hear the actions and also note down the times at which they occur (as demonstrated in the example). They may have to listen a few times.

Answers
f, 11 Uhr, e, 11.15, b, 11.30, h, 12 Uhr, c 12.30, a, 6 Uhr, d, 7 Uhr, g, 12 Uhr

Interviewer: Und wie ist es am Wochenende, Fatima?
Fatima: Am Wochenende ist es ganz anders! Mein Wecker klingelt gar nicht! Ich wache um elf Uhr auf. Ich dusche um Viertel nach elf und dann frühstücke ich um halb zwölf. Ich putze mir um zwölf Uhr die Zähne und ich verlasse das Haus um halb eins. Meistens hänge ich in der Stadt 'rum oder gehe zu Freunden. Abendessen gibt's um sechs Uhr, wie immer. Dann gehe ich um sieben wieder in die Stadt, entweder in die Kneipe oder ins Kino. Manchmal gibt's eine Party, wie letzten Samstag zum Beispiel. Meistens bin ich um Mitternacht zu Hause und dann wasche ich mich und gehe schlafen.

2b Was sagt Fatima? Schreib Sätze. (Writing)
Students write out the answers to exercise 2a in full sentences, thus constructing a paragraph about Fatima's day.

Answers
Ich wache um 11 Uhr auf. Ich dusche um Viertel nach elf. Ich frühstücke um 11.30 Uhr. Ich putze mir die Zähne um 12 Uhr. Ich verlasse das Haus um 12.30 Uhr. Ich esse Abendbrot um 6 Uhr. Ich gehe um 7 Uhr in die Stadt. Ich gehe schlafen um 12 Uhr.

3 Partnerarbeit. A (▲) stellt Fragen B (●) erfindet Antworten. (Speaking)
Students work in pairs to practise giving times and talking about daily routine. Students should take it in turns to ask and answer questions.

4 Jetzt schreib die Information über *deine* tägliche Routine auf. (Writing)
Students must write a paragraph about their own daily routine, both on weekdays and at the weekend. Encourage them to make their paragraph as detailed and as adventurous as possible.

Tip box
Students should use lots of time expressions when writing about their daily routine (exercise 4). When a sentence starts with a time expression, the verb comes next.

Grammatik: Reflexive Verben (reflexive verbs)
An explanation of the *ich* and *er / sie* forms of reflexive verbs, both in the present and perfect tense. These can be practised with simple mimes to illustrate expressions like *Ich habe mich rasiert, er hat sich gewaschen*, etc.

5 Lies den Text und wähle die richtige Antwort. Schreib die Sätze auf.
(Reading / Writing)

Students read this story, which demonstrates how to use the perfect tense to talk about daily routine in the past, and carry out a multiple-choice activity which students write out in full sentences.

Answers

1 Rikki ist früh aufgestanden. 2 Er hat sich nicht rasiert. 3 Er hat eine dunkle Brille getragen. 4 Er hat ein großes Frühstück gegessen. 5 Er ist nicht zu Fuß in die Stadt gegangen. 6 Er ist am Vormittag wieder ins Bett gegangen.

6 Partnerarbeit. Macht ein Interview mit Rikki Räuber. Rikki Räuber muss lügen!
(Speaking)

Students use the cues provided to make up questions for Rikki Räuber. Partner B pretends to be Rikki Räuber but must give untruthful answers. Partner A must make notes about what Rikki replies, ready for the next exercise.

7 Was hast du gestern gemacht? Schreib Sätze.
(Writing)

Now students write about their own routines in the past, providing as much detail as possible.

Further practice of the language and vocabulary of this unit is given on the following pages.
Speaking: p. 141, Gespräch 1 + 2
Workbook: p. 54

Logo! 4 8 Mein Leben zu Hause

2 Essen (pp. 126–127)

Students will learn how to:
- talk about meals at home

Key language
Ich esse gern / lieber / am liebsten Toast / Brötchen / Käse usw.
Ich trinke gern / lieber / am liebsten Tee / Kaffee / Wasser.
Was isst / trinkst du zum Frühstück / Mittagessen / Abendessen / Abendbrot?
Zum Frühstück / Mittagessen / Abendessen esse / trinke ich …
Ich habe gestern … gegessen / getrunken.

Grammar focus
- *gern, lieber, am liebsten*
- *essen, trinken* (present and perfect tense)

Resources
- Cassette C, Side A
- Workbook p. 55
- Sprechen p. 141, Gespräch 3

Start this spread by brainstorming items in German that people might eat for breakfast. Remind students about the German breakfast, very different from an English one, with *Wurst*, cheese, etc.

1 Lies den Artikel und beantworte die Fragen auf Deutsch (ganze Sätze, bitte!). (Reading / Writing)
Students read a magazine article and answer German questions in full sentences. There is leeway for variations in the answers.

Answers
1 Er braucht viel Energie, weil er Sportler ist. 2 Er hat gestern mindestens vier Dosen Cola getrunken. 3 Am Abend isst er gern Fleisch mit Kartoffeln und Gemüse. 4 Weil er nicht gern Fett / Bratwurst isst. 5 Weil sie schlank bleiben muss. 6 Nein, weil sie Schokolade nicht essen darf. 7 Sie isst normalerweise ein Stück Knäckebrot und trinkt ein Glas Wasser. 8 Sie hat eine Praline gegessen.

2 Partnerarbeit. (Speaking)
Working in pairs, students use the picture prompts to say what they like, prefer and most like eating and drinking. Make sure students take it in turns to ask and answer questions, otherwise partner B will do all the work!

Grammatik: gern, lieber, am liebsten (like, prefer, like most)
An explanation of the meaning of *gern, lieber, am liebsten* plus a reminder that they all come after the verb.

3 Hör zu! Was isst und trinkt Olli gern und nicht gern? Schreib Sätze. (Listening)
Students listen to a youngster being interviewed by his teacher, prior to an exchange visit, about what he likes and doesn't like eating and drinking. They make notes and then write down what they have found out.

Answers
Er isst gern Obst und Fleisch. Er isst nicht gern Fisch und Gemüse. Er trinkt gern Cola und Limonade. Er trinkt nicht gern Kaffee und Wasser.

Lehrer: So, Olli, du möchtest an dem Englandaustausch teilnehmen? Prima! Aber Essen ist oft ein Problem, also muss ich ein paar Fragen stellen und ein Formular ausfüllen.
Olli: Alles klar, Herr Schlüter!
Lehrer: So, Olli, was isst du denn gern?
Olli: Also, ich esse ganz gern Obst und Fleisch.
Lehrer: Moment … Na, und was isst du nicht so gern?
Olli: Ich esse nicht gern Fisch und Gemüse. Igitt! So was mag ich nicht!
Lehrer: Und was trinkst du gern, Olli?
Olli: Ich trinke ganz besonders gern Cola und Limonade.
Lehrer: Natürlich doch! Aber was trinkst du denn nicht gern?
Olli: Nicht gern? Ach, ich trinke nicht gern Kaffee und Wasser.

4 Partnerarbeit. (Speaking)
In pairs, students interview each other about what they eat at various mealtimes and what they ate yesterday. Remind them that these are questions which frequently crop up in Speaking Tests. It may be useful to remind students of present and perfect tenses at this point by referring them to the appropriate pages in the Grammar reference section.

5 Schreib einen Brief an deinen neuen Austauschpartner / deine neue Austauschpartnerin. (Writing)
Students write a letter in German giving details about their eating habits. As well as following all the instructions, encourage them to add in as many extra details and opinions as they can.

Further practice of the language and vocabulary of this unit is given on the following pages.
Speaking: p. 141, Gespräch 3
Workbook: p. 55

3 Gesundheit (pp. 128–129)

Students will learn how to:
- talk about a healthy lifestyle

Key language
Um gesund zu bleiben,
...
spiele ich Fußball.
gehe ich schwimmen /
ins Fitnesszentrum.
laufe ich Ski.
rauche ich nicht.
esse ich kein Fastfood /
vegetarisch.

Grammar focus
- *um ... zu ...*

Resources
- Cassette C, Side A
- Workbook p. 56
- Lesen / Schreiben A p. 200

Start this spread by introducing the idea of *gesund* and *ungesund* by listing some food items and activities. Students must say they think they are *gesund* or *ungesund*.

1 Schreib die Sätze ab und trag die Namen ein: Oliver, Sabine oder Robert. (Reading)

Students copy out the sentences and insert the appropriate names.

Answers
1 Oliver isst Toast mit Wurst und Käse. 2 Robert isst gern Fastfood. 3 Sabine isst nur Obst zum Frühstück. 4 Sabine isst sehr gesund. 5 Robert isst total ungesund. 6 Oliver isst ziemlich gesund.

2 Wo klickt man, um diese Informationen zu finden? Schreib „blau", „grün" oder „rot". (Reading)

Students look at the homepage for a health website, decide where to find the information depicted and write down the colour of the button to click on.

Answers
1 Rot. 2 Blau. 3 Grün. 4 Grün. 5 Rot. 6 Blau.

3 Hör die Interviews an und schreib „gesund" oder „ungesund". Dann schreib den Grund auf Englisch auf (1–6). (Listening)

Students listen to six brief interviews about lifestyles, write down in German whether they are healthy or not, then note down in English the reasons.

Answers
1 ungesund (watches TV all evening), 2 gesund (plays squash), 3 ungesund (drinks beer at the pub), 4 ungesund (smokes 20 cigarettes a day), 5 gesund (jogs about 4 km a day), 6 ungesund (eats chips every day, sits in front of computer)

1 – Otto, was machst du am Abend?
– Also, wenn ich nach Hause komme, setze ich mich gleich vor den Fernseher und gucke bis zehn Uhr.
2 – Sascha, guckst du auch viel fern?
– Nee, ich gehe lieber zum Squashklub.
3 – Bist du sportlich, Ali?
– Nicht besonders, nein. Ich gehe aber ganz gern in die Kneipe und trinke Bier.
4 – Hmmm ... gehst du auch oft in die Kneipe, Roland?
– Nein, Alkohol mag ich nicht, aber ich muss zugeben, dass ich rauche. Ich rauche etwa 20 Zigaretten pro Tag.
5 – Sylvia, rauchst du denn?
– Um Gotteswillen, nein! Das finde ich dumm. Ich gehe jeden Abend joggen, ungefähr vier Kilometer.
6 – Und zum Schluss noch Jutta. Joggst du auch?
– Nein, leider nicht, dazu habe ich keine Zeit. Mein Leben ist zu stressig. Nach der Arbeit gehe ich zum Imbiss, wo ich eine Tüte Pommes esse. Dann setze ich mich vor den Computer.

Grammatik: um ... zu ... (in order to ...)

An explanation of the meaning of the structure and how to use it.

4 Was machst du, um fit zu bleiben? Schreib Sätze. (Writing)

Students practise using the *um ... zu ...* construction by converting phrases into full sentences, following the example provided.

Answers
1 Um fit zu bleiben, spiele ich Squash. 2 Um schlank zu bleiben, esse ich vegetarisch. 3 Um Geld zu verdienen, mache ich Babysitting. 4 Um nach Hamburg zu fahren, nehme ich den Zug. 5 Um gesund zu bleiben, gehe ich schwimmen. 6 Um stark zu werden, gehe ich ins Fitnesszentrum. 7 Um Sport zu treiben, rauche ich nicht.

5 Hör zu und beantworte die Fragen mit „ja" oder „nein". (Listening)

Students listen to an interview with a 'couch potato' and answer simple *ja oder nein* questions. More able students can then convert the answers into full sentences if wished.

Answers
1 Nein. 2 Ja. 3 Nein. 4 Nein. 5 Ja. 6 Ja. 7 Ja. 8 Nein.

Interviewerin: Herr Becker, was machen Sie, um gesund zu bleiben?
Herr Becker: Ich muss echt sagen, ich mache nicht sehr viel für meine Gesundheit. Zum Beispiel könnte ich vegetarisch essen, aber ich tu's nicht. Ich mag einfach zu gern Fleisch. Also esse ich Wurst zum Frühstück, zum Mittagessen und auch zum Abendbrot! Gemüse mag ich überhaupt nicht: Salat, Spinat, Brokkoli, das ist alles Kaninchenfutter. Das ist doch nichts für einen echten Mann!
Interviewerin: Treiben Sie denn keinen Sport?
Herr Becker: Was? Sport? Natürlich doch! Ich gehe zu Fuß in die Kneipe! Und wenn ich in der Kneipe bin, bewege ich meinen rechten Arm, um mein Bier zu trinken. Und ich bewege meinen linken Arm, um meine Zigarette an meine Lippen zu bringen! Na ja, so schlimm ist es natürlich nicht. Ich interessiere mich zum Beispiel für Fußball …
Interviewerin: Aha, Sie spielen Fußball?
Herr Becker: Was? Spielen? Nein, ich sehe gern Fußball im Fernsehen!
Interviewerin: Oha, mit Ihnen ist es hoffnungslos, Herr Becker. Denken Sie nie an Ihren Herzen? Sie könnten sehr jung sterben.
Herr Becker: Unsinn! Mein Vater hat jeden Tag zehn Bier getrunken und vierzig Zigaretten geraucht und er ist erst mit neunzig Jahren gestorben. Mein Motto ist: ungesund, aber glücklich!

6 Jetzt du! Was machst du (und was machst du nicht), um fit zu bleiben? Was hast du letzte Woche gemacht, um fit zu bleiben? (Writing)

Students sum up the contents of this unit by writing about their own lifestyles. Make sure they use both present and perfect tenses and write as much as they can. A few phrases have been provided as suggestions.

Further practice of the language and vocabulary of this unit is given on the following pages.
Reading and Writing A: p. 200
Workbook: p. 56

4 Aua! (pp. 130–131)

Students will learn how to:
- talk about illness and injury

Key language	Er / Sie hat ...
Ich habe Ohrenschmerzen / Bauchschmerzen / Kopfschmerzen / Halsschmerzen / Rückenschmerzen / Zahnschmerzen.	Durchfall / Fieber / Schnupfen / eine Grippe / einen Sonnenbrand.
Mein Arm / Finger / Fuß / Knie / Bein tut weh.	Ich bin müde Er / Sie ist krank.
Ich habe mich / meine Hand / meinen Fuß verletzt.	**Skill focus** • *es geht mir (nicht) gut / schlecht* • *weil*
Ich habe mein Bein / meinen Arm gebrochen. Ich habe ...	**Resources** • Cassette C, Side A • Workbook p. 57

Start this unit by revising the words for the various parts of the body. Can students remember how to complain about ailments?

1 Hör zu! Wer hat welches Problem? Schreib a, b, c usw. (Listening)

Students listen to a tape of ten school pupils telling their teacher what is wrong with them. By looking at the illustration, students work out who is who and write down letters.

Answers

1 d, 2 i, 3 f, 4 h, 5 e, 6 b, 7 g, 8 j, 9 a, 10 c

 1 – Herr Klein, mein Bein tut weh! Ich kann nicht laufen.
 2 – Es tut mir Leid, Herr Klein, mein Finger tut weh.
 3 – Oh, Herr Klein, ich habe mein Knie verletzt!
 4 – Ich kann keinen Sport treiben. Mein Fuß tut weh.
 5 – Meine Hand tut weh, Herr Klein! Volleyball ist für mich heute unmöglich.
 6 – Ich kann nicht mitspielen, weil ich Halsschmerzen habe!
 7 – Entschuldigen Sie, Herr Klein, ich habe Bauchschmerzen. Darf ich nach Hause gehen?
 8 – Aua, ich habe furchtbare Kopfschmerzen. Haben Sie vielleicht eine Kopfschmerztablette für mich?
 9 – Meine Ohrenschmerzen sind schrecklich! Was haben Sie gesagt?
 10 – Ich kann heute keinen Sport treiben, weil ich Rückenschmerzen habe.

2 Partnerarbeit. (Speaking)

In pairs, students conduct an information gap activity. Partner A chooses a picture and answers questions about the symptoms. Partner B works out which picture is being referred to. Students should take it in turns to ask and answer questions, and more examples can be thought up if wished. (Students can sketch their own pictures.)

3 Lies die E-Mail. Wer hat welches Problem? Schreib Sätze. (Reading / Writing)

Students read an e-mail, work out who is who and write out the answers in full sentences.

Answers

1 Tanita ist müde. 2 Klaus hat Schnupfen. 3 Frank hat Fieber. 4 Susanne hat Durchfall. 5 Frank hat eine Grippe. 6 Tanita hat einen Sonnenbrand.

Tip box
The easiest way to say you feel well or unwell is to use *Es geht mir (nicht) gut*.

4 Schreib an die Schule. (Writing)

Students practise using the *weil* construction to write notes (e.g. as in a fax) explaining why they aren't in school. Ask the more able students to write them out in the imperfect tense as well (using *konnte* and *hatte*).

Answers

1 Ich kann nicht in die Schule kommen, weil ich Fieber habe. 2 Ich kann nicht in die Schule kommen, weil ich Zahnschmerzen habe. 3 Ich kann nicht in die Schule kommen, weil ich Bauchschmerzen habe. 4 Ich kann nicht in die Schule kommen, weil ich mein Bein gebrochen habe. 5 Ich kann nicht in die Schule kommen, weil ich meinen Kopf verletzt habe.

Tip box
A reminder that *weil* sends the verb to the end of the sentence.

5 Schreib eine E-Mail wie in Übung 3. Du kannst nicht mit deiner Familie zur Party gehen. (Writing)

Following the example provided in exercise 3, students write an e-mail explaining why they and their family can't attend a party. Ask them to embroider it as much as they like – e-mails are cheap!

Further practice of the language and vocabulary of this unit is given on the following page.
Workbook: p. 57

Logo! 4 8 Mein Leben zu Hause

5 Beim Arzt (pp. 132–133)

Students will learn how to:
- visit the doctor

Key language
Ich habe Kopschmerzen / Zahnschmerzen / Husten / Schnupfen / Grippe.
Mein Kopf tut weh.
Haben Sie etwas gegen Zahnschmerzen?
Ich habe Tabletten / Hustensaft / eine Salbe.
Sie müssen im Bett bleiben / Tabletten nehmen.

Grammar focus
- the imperative (*du* and *Sie* forms)

Skill focus
- recognising imperfect forms in a text

Resources
- Cassette C, Side A
- Workbook pp. 58–59
- Sprechen p. 141, Rollenspiel 1

Start the spread by explaining the health system in Germany. There is no National Health Service as we know it in the UK. All medicine is private and each citizen has an insurance policy to cover illness. Ask students if they can remember how to ask for items in a chemist's shop.

1 Schau die Schilder an. Welcher Arzt / Welche Ärztin ist am besten? (Reading)

Students look at some signs from outside doctors' surgeries and write down the names of the doctors being referred to.

Answers
1 Andreas Müller, 2 Ute Heine-Rostock, 3 Rolf Schenker, 4 Dr. med. B. Kaiser, 5 Ute Heine-Rostock, 6 Andreas Müller

2a Hör zu! Was hat Christine und was hat sie nicht? Schreib ✔ oder ✘. (Listening)

Students listen to Christine explaining her ailments to her mother, and put ticks or crosses according to whether Christine has the particular problem or not.

Answers
1 ✔, 2 ✔, 3 ✔, 4 ✘, 5 ✘, 6 ✔, 7 ✘, 8 ✘

Christine: Mutti, es geht mir nicht sehr gut.
Mutter: Tatsächlich? Ist es nicht nur, dass du keine Lust hast, die Klassenarbeit zu schreiben?
Christine: Nein, Mutti, wirklich nicht! Ich hab' wirklich ganz dolle Halsschmerzen und Bauchschmerzen auch. Hast du vielleicht etwas gegen Bauchschmerzen? Ich glaube, ich hab' Fieber.
Mutter: Komm mal her, wir messen mal Fieber. Hmmm … Oh ja, es stimmt, neununddreißig Grad. Du musst sofort ins Bett.
Christine: Aber Mutti, ich geh' doch heute Abend mit Olli ins Kino.
Mutter: Heute Abend darfst du nicht ins Kino gehen, Christine! Du bist doch krank.
Christine: Jetzt fang' ich auch noch an zu husten. Hast du etwas gegen Husten?
Mutter: Moment, ich schaue mal im Schrank nach. Ich war doch gestern in der Apotheke … Ja, Hustensaft haben wir, und … Was ist das denn hier? „Magen-Fix, Tabletten gegen Bauchschmerzen". Hier, nimm mal.
Christine: Ooh! Mutti! Das schmeckt furchtbar!
Mutter: So, und jetzt rufe ich den Arzt an …

2b Schreib jetzt für jedes Wort aus Übung 2a einen Satz. Schreib entweder „… hat sie" oder „… hat sie nicht". (Writing)

A brief additional written exercise in which students write out the information gleaned in exercise 2a.

Answers
1 Bauchschmerzen hat sie. 2 Halsschmerzen hat sie. 3 Fieber hat sie. 4 Ohrenschmerzen hat sie nicht. 5 Grippe hat sie nicht. 6 Husten hat sie. 7 Kopfschmerzen hat sie nicht. 8 Rückenschmerzen hat sie nicht.

3 Partnerarbeit. (Speaking)

Working in pairs, students use picture prompts to help them construct short dialogues at a chemist's shop.

4 Lies den Text und finde die Wörter. Schreib sie auf Deutsch auf. (Reading)

Students read a phone conversation between Christine's mother and the doctor and find and write down the German equivalents for some English expressions.

Answers
1 Bauchschmerzen, 2 Arztpraxis, 3 Fieber, 4 Termin, 5 Sprechstunden

5 Hör zu, lies den Dialog und beantworte die Fragen (ganze Sätze, bitte!). (Listening / Reading / Writing)

Students listen to a dialogue between Christine and her doctor and answer some questions in full sentences. The script is printed on the page, but the more able can attempt the exercise without reading it. This dialogue can be read aloud and used for a substitution exercise.

Answers
1 Christines Bauch tut weh. 2 Sie hustet nicht mehr. 3 Sie hat noch Fieber. 4 Sie muss drei Tage im Bett bleiben. 5 Sie muss dreimal pro Tag Tabletten mit Wasser nehmen.

Arzt: So, Christine, komm herein. Geht es dir jetzt besser?
Christine: Ein bisschen besser, Herr Doktor.
Arzt: Wie sind deine Bauchschmerzen?
Christine: Mein Bauch tut immer noch weh, aber ich huste nicht mehr.
Arzt: Darf ich mal Fieber messen? Ach ja, du hast noch Fieber.
Christine: Was muss ich tun?
Arzt: Folgendes. Geh nach Hause und bleib für drei Tage im Bett. Ich verschreibe dir ein Rezept für Tabletten. Nimm die Tabletten dreimal pro Tag mit Wasser. Komm dann wieder zu mir.
Christine: Okay, Herr Doktor. Hoffentlich geht es mir bald besser.

Grammatik: Der Imperativ (the imperative)
An explanation of how to form the *du* and *Sie* forms of the imperative.

6 Lies den Text. Schreib „richtig" oder „falsch". (Reading)
Students read a text about a past visit to a dentist and answer some straightforward true or false questions.

Answers
1 Falsch. 2 Richtig. 3 Richtig. 4 Falsch. 5 Falsch.

Tip box
The imperfect forms of verbs in the text are pointed out for students. There is more information about the imperfect in the next spread.

7 Schreib eine ähnliche Geschichte wie in Übung 6. Ersetze die folgenden Wörter. (Writing)
Students are invited to write a similar tale of woe. Little help is provided, apart from suggestions of words and phrases to alter, so it is up to them to invent symptoms, remedies, etc. Teacher support may well be needed. Encourage pupils to be adventurous and humorous.

Further practice of the language and vocabulary of this unit is given on the following pages.
Speaking: p. 141, Rollenspiel 1
Workbook: pp. 58–59

Logo! 4 8 Mein Leben zu Hause

6 Unfall! (pp. 134–135)

Students will learn how to:
- cope with a breakdown or accident

Key language
Mein Auto ist kaputt.
Mein Motorrad hat kein Benzin mehr.
Ich habe eine Panne.
Der Motor / Die Batterie ist / Die Bremsen / Lampen sind nicht in Ordnung.
Wo ist die nächste Reparaturwerkstatt / Tankstelle?
Könnten Sie mir helfen / einen Mechaniker herschicken / mein Auto reparieren / die Polizei rufen?
Mein Auto steht auf der Bundesstraße …, … Kilometer von …
Ich habe einen Unfall gehabt.
Ich habe mich verletzt.
Können Sie einen Krankenwagen rufen?

Grammar focus
- imperfect forms used in reports and stories
- *Können / Könnten Sie …?*

Skill focus
- expressions for calling emergency services

Resources
- Cassette C, Side A
- Sprechen p. 141, Rollenspiel 2

Start this unit by explaining that, while students may not be driving in Germany yet, this topic is in the syllabus because it may come in useful in the future. Or else they may be able to help their parents out of a scrape. Can students suggest what kinds of problem might arise?

1 Lies den Artikel. Schreib „Herr Schneider" oder „Herr Klein". (Reading)
Students read a news item about a traffic accident (of a type typical of GCSE reading texts) and write either *Herr Schneider* or *Herr Klein* in answer to the questions.

Answers
1 Herr Schneider, 2 Herr Klein, 3 Herr Klein, 4 Herr Schneider, 5 Herr Klein

2 Schreib einen ähnlichen Bericht wie in Übung 1 über einen anderen Unfall. Ersetze die Ausdrücke im Text wie folgt. (Writing)
Students write a report similar to that in exercise 1, substituting different words as suggested on the page.

Grammatik: Das Imperfekt (imperfect)
A list of imperfect forms that might be used in a newspaper report or story. Ask students to write out a little report of their own invention about anything they like, using some of these verbs.

3 Hör zu! Verbinde die Satzteile. (Listening / Reading)
Students listen to a phone call from a motorist to a garage and link parts of sentences.

Answers
1 e Könnten Sie mir bitte helfen? 2 d Der Motor ist nicht in Ordnung. 3 a Mein Auto steht auf der Bundesstraße. 4 b Könnten Sie einen Mechaniker herschicken? 5 c Ich habe eine Panne.

> Hallo, ist das die Reparaturwerkstatt? Guten Tag. Ich habe eine Panne. Mein Auto steht auf der Bundesstraße 3, fünf Kilometer von Delmenhorst. Der Motor ist nicht in Ordnung. Er ist kaputt. Könnten Sie mir bitte helfen? Könnten Sie einen Mechaniker herschicken? Vielen Dank!

Tip box
This explains the difference between *Können Sie …?* and *Könnten Sie …?*

4a Partnerarbeit. (Speaking)
Working in pairs, students use the prompts to make a phone conversation following a breakdown.

4b Partnerarbeit. Erfindet ein ähnliches Telefongespräch wie in Übung 4a. Beschreibt das Problem, bittet um Hilfe und beschreibt, wo ihr seid. (Speaking)
Now students make up a similar conversation, but making up the information themselves.

Tip box
This provides a list of useful expressions to use when calling the emergency services.

5 Partnerarbeit. (Speaking)
Based on the final Tip box, students practise using more useful expressions for use in an accident situation. Explain that the majority of work on this spread is oral because this is what they would need in real life.

Further practice of the language and vocabulary of this unit is given on the following page.
Speaking: p. 141, Rollenspiel 2

7 Problemseite (pp. 136–137)

Students will learn how to:
- read and interpret information about typical teenage problems

Key language	Skill focus
Ich bin zu schüchtern.	• reading strategies
Ich habe Pickel und trage eine Brille.	
Ich kann noch nicht sehr gut Deutsch sprechen.	**Resources**
Meine Noten sind nicht sehr gut.	• Cassette C, Side A
Ich will mit meiner Clique nach … fahren.	• Lesen / Schreiben B p. 201
Meine Kleidung ist nicht modern und modisch.	
Ich war total betrunken.	

The main aim of this spread is to provide the opportunity for more extended reading and to help students to develop their reading strategies.

1a Lies die Briefe und die Antworten. Welche Antwort passt zu welchem Brief? (Reading)
Students read through the problem page letters and match each letter to the appropriate reply.

Answers
1 E, 2 B, 3 D, 4 C, 5 F, 6 A

1b Diese Sätze sind alle falsch. Korrigiere sie (ganze Sätze, bitte!). (Writing / Reading)
Based on the same letters, students look at a list of incorrect sentences and write out corrected versions.

Suggested answers

(There are plenty of other correct possibilities.)
1 Joschka hat Pickel und trägt eine Brille. 2 Karin antwortet: Frag sie einfach. 3 Stefan hat Wodka mit Cola getrunken. 4 Karin antwortet: Du musst die Vase bezahlen. 5 Lydia fährt nicht gern an die Nordsee. 6 Karin antwortet: Fahr mit deinen Eltern. 7 Samiras Zeugnis ist schlecht. 8 Karin antwortet: Die Lehrer müssen langsamer sprechen. 9 Björn trägt keine Designer-Klamotten. 10 Karin antwortet: Kauf dir keine neuen Adidas-Schuhe. 11 Jana hat Dennis geküsst. 12 Karin antwortet: Jana ist keine gute Freundin / Finde eine neue Freundin.

Tip box
This suggests strategies to help students save time in the Reading Test: concentrate on the necessary words, make intelligent guesses and look for 'cognate' words. Work through these with students, using the passages to help them to cope better with Higher Level texts in the exam.

1c Lies die Briefe und Antworten nochmal. Finde diese Ausdrücke. (Reading)
Students consult the problem page for a final time and identify and write down the German equivalents of some English expressions.

Answers

1 Du wirst bezahlen müssen. 2 Nur weil sie toll aussieht … 3 Das ist wichtiger. 4 Ich bin zu schüchtern. 5 Das wäre peinlich. 6 Es ist hoffnungslos. 7 Ich würde sagen … 8 Es tut mir Leid.

2 Partnerarbeit. A (▲) beschreibt ein Problem und fragt, was er / sie tun sollte. B (●) gibt Rat. (Speaking)
Students will require plenty of time to prepare this little counselling session in pairs. Each person needs to invent a problem and explain it. The partner should then offer some good advice. The results should be performed to the rest of the class.

Tip box
A reference to the section on imperatives.

3 Schreib einen Brief an Dr. Karin Koppe. Hast du kein Problem? Erfinde eins! Dein Partner / Deine Partnerin ist Karin. Schreib eine Antwort. (Writing)
Each student invents a problem and writes to Dr. Karin Koppe to ask for advice. When ready, the letter should be swapped with another member of the class. Everyone should then write a reply containing advice as to what to do. Encourage imagination and good humour.

Further practice of the language and vocabulary of this unit is given on the following page.
Reading and Writing B: p. 201

All the vocabulary and structures from this chapter are listed on the *Wörter* pages at the end (pp. 138–139). These can be used for revision by covering up either the English or the German. Students can check here to see how much they remember from the chapter.

For more speaking practice to do with this chapter, use p. 141.

Further grammar and speaking practice on the language of this chapter is provided on pp. 60–61 of the Workbook.

Assessment materials for Chapters 7 and 8 are available after Chapter 8.

Workbook (pp. 54–61)

Logo! 4 8 Mein Leben zu Hause

p. 54

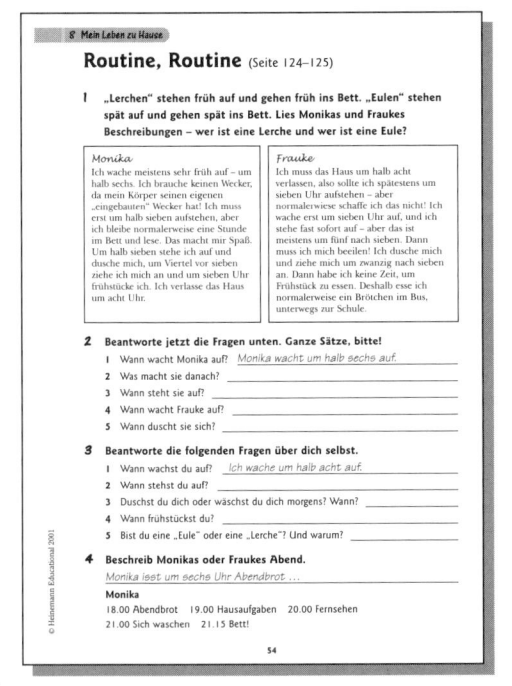

p. 55

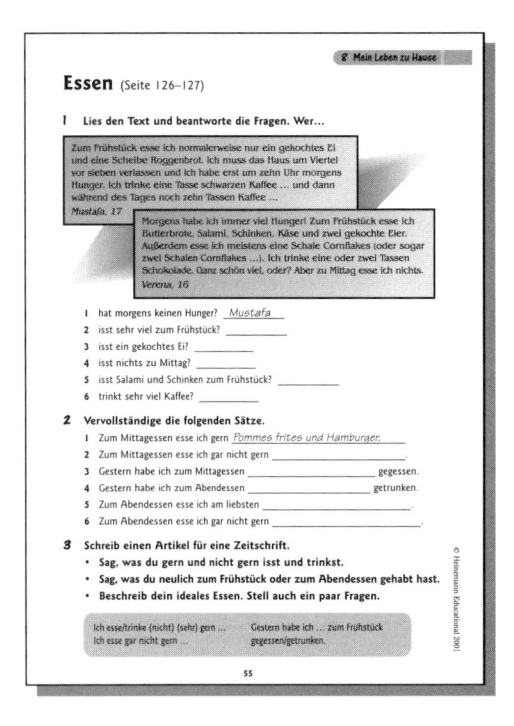

1 Monika ist eine Lerche und Frauke ist eine Eule.
2 1 Monika wacht um halb sechs auf. **2** Sie bleibt im Bett und liest. **3** Sie steht um halb sieben auf. **4** Frauke wacht um sieben Uhr auf. **5** Sie duscht sich um fünf nach sieben.
3 open-ended
4 open-ended

1 1 Mustafa, **2** Verena, **3** Mustafa, **4** Verena, **5** Verena, **6** Mustafa
2 open-ended
3 open-ended: overlook minor errors

p. 56

p. 57

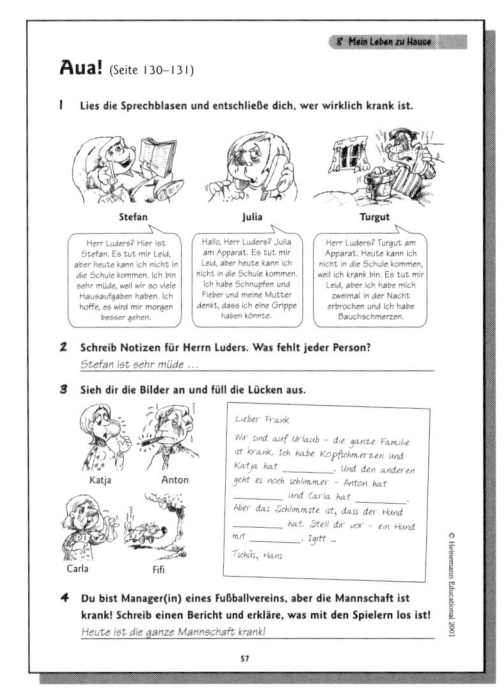

1 a G, **b** G, **c** NG, **d** NG, **e** NT, **f** G, **g** NT
2 open-ended

1 Julia und Turgut.
2 open-ended: information may be given in any way wished
3 Lieber Frank
Wir sind auf Urlaub – die ganze Familie ist krank. Ich habe Kopfschmerzen und Katja hat <u>Zahnschmerzen</u>. Und den anderen geht es noch schlimmer – Anton hat <u>Fieber</u> und Carla hat <u>Schnupfen</u>. Aber das Schlimmste ist, dass der Hund <u>Durchfall</u> hat. Stell dir vor – ein Hund mit <u>Durchfall</u>. Igitt …

Tschüs, Hans

4 open-ended

147

p. 58

1 Gisela

Ich bin wütend! Gestern <u>musste</u> ich nochmal zum Arzt gehen, weil mein Problem wieder ganz schlimm war (du erinnerst dich ohne Zweifel daran – die Kopfschmerzen und Bauchschmerzen, die ich nur werktags bekomme).

Es hat nicht gut angefangen – der Termin war um eins, aber ich <u>musste</u> bis halb zwei warten (zu spät, um nachher wieder ins Büro zu gehen). Außerdem gab es im Warteraum nichts Interessantes zum Lesen. Ich <u>musste</u> Zeitschriften über Baumaterial lesen. Zum Einschlafen!

Als der Arzt mich endlich gesehen hat, hat er nichts gemacht! Gar nichts! Er hat mir keine Tabletten gegeben und er <u>wollte</u> mir auch keinen Krankenschein geben. Er sagt, dass ich nicht krank sein <u>kann</u>! Ich! Nicht krank – sag' ich dir! Jetzt <u>kann</u> ich für gestern Nachmittag keinen Lohn bekommen.

Tschüs

Helga

2 a Sie hatte Kopfschmerzen und Bauchschmerzen. **b** Sie bekommt nur werktags Kopfschmerzen. **c** Der Termin war gestern um ein Uhr. **d** Sie musste bis halb zwei warten. **e** Sie musste Zeitschriften über Baumaterial lesen. **f** Der Arzt hat nichts für Helga gemacht. **g** Helga bekommt kein Geld für den Nachmittag.

p. 59

1 1 c, 2 b, 3 d, 4 a
2 open-ended

p. 60

no answers – *Sprechen*

p. 61

1 open-ended
2 Meine Mutter ist nicht sehr streng, und ich muss ihr nicht viel helfen. Zum Beispiel muss ich nicht Staub saugen und bügeln und ich muss mein Zimmer nicht jeden Tag aufräumen. Ich muss aber einkaufen gehen (schade!!) und außerdem muss ich abends abwaschen. Und am Abend darf ich nicht spät ins Bett gehen.
3 open-ended

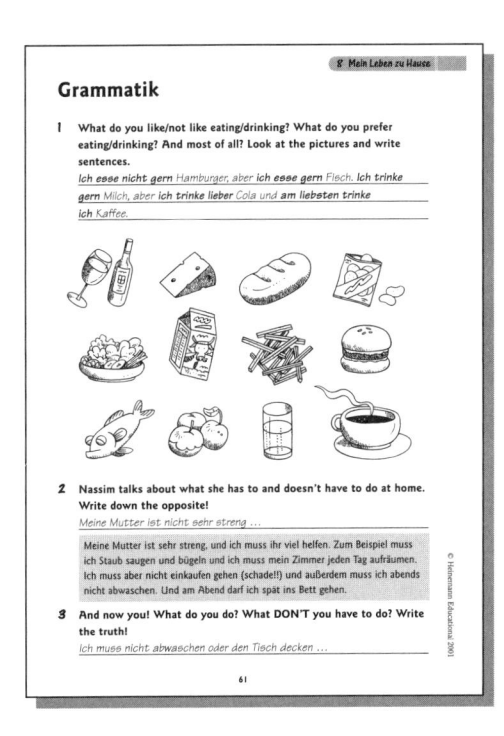

9 Die Arbeit (Student's Book pp. 142–157)

Topic area	Key language	Grammar	Skills
9.1 Die Arbeit (pp. 142–143) Part-time work	*Ich habe keinen Job.* *Ich arbeite … Er / Sie arbeitet jeden Tag / am Wochenende / einmal / zweimal in der Woche in einem Büro / Supermarkt / in einer Fabrik / an einer Tankstelle / auf einem Bauernhof / als Babysitter.* *Ich trage Zeitungen aus.* *Ich arbeite … Stunden. Ich verdiene € … Die Arbeit macht Spaß / ist schwer / langweilig / gut bezahlt / schlecht bezahlt.*		Strategies for listening
9.2 Was machst du? (pp. 144–145) General jobs	*Ich bin … Er / Sie ist …* *Arzt / Ärztin, Beamter / Beamtin (usw.). Ich arbeite …* *Er / Sie arbeitet … in einer Schule / bei der Polizei / in einem Krankenhaus / Büro / Geschäft / Restaurant / zu Hause. Er / Sie mag die Arbeit (nicht), weil sie (schwer) ist.*	The passive No articles with jobs	*Das stimmt nicht!* Strategies for extended writing
9.3 Arbeitssuche (pp. 146–147) Look for a job	*Ich möchte … mich um die Stelle als … bewerben / für eine Firma aus … arbeiten / gern zu Hause arbeiten.* *Ich habe einen Führerschein. Ich will Teilzeit arbeiten.* *Ich kann gut Englisch sprechen und schreiben.*		*doch* Expressions to use when applying for jobs
9.4 Am Apparat (pp. 148–149) Make and understand phone calls	*Wie ist deine Telefonnummer? Kann ich bitte Herrn / Frau … sprechen? Kann ich etwas ausrichten? Wie schreibt man …?* *Können Sie Herrn / Frau … bitten, mich zurückzurufen?* *Ich sage Bescheid. Auf Wiederhören.*		How to say phone numbers Speaking on the phone Expressions for formal phone conversations
9.5 Das Betriebspraktikum (pp. 150–151) Talk about work experience	*Ich war bei der Firma … Ich habe in einer Fabrik / in einem Büro gearbeitet. Ich bin mit dem Bus / Rad dorthin gefahren.* *Der Arbeitstag hat um … Uhr begonnen. Der Arbeitstag war um … Uhr zu Ende. Ich habe die Arbeit (schwer) gefunden.*	Revision of perfect tense Imperfect of *müssen: musste, mussten*	Advice on extended writing
9.6 Pläne für die Zukunft (pp. 152–153) Career plans	*Was willst / möchtest / wirst du werden?* *Ich will / möchte / werde … zur Universität gehen / … studieren / eine Lehre machen / Arzt / Ärztin werden / reisen / heiraten / Kinder haben.*	Different ways of talking about the future	Adding extra details to written work
9.7 Die Arbeitswelt (pp. 154–155) Work-related issues	*Ich könnte gleich studieren / eine Arbeit suchen.* *Ich möchte Pause machen.* *Ich werde … / ein bisschen reisen / ein halbes Jahr in … verbringen / hier arbeiten, um Geld zu verdienen.* *Ich kann da meine …kenntnisse verbessern.*	*hoffentlich …* + future tense	Learning personal job information for use in the Speaking Test

- The vocabulary and structures taught in Chapter 9 are summarised on the *Wörter* pages of the Student's Book, 156–157.
- Further speaking practice on the language of this chapter is provided on p. 174.
- Coursework pages relating to this chapter can be found on pp. 184–185.
- Further reading and writing practice on the language of this chapter is provided on pp. 202–203.
- For a selection of assessment tasks for Chapters 9 and 10, please refer to the separate Assessment Pack for your chosen examination board: AQA, OCR or Edexcel.

Logo! 4 9 Die Arbeit

1 Teilzeitjobs (pp. 142–143)

Students will learn how to:
- talk about part-time work

Key language
Ich arbeite …
Er / Sie arbeitet jeden Tag / am Wochenende / einmal / zweimal in der Woche …
  in einem Büro / Supermarkt.
  in einer Fabrik.
  an einer Tankstelle.
  auf einem Bauernhof.
  als Babysitter.
Ich trage Zeitungen aus.
Ich arbeite … Stunden.
Ich verdiene € …

Die Arbeit …
  macht Spaß.
  ist schwer / langweilig / leicht / gut bezahlt / schlecht bezahlt.
Ich habe keinen Job.

Skill focus
- strategies for listening

Resources
- Cassette C, Side B
- Workbook p. 62
- Sprechen p. 174, Gespräch 1

Start this spread by asking how many students have part-time jobs, how much they earn, how many hours they work and how many of them can explain these details in German!

1a Hör zu! Wer macht was und wann? (Listening)

Students listen to six youngsters talking about their jobs. After looking at the pictures, they select, in each case, one letter to identify the job and one phrase to say when they do it. Mention that one person will not have a job at all.

Answers
1 Katharina: d, am Samstag, 2 Ines: f, am Wochenende, 3 Felix: e, zweimal in der Woche, 4 Lars: c, 5 Wiebke: b, dreimal in der Woche, 6 Björn: a, jeden Tag

1 **Interviewer:** Guten Abend, meine Damen und Herren. Hier spricht Jürgen Schiller. Herzlich willkommen bei Jugend Heute im Radio 118. Hallo, wer ist dran?
Katharina: Hallo, Jürgen! Hier spricht die Katharina aus Nordenham.
Interviewer: Hast du einen Teilzeitjob, Katharina?
Katharina: Ja, ich arbeite am Samstag in einem Büro. Das macht Spaß und ich verdiene auch ganz gut.
2 **Interviewer:** Und du, Ines, hast du auch einen Job?
Ines: Ja, ich arbeite auch. Ich arbeite am Wochenende in einem Supermarkt. Es ist ziemlich langweilig, aber ganz gut bezahlt. Letztes Wochenende habe ich zum Beispiel fünfzig Euro verdient.
3 **Interviewer:** Nicht schlecht. Wie ist es mit dir, Felix?
Felix: Ich habe auch einen Job. Ich arbeite zweimal in der Woche in einer Fabrik. Das ist unheimlich schwer! Bald will ich einen besseren Job suchen.
4 **Interviewer:** Arbeitest du auch, Lars?

Lars: Nein, ich habe keine Zeit. Ich muss so viele Hausaufgaben machen. Leider!
5 **Interviewer:** Und du, Wiebke?
Wiebke: Ich arbeite dreimal in der Woche als Babysitter. Das ist ganz interessant, aber letzte Woche hatte ich Ärger mit dem Baby. Es hat den ganzen Abend geheult!
6 **Interviewer:** Und zum Schluss noch …
Björn: Hallo, hier spricht Björn.
Interviewer: Tag, Björn. Machst du auch Babysitting?
Björn: Ich? Nee, so was mach' ich nicht! Ich trage Zeitungen aus.
Interviewer: So, wie oft?
Björn: Jeden Tag! Ich muss sehr früh aufstehen. Heute Morgen bin ich schon um sechs Uhr aufgestanden.

Tip box
A reminder to students to look at the questions before listening and to concentrate on just the answers they need. In the exam, if they look carefully at the questions before they listen, they will get a good idea of the subject matter and will be better prepared to cope with the tape.

1b Schreib die Sätze aus Übung 1a auf. (Writing)

Students now write out the answers from the previous exercise in full sentences, following the example provided.

Answers
1 Katharina arbeitet am Samstag in einem Büro. 2 Ines arbeitet am Wochenende im Supermarkt. 3 Felix arbeitet zweimal in der Woche in einer Fabrik. 4 Lars arbeitet nicht / macht seine Hausaufgaben. 5 Wiebke arbeitet dreimal in der Woche als Babysitter. 6 Björn trägt jeden Tag Zeitungen aus.

2 Lies den Text und schreib die Prozentzahl auf. (Reading)

Students read a short article and look at a pie-chart, before writing down the answers in the form of percentages.

Answers
1 10%, 2 23%, 3 5%, 4 30%, 5 15%, 6 17%

3 Hör zu! Wie lange arbeiten diese Personen und wie viel verdienen sie? (Listening)

Students listen to young people talking about their jobs and note down how long they work for and how much they earn. As follow-up, they could write out the answers in full sentences.

Answers
1 Katharina: 6 Stunden, €30,00, 2 Ines: 8 Stunden, €40,00, 3 Felix: 6 Stunden, €36,00, 4 Lars: 20 Stunden, nichts, 5 Wiebke: 12 Stunden, €60,00, 6 Björn: jeden Tag, €30,00

1 **Interviewer:** Wie viel verdienst du, Katharina?
  Katharina: Ich bekomme €5,00 die Stunde und ich arbeite für sechs Stunden.
2 **Interviewer:** Ines?
  Ines: Ich arbeite für acht Stunden und ich bekomme €5,00 die Stunde.
3 **Interviewer:** Und du, Felix?
  Felix: Ich arbeite für sechs Stunden in der Fabrik. Ich kriege nur €6,00 die Stunde. Das finde ich furchtbar!
4 **Interviewer:** Lars?
  Lars: Für meine Hausaufgaben verdiene ich natürlich nichts! Eigentlich ist das unfair, weil ich zwanzig Stunden arbeite.
5 **Interviewer:** Wie viel bekommst du als Babysitter, Wiebke?
  Wiebke: Es ist nicht schlecht. Gestern habe ich €5,00 die Stunde bekommen, aber ich habe zwölf Stunden gearbeitet.
6 **Interviewer:** Und Björn?
  Björn: Na ja, Zeitungen austragen ist nicht gut bezahlt. Ich arbeite jeden Tag, aber ich verdiene nur €30,00 in der Woche. Ich muss mir bald einen neuen Job suchen.

4 Lies den Artikel. Wer sagt was? Schreib Frank, Irena oder Sonja. (Reading)

Students read a detailed magazine article in which three people talk about their part-time jobs. The answers must be written in the form of the name of the person being described in each sentence.

More able students can be asked to write out the answers in full sentences in the third person singular: *Sonja verdient oft kein Geld.* This activity is useful as classwork or for homework.

Answers

1 Sonja, 2 Frank, 3 Frank, 4 Sonja, 5 Frank, 6 Frank, Sonja, 7 Sonja, 8 Irena, 9 Frank, 10 Irena

5 Partnerarbeit. (Speaking)

Working in pairs, students create conversations based on the information contained in the speech bubbles.

6 Und du? Hast du einen Job? Schreib die Informationen auf. (Writing)

Students must write a piece about their own part-time jobs, based on the questions provided. If they don't have one, they should pretend they have! As this is a popular exam topic, this piece should have as much in the way of tenses, opinions and details as possible, and be marked by the teacher.

Further practice of the language and vocabulary of this unit is given on the following pages.
Speaking: p. 174, Gespräch 1
Workbook: p. 62

Logo! 4 9 Die Arbeit

2 Was machst du? (pp. 144–145)

Students will learn how to:
- talk about general jobs

Key language
Ich bin …
Er / Sie ist …
   Arzt / Ärztin.
   Beamter / Beamtin.
   Hausmann / Hausfrau.
Ich arbeite …
Er / Sie arbeitet …
   in einer Schule.
   bei der Polizei / Zeitung.
   in einem Krankenhaus / Büro / Geschäft / Restaurant.
   zu Hause.
Er / Sie mag die Arbeit (nicht), weil sie schwer ist.
Mein Vater / Bruder / Onkel / Meine Mutter / Schwester / Tochter ist …
   Ingenieur / Ingenieurin, Kellner / Kellnerin, Krankenpfleger / Krankenschwester, Lehrer / Lehrerin, Manager / Managerin, Mechaniker / Mechanikerin, Polizist / Polizistin, Schüler / Schülerin, Student / Studentin, Sekretär / Sekretärin, Verkäufer / Verkäuferin, Zahnarzt / Zahnärztin, Journalist / Journalistin / arbeitslos.

Grammar focus
- the passive
- no articles with jobs

Skill focus
- *das stimmt nicht!*
- extended writing

Resources
- Cassette C, Side B
- Workbook p. 63
- Sprechen p. 174, Gespräch 2

Start this spread by asking students whether they know the German words to describe the jobs done by their parents and what they themselves hope to do in the future.

1 Lies diesen Artikel. Was für Berufe haben die Personen? (Reading)

Students read a magazine article which gives clues about people's jobs without actually specifying them. They work out who does which job (the people are numbered within the text) and write out the answers in full sentences.

Answers

1 Frau Kutchinski ist Hausfrau. 2 Daniela Braun ist Sekretärin. 3 Luigi Fettini ist Kellner. 4 Herr Meyer ist Lehrer. 5 Karin Fritz ist Mechanikerin. 6 Herr Thiel ist Polizist. 7 Frau Dr. Klein ist Ärztin. 8 Gabriela Steuder ist Krankenschwester. 9 Wolfgang Holle ist Verkäufer. 10 Frau Dr. Schneider ist Zahnärztin.

Tip box

This provides an explanation of the passive. Students then look through the text for examples of the passive.

Grammatik: Jobs

In German, you don't need an article with a job. Most words for jobs add *-in* to describe a woman doing the job.

2a Hör zu! Wer spricht? (1–10) (Listening / Writing)

Students listen to ten short dialogues which give clues as to the job of the main person speaking. They write down the jobs.

Answers

1 Sie ist Ärztin. 2 Er ist Kellner. 3 Sie ist Sekretärin. 4 Er ist Zahnarzt. 5 Sie ist Polizistin. 6 Sie ist Verkäuferin. 7 Er ist Mechaniker. 8 Er ist Lehrer. 9 Sie ist Krankenschwester. 10 Sie ist Hausfrau.

1 – Guten Tag! Mein Name ist Eva Krüger und ich arbeite im Krankenhaus.
   – Sind Sie Krankenschwester?
   – Nein, nein, mein Name ist Frau Dr. Krüger.
2 – Herr Ober!
   – Ja, Moment! Ich komme gleich! Meinen Sie, ich habe acht Beine und zehn Arme?
   – Aber wir haben Durst!
3 – Hallo! Ich bin Brigitte und ich arbeite in einem Büro. Meine Chefin diktiert Briefe und ich tippe sie ein. Ehrlich gesagt, mag ich meine Arbeit nicht sehr gern. Meine letzte Stelle war besser.
4 – Hmm … Ja, leider haben Sie ein Loch im Zahn. Es tut mir Leid, aber ich muss bohren.
   – Nein, bitte nicht!
5 – Guten Tag. Was machen Sie hier? Sie haben falsch geparkt. Da müssen Sie leider eine Geldstrafe von €40,00 bezahlen.
   – Ach, das ist unfair!
6 – Hier im Kaufhaus haben wir viele Angebote zu Weihnachten, zum Beispiel Schoko-Leck-Pralinen für nur €1,75.
7 – Können Sie mir sagen, was das Problem ist?
   – Oha, das wird teuer! Der Motor ist kaputt! Was haben Sie bloß gemacht? Das wird mindestens €500,00 kosten.
8 – Kevin, was ist acht mal fünf?
   – Fünfzig, Herr Klein.
   – Was??
9 – Ich arbeite im Krankenhaus und trage eine Uniform. Die Arbeit ist schwer und nicht sehr gut bezahlt.
10 – Jeden Morgen bügle ich und mache das Haus sauber. Es ist ziemlich langweilig. Bald werde ich mir eine neue Stelle suchen, die interessanter ist.

2b Hör nochmal zu und notiere auf Englisch mehr über die Personen. (Listening)

Students listen to the tape again and note down, in

153

English, as much extra information as they can understand.

Suggested answers

1 She works in a hospital. 2 He is busy and the customers are impatient. 3 She liked her last job better. 4 He has just found a hole that needs filling, so he will have to use the drill. 5 She fines the driver €40,00. 6 Chocolates are on special offer for €1,75. 7 The engine is broken and the repair will cost at least €500,00. 8 Kevin can't multiply 8 × 5. 9 Her work is hard and not very well paid. 10 Her job is boring and she is going to look for a more interesting one.

Tip box

This tells us how to say something is not true and how to contradict someone.

3 Korrigiere diese Sätze (ganze Sätze, bitte!). (Writing / Reading)

Students write out corrected versions of some incorrect sentences, starting them with the useful expression *Das stimmt nicht!*

Answers

1 Eine Krankenschwester arbeitet in einem Krankenhaus. 2 Eine Sekretärin arbeitet in einem Büro. 3 Ein Kellner arbeitet in einem Restaurant. 4 Eine Hausfrau arbeitet zu Hause. 5 Ein Polizist arbeitet bei der Polizei. 6 Eine Lehrerin arbeitet in einer Schule.

4 Partnerarbeit. (Speaking)

Students work in pairs to create dialogues about people's jobs, based on the prompts provided. As is appropriate at this level, the sentences which they must produce are quite complex, saying where the people work, whether they like it and why. Students should take it in turns to ask and answer questions and the exercise can be extended by making up further similar conversations.

5a Partnerarbeit. Und jetzt die Wahrheit über deine Familie. (Speaking)

Point out that this is a topic which might well come in useful in the Speaking or Writing tests. Students ask and answer questions about the jobs of their own family members.

This is an area where students are very likely to ask you for words to describe various obscure jobs which their relations do. Tell them to use the nearest equivalent provided. The examiner won't come round to check that they are telling the exact truth!

5b Schreib die Informationen (über mindestens vier Personen) aus Übung 5a auf. (Writing)

Students write out the information from the previous exercise.

Tip box

An example to show students how to include as much detail as possible in their writing. Remind them that, if they are to gain a top grade, they must produce longer, more complex sentences.

Further practice of the language and vocabulary of this unit is given on the following pages.
Speaking: p. 174, Gespräch 2
Workbook: p. 63

Logo! 4   9 Die Arbeit

3 Arbeitssuche (pp. 146–147)

Students will learn how to:
- look for a job

Key language
Ich möchte …
  mich um die Stelle als … bewerben.
  für eine Firma aus … arbeiten.
  gern zu Hause arbeiten.
Ich habe einen Führerschein.
Ich will Teilzeit arbeiten.
Ich kann gut Englisch sprechen und schreiben.

Skill focus
- *doch*
- expressions to use in job applications

Resources
- Cassette C, Side B
- Workbook p. 64
- Lesen / Schreiben A p. 202

Start this spread by explaining that the reading material on the first page consists of genuine advertisements taken directly from a German newspaper and not sanitised at all. Remind students that if they pursue their languages, a job elsewhere in Europe could easily be a reality.

1 Finde Stellen für diese Personen. Schreib die Telefonnummern oder Adressen auf. (Reading)

Students read the job advertisements, find jobs for the people in the speech bubbles and note down the phone number for them to ring. (One of them has no number and therefore they will have to write *keine Nummer*). They will need to study the advertisements carefully and make good use of the glossary and a dictionary. Point out to students that this is a good example of a reading activity filled with 'distracters', or words which have no relevance to the task and can be safely skipped over in the search for the essence of the meaning. This activity is best carried out as a silent activity or a homework task.

Answers
1 0221 240595, 2 069 152420, 3 78 090800, 4 05344 902097, 5 keine Nummer, 6 069 34 55 62, 7 06174 33 56, 8 069 13 38 77, 9 069 13 38 70, 10 06174 61095

2 Hör zu und finde gute Stellen für die Personen auf Seite 146. (Listening)

Students listen to some people looking at the same job adverts and find out who is interested in which job. They note down the letter applying to the appropriate advert on p. 146.

Answers
1 c, 2 k, 3 i, 4 h, 5 j, 6 g, 7 d, 8 e, 9 f, 10 b

1 – Moment mal … Gibt es Stellen in Friedberg und Gegend? Ach ja! Nicht schlecht, fünfzehn Stellen!
2 – Guck mal, Anni, das ist doch perfekt. Ich habe ein Auto und ich interessiere mich für Wein.
  – Dann ruf doch an!
3 – Mein bestes Fach in der Schule war Kunst, aber es gibt nicht viele Stellen, wo man Kunstkenntnisse braucht. Diese Stelle ist vielleicht gut für mich.
4 – Ich will sehr schnell sehr viel Geld verdienen. Hey! Guck mal! Das hört sich wunderbar an!
5 – Also, ich suche eine Stelle, wo ich in einem Büro am Computer arbeiten kann. Ich kann auch ganz gut Englisch. Aha! Vielleicht habe ich was gefunden.
6 – Arbeit in einem Supermarkt … ja, ich möchte mich bewerben.
  – Dann ruf doch an.
  – Ja, mache ich … ach, es gibt keine Telefonnummer. Ich muss einen Brief schreiben.
7 – Ob ich was finde? Ich will nur Teilzeit arbeiten und ich kann nicht vor November anfangen.
8 – Ich brauche sofort Arbeit. Aha, was haben wir hier?
  – Ist das eine Stelle für einen Heizungsingenieur?
  – Ich glaube ja!
9 – Ich habe keine Lust, in einem Büro oder in einer Fabrik zu arbeiten. Ich möchte lieber zu Hause Geld verdienen. Ist das möglich?
10 – Gibt es irgendwo in der Zeitung eine Stelle für einen Elektro-Ingenieur?
  – Nee … ach, Moment, doch! Hier gibt's etwas!

Tip box
How to use *doch* to contradict something negative that has been said. Practise this by making a few preposterous statements to which the only reaction can be *doch*:
Mädchen sind nicht so intelligent wie Jungen.
Deutschland ist nicht in Europa.

3 Widersprich diesen Sätzen. Schreib Sätze mit „nein" oder „doch". (Writing)

Students respond to some statements by using *nein* or *doch* (if the original statement is a negative).

Answers
1 Nein, Berlin ist in Deutschland. 2 Doch, Paris ist in Frankreich. 3 Doch, Eis schmeckt gut. 4 Nein, Steffi Graf spielt Tennis. 5 Doch, Hamburg ist in Norddeutschland.

4 Partnerarbeit. (Speaking)

Again, this activity is based on the job adverts on p. 146. Student A selects a job and says he / she would like to apply for it. Student B looks at the adverts and identifies which job it is. They should take it in turns.

5 Schreib Bewerbungen um diese Stellen. (Writing)

Following the example letter provided, students practise writing letters of application for some or all of the jobs advertised. Emphasise that this sort of activity is common in the Higher Level Writing Test, so this work must be taken in and corrected.

Tip box

This lists expressions to use when applying for jobs. Encourage students to use these expressions when carrying out exercise 5

> Further practice of the language and vocabulary of this unit is given on the following pages.
> Reading and Writing A: p. 202
> Workbook: p. 64

Logo! 4 9 Die Arbeit

4 Am Apparat (pp. 148–149)

Students will learn how to:
- make and understand phone calls

Key language	Skill focus
Wie ist deine Telefonnummer?	• how to say phone numbers
Kann ich bitte Herrn / Frau ... sprechen?	• speaking on the phone
Kann ich etwas ausrichten?	• expressions for formal phone conversations
Wie schreibt man ...?	
Können Sie Herrn / Frau ... bitten, mich zurückzurufen?	**Resources**
Ich sage Bescheid.	• Cassette C, Side B
Auf Wiederhören.	• Workbook p. 65
	• Sprechen p. 174, Rollenspiel

Introduce this spread by asking students to give their own telephone (and mobile) numbers in the German format. They may well think that this is a very easy activity, but they are probably in for a shock, especially from the point of view of understanding numbers given fast, as in exercise 1.

Tip box
This shows how to give phone numbers in German.

1 Hör zu! Schreib die Telefonnummern auf. (Listening)
Students listen to some people giving phone numbers in German and note them down. If students think this activity is easy, ask them to complete it correctly after just one hearing. Point out to them that this is very likely to happen in real life. Maybe they might meet someone they would really like to see again. At the last moment, as the train departs, they suddenly remember that they haven't asked for their phone number. They have only one chance to write it down or never see the person again. This wouldn't present a problem in English, but it would in German because the format for giving a phone number is so different.

Answers
1 04221–62 41 94 21, 2 09832–28 42 93 76,
3 07623–71 45 20 72, 4 03355–88 23 19 12,
5 04467–44 43 28 11, 6 06225–98 89 42 24,
7 01331–73 62 39 49, 8 09227–31 24 63 82,
9 07882–15 16 12 99, 10 04862–21 41 38 90

1 – Meine Telefonnummer ist 04221–62 41 94 21.
2 – Wie ist deine Telefonnummer? 09832–28 42 93 76? Alles klar!
3 – Die Telefonnummer vom Bahnhof ist 07623–71 45 20 72.
4 – Julias Telefonnummer? Moment ... ach ja, 03355–88 23 19 12.
5 – Meine Telefonnummer ist 04467–44 43 28 11.
6 – Dieters Rufnummer ist 06225–98 89 42 24.
7 – Die Telefonnummer vom Krankenhaus ist 01331–73 62 39 49.
8 – Die Telefonnummer vom Stadion ist 09227–31 24 63 82.
9 – Meine Telefonnummer ist 07882–15 16 12 99.
10 – Brauchst du Silkes Telefonnummer? Hast du was zu schreiben da? Also, pass auf: 04862–21 41 38 90.

2a Partnerarbeit. (Speaking)
A simple activity in which student A provides a phone number while student B notes it down. Student B must not look at the page.

2b Partnerarbeit. Jetzt erfindet die Nummern und macht Dialoge wie in Übung 2a. (Speaking)
Students now repeat the previous activity, but this time make up the phone numbers themselves.

Tip box
Students should write down the phone numbers they make up so that they can be checked.

3 Hör zu und beantworte die Fragen auf Englisch. (Listening)
Students listen to two office phone conversations and write answers to the questions in English.

Answers
1 He has gone to Frankfurt. 2 Tomorrow. 3 Herr Richter, 49 32 66 14. 4 He should ring back. 5 She's a teacher. 6 She is teaching. 7 At break (11.20). 8 Frau Sieghart, 52 82 69 12.

Konversation 1
Sekretärin: Meyer.
Kunde: Ach, guten Tag. Ist das die Firma Gottlieb?
Sekretärin: Ja.
Kunde: Kann ich bitte Herrn Schulz sprechen?
Sekretärin: Leider ist Herr Schultz nicht im Büro. Er ist heute nach Frankfurt gefahren. Er wird morgen wieder hier sein. Kann ich etwas ausrichten?
Kunde: Ja. Also, mein Name ist Richter. R.I.C.H.T.E.R. Meine Telefonnummer ist 49 32 66 14. Können Sie Herrn Schultz bitten, mich zurückzurufen?
Sekretärin: Gut, Herr Richter. Geht in Ordnung. Ich werde Bescheid sagen. Auf Wiederhören.

Konversation 2
Sekretärin: Gerhard-Rolfs-Gymnasium, guten Tag.
Mutter: Ach, guten Tag. Kann ich bitte Frau Thülig sprechen?
Sekretärin: Leider ist das im Moment unmöglich, weil sie unterrichtet. Sie können in der Pause um elf Uhr zwanzig anrufen.
Mutter: Können Sie für mich etwas ausrichten? Mein Name ist Sieghart. S.I.E.G.H.A.R.T. Meine Telefonnummer ist 52 82 69 12. Meine Tochter Sigrid ist in Frau Thüligs Klasse und ich möchte sie etwas fragen. Können Sie Frau Thülig bitten, mich zurückzurufen?
Sekretärin: Gut, Frau Sieghart. Geht in Ordnung. Ich werde Bescheid sagen. Auf Wiederhören.

4a Partnerarbeit. Partner(in) A (▲) ist der Sekretär / die Sekretärin. Partner(in) B (●) ist der Kunde / die Kundin. (Speaking)

Based on a sample dialogue provided, students use the cues to make up three further telephone conversations.

Tip boxes

These provide assistance on how to speak on the phone in German and list some useful expressions for formal phone conversations.

4b Schreib Notizen für den Chef. Benutze die Informationen aus Übung 4a. (Writing)

Students write notes for the boss based on having taken the messages in the previous activity.

Suggested answers

1 Herr Kolinski hat angerufen. Rufen Sie bitte zurück. Seine Telefonnummer ist 33 44 26 20. 2 Herr / Frau Schlitz hat angerufen. Rufen Sie bitte zurück. Seine / Ihre Telefonnummer ist 26 14 93 19. 3 Herr / Frau Haasemann hat angerufen. Rufen Sie bitte zurück. Seine / Ihre Telefonnummer ist 69 96 44 32. 4 Herr / Frau Siebels hat angerufen. Rufen Sie bitte zurück. Seine / Ihre Telefonnummer ist 72 18 42 41.

5 Lies die E-Mail und beantworte die Fragen auf Englisch. (Reading)

Students read a formal e-mail and answer questions about it in English.

Answers

1 Frank first tried to phone Frau Trimmer. 2 No. 3 The phone line was continuously engaged. 4 He wants to tell Frau Müller that he has repaired her radio. 5 He has mislaid her phone number. 6 He knows that Frau Trimmer knows how to contact Frau Müller.

Further practice of the language and vocabulary of this spread is given on the following pages.
Speaking: p. 174, Rollenspiel
Workbook: p. 65

Logo! 4 9 Die Arbeit

5 Das Betriebspraktikum
(pp. 150–151)

Students will learn how to:
- talk about work experience

Key language
Ich war bei der Firma …
Ich habe in einer Fabrik / Schule / in einem Geschäft / in einem Büro gearbeitet.
Ich bin mit dem Bus / Rad dorthin gefahren.
Der Arbeitstag hat um … Uhr begonnen.
Der Arbeitstag war um … Uhr zu Ende.
Ich habe die Arbeit leicht schwer / langweilig / interessant gefunden.

Grammar focus
- revision of the perfect tense
- imperfect of *müssen*: *musste, mussten*

Skill focus
- advice on extended writing

Resources
- Cassette C, Side B
- Workbook p. 66
- Sprechen p. 174, Gespräch 3
- Kursarbeit pp. 184–185

Start the spread by explaining that the German *Betriebspraktikum* is the equivalent of the UK work experience. This topic is included in the GCSE syllabus and thus is liable to crop up in any part of the exam. Could your students describe their own work experience in German?

1 Lies den Artikel und beantworte die Fragen (ganze Sätze, bitte!). (Reading / Writing)
Students read a magazine article in which Robert talks about his work experience and answer German questions in full sentences. This is suitable either for classwork or homework.

Suggested answers

1 Er war bei der Firma Gottschalk. 2 Das war eine Möbelfirma / eine Möbelfabrik / eine Firma, die Möbel produziert. 3 Er ist mit dem Bus zur Arbeit gefahren. 4 Die Fahrt hat 20 Minuten gedauert. 5 Der Arbeitstag hat um 8 Uhr begonnen. 6 Er hat Möbel gebaut. 7 Er hat Telefonanrufe beantwortet und Briefe getippt. 8 Der Chef war ein bisschen blöd. 9 Der Arbeitstag war um 4 Uhr zu Ende. 10 Die Arbeit war anstrengender als die Schule.

2 Hör zu! Welche Wörter fehlen? Schreib Martinas Text ab und trag die Wörter ein. (Listening / Writing)
Students copy out Martina's note, leaving space to write in the missing words and phrases, which they can do on the basis of listening to the interview on tape as many times as necessary.

Answers

Krankenhaus, Rad, (mindestens) 30, 7.45, 1, gemacht, gekocht, gesprochen, ziemlich schwer (aber auch ganz lustig)

Udo: Wo hast du dein Betriebspraktikum gemacht, Martina?
Martina: Ich habe in einem Krankenhaus gearbeitet.
Udo: So? Welches Krankenhaus denn?
Martina: Die Universitätsklinik in Finndorf.
Udo: So? Und wie bist du denn dahin gekommen?
Martina: Ich bin mit dem Rad gefahren. Das war doof, weil ich am frühen Morgen anfangen musste und die Uni-Klinik ist ganz schön weit weg.
Udo: Wie lange hat die Fahrt gedauert?
Martina: Mindestens eine halbe Stunde, oft noch mehr. Und der Verkehr war furchtbar, ich konnte kaum atmen.
Udo: Wann hat der Arbeitstag begonnen?
Martina: Um 7.45 Uhr. Fürchterlich, nicht wahr?
Udo: Und wann war der Tag zu Ende?
Martina: Na ja, wenigstens konnte ich verhältnismäßig früh nach Hause fahren. Um ein Uhr war ich schon fertig.
Udo: Was musstest du alles machen?
Martina: Ich habe sauber gemacht, Kaffee gekocht und mit den Patienten gesprochen.
Udo: Wie fandest du die Arbeit?
Martina: Die Arbeit war ziemlich schwer, aber manchmal auch ganz lustig.

Grammatik: müssen (Imperfekt) (have to – imperfect)
The *ich*, *er / sie* and *wir* forms of *müssen* with examples from the text on p. 150. Remind students that the imperfect is normally used in a written narrative in the past, such as a newspaper report. However, they will need to recognise the imperfect (e.g. in the Reading Test) and will need to actually use *war, hatte, wollte, musste* and, in particular, *es gab*.

Wiederholung: Das Perfekt (perfect tense)
A reminder of the perfect tense with examples taken from the text on p. 150. Tell students that there is a tendency just to learn the perfect forms of very common verbs. However, when talking about a specialist area such as work experience, more unusual verbs, such as those given here, may be required.

3a Partnerarbeit. Interviewe deinen Partner / deine Partnerin. Benutze die Informationen unten. (Speaking)
Students, working in pairs, simulate a situation in a Speaking Test where an examiner is asking questions about work experience. They should read out the sample dialogue, then do the other two, swapping roles.

3b Jetzt du? Wie war dein Betriebspraktikum? Schreib *deine* Antworten auf die Fragen in Übung 3a auf. (Writing)
Finally, students write down their own answers to the questions posed in the previous exercise. This will accumulate into a useful paragraph about their own work experience, which should be taken in and marked. The teacher may well have to provide specialist vocabulary about various unusual work experience placements.

Tip box
A quick reference to the coursework spread on work experience.

> Further practice of the language and vocabulary of this unit is given on the following pages.
> Speaking: p. 174, Gespräch 3
> Workbook: p. 66

Kursarbeit
Further extended writing practice about a work experience placement is contained in the coursework section, pp. 184–185.

Logo! 4 9 Die Arbeit

6 Pläne für die Zukunft
(pp. 152–153)

Students will learn how to:
- talk about career plans

Key language
Was willst / möchtest / wirst du werden?
Ich will / möchte / werde …
zur Universität / Hochschule / technischen Hochschule / zum Bund gehen.
studieren.
eine Lehre machen.
Arzt / Ärztin /
Beamter / Beamtin /
Lehrer / Lehrerin /
Programmierer / Programmiererin werden.
reisen.
heiraten.
Kinder haben.

Grammar focus
- different ways of talking about the future

Skill focus
- adding details to writing work

Resources
- Cassette C, Side B
- Sprechen p. 174, Gespräch 4

Start this spread by asking, in English, how many students in the class already have firm career intentions. Would they be able to describe these in German?

1 Lies den Text und beantworte die Fragen (ganze Sätze, bitte!). (Reading / Writing)
Students read the text of a conversation about career plans and answer some German questions in full sentences. Tell them to begin the answers as suggested on the page.

Answers
1 Sie wird Medizin studieren. 2 Sie möchte Ärztin werden. 3 Er will eine Stelle suchen. 4 Er will Programmierer werden. 5 Er will eine Lehre machen. 6 Er wird in einer Autowerkstatt arbeiten. 7 Er will Fremdsprachen studieren. 8 Er möchte eine Lehrerausbildung machen / Lehrer werden.

Grammatik: Das Futur (future tense)
A reminder that *wollen, mögen* and *hoffen* can be used with an infinitive to express the future. The formation of the future tense with *werden* is then explained.

The exam criteria specify that students must be able to express future intentions. This they can do in any of the ways laid out here (in particular, by the use of the present tense) but, at Higher Level, it will be impressive if students demonstrate use of the 'real' future, i.e. with *werden*.

2a Hör zu und trag die Namen ein: Dorit, Anton oder Birte. (Listening)
Students listen to a conversation about career plans and write down names to complete the sentences provided. They may have to listen to the tape several times, because the sentences aren't in the same order as they are heard. Besides, identifying who is speaking is not an easy task. They will have to listen carefully for the names of the speakers.

Answers
1 Birte will in einem Büro arbeiten. 2 Birte wird Informatik studieren. 3 Anton will in einem Geschäft arbeiten. 4 Dorit möchte als Lehrerin arbeiten. 5 Dorit will an der Universität studieren. 6 Anton wird eine Lehre machen.

> Interviewer: Hast du schon eine Idee, was du nächstes Jahr machen wirst, Dorit?
> Dorit: Ja, eigentlich schon. Wenn meine Noten gut genug sind, werde ich an der Universität Hamburg Französisch studieren. Dann möchte ich gern für ein paar Jahre in Südfrankreich in einer Schule als Lehrerin arbeiten.
> Interviewer: Und du, Anton?
> Anton: Ich hoffe, bei der Firma McNamara eine Lehre zu machen und dann später möchte ich eventuell in Bonn in einem Geschäft arbeiten, vielleicht als Verkäufer.
> Interviewer: Und zum Schluss noch Birte. Hast du schon eine Ahnung, was du machen möchtest?
> Birte: Ja, ich weiß ganz genau! Ich werde an der technischen Hochschule in Berlin Informatik studieren, weil ich mich sehr für das Internet interessiere. Dann will ich in Berlin in einem Büro arbeiten, hoffentlich für eine Software-Firma.

2b Hör nochmal zu und notiere auf Englisch mehr über die Personen. (Listening)
Students listen to the tape again and note down, in English, any further information they can glean.

Suggested answers
Dorit: would like to work in a school in southern France as a teacher. **Anton:** would like to work in Bonn later, maybe as a salesman. **Birte:** interested in the Internet; would like to work for a software firm.

3a Partnerarbeit. (Speaking)
Using various future forms, students conduct interviews with each other about career plans, using the information provided.

3b Schreib die detaillierten Antworten aus Übung 3a auf. (Writing)
Students now write out the information provided in the previous exercise, using the third person singular form.

Answers

> 1 Wenn sie 18 ist, wird Ursel zuerst reisen. Dann möchte sie Politik studieren. Später hofft sie, Politikerin zu sein. 2 Wenn sie 18 ist, wird Yesim zuerst ins Ausland fahren. Dann möchte sie Deutsch studieren. Später hofft sie, Lehrerin zu sein. 3 Wenn er 18 ist, wird Klaus zuerst ein Jahr arbeiten. Dann möchte er zur Universität gehen. Später hofft er, Arzt zu sein.
> 4 Wenn sie 18 ist, wird Sabine zuerst in einem Geschäft arbeiten. Dann möchte sie heiraten. Später hofft sie, Kinder zu haben.

Tip box
Advice to students about how to add detail to their writing (and so get better marks).

4 Beschreib *deine* Pläne für die Zukunft. (Writing)
Students finally write out their own career hopes and plans. This will need to be a substantial paragraph, taken in and marked by the teacher. Suggestions for content are provided.

This would be a good point for the teacher to introduce and explain the use of *hoffentlich* (explained in detail in the next spread): *Hoffentlich werde ich im Ausland arbeiten.*

Further practice of the language and vocabulary of this unit is given on the following page.
Speaking: p. 174, Gespräch 4

Logo! 4 9 Die Arbeit

7 Die Arbeitswelt (pp. 154–155)

Students will learn how to:
- talk about work-related issues

Key language	Grammar focus
Ich könnte gleich studieren / eine Arbeit suchen.	• *hoffentlich* + future tense
Ich möchte Pause machen.	**Skill focus**
Ich werde …	• learning job information for use in Speaking Test
ein bisschen reisen.	
ein halbes Jahr in … verbringen.	**Resources**
hier arbeiten, um Geld zu verdienen.	• Cassette C, Side B
Ich kann da meine …kenntnisse verbessern.	• Sprechen p. 174
	• Lesen / Schreiben B p. 203

Start the spread by explaining that it consists mainly of listening and reading activities going into more detail about the world of work.

1 Lies den Text, bring die Sätze in die richtige Reihenfolge und schreib sie auf. (Es gibt mehrere Möglichkeiten.) (Listening / Reading)

Students listen to the teacher reading out an interview with a soap star, while reading the interview on the page. The task is to put the sentences provided into the correct order (there are possibilities for variations; the teacher should judge which compilations are acceptable).

The more able can do this activity as a 'pure' listening activity, i.e. without referring to the printed text. This will be quite a taxing task!

Suggested answer

Ayse hatte eine große Familie. Sie musste oft auf ihre Geschwister aufpassen. Ihre Mutter konnte nicht aufpassen, weil sie immer so viel zu tun hatte. Und ihr Vater war oft arbeitslos. Also war die Familie sehr arm. Deswegen musste Ayse Nebenjobs machen. Einer von diesen Jobs war in einer Kneipe. Dort musste sie die schmutzigen Gläser abwaschen. Diese Stelle war schlecht bezahlt. Nach der Schule wollte sie eigentlich Kunst studieren. Aber eines Abends kam ein Fernsehregisseur in das Lokal. Er hat Ayse ins Studio eingeladen. Jetzt ist Ayse Fernsehstar. Sie ist zwar keine Kindergärtnerin, aber sie spielt die Rolle einer Kindergärtnerin.

2 Lies den Artikel, finde die Sätze und schreib sie auf Deutsch auf. (Reading)

Students read another interview, this time with a young male *Abiturient*, identify some German sentences from their English equivalents and write them out.

Answers

1 Du könntest an jeder Universität studieren. 2 Ich kann da meine Spanischkenntnisse verbessern. 3 Ich möchte mal Pause machen. 4 Jetzt muss er sich entscheiden, was er nächstes Jahr macht. 5 Natürlich möchte ich gern studieren. 6 Ich werde wohl ein halbes Jahr in Südamerika verbringen. 7 Ich werde nächstes Jahr ein bisschen reisen. 8 Deine Noten sind toll. 9 Ich könnte gleich studieren. 10 Ehrlich gesagt, bin ich ziemlich müde.

Tip box

Use *hoffentlich* followed by a verb in order to express a hope for the future.

3 Schreib einige Sätze über deine Teilzeitjobs. (Writing)

Students write a paragraph about part-time jobs, using past, present and future. They should include as much detail as possible and have their work marked by the teacher.

Tip box

Advice to learn their answer to exercise 3 by heart and then use it for the Speaking Test.

Further practice of the language and vocabulary of this unit is given on the following pages.
Speaking: p. 174
Reading and Writing B: p. 203

All the vocabulary and structures from this chapter are listed on the *Wörter* pages at the end (pp. 156–157). These can be used for revision by covering up either the English or the German. Students can check here to see how much they remember from the chapter.

For more speaking practice to do with this chapter, use p. 174.

Further grammar and speaking practice on the language of this chapter is provided on pp. 67–68 of the Workbook.

Assessment materials for Chapters 9 and 10 are available after Chapter 10.

Kursarbeit

9 Betriebspraktikum
(pp. 184–185)

The coursework spreads in *Logo! 4* give regular, guided practice in preparing for the coursework element of the GCSE exam.

The spreads always start with a model text on each theme (at a higher level than that expected by the student) which acts as a stimulus to give students ideas of what they might include in their own piece of work. Students are encouraged to look at the detail of the text through the guided reading activities. They are gradually guided to produce good German sentences in the tasks through to the final task, which is to produce an extended piece of writing. The *Hilfe* column is a feature on all the spreads. It reminds students of language they might include and particular structures that will raise the level of their writing. Remind students who are capable of achieving a Higher grade that they should always include examples of two or three tenses in their writing.

This spread guides students to produce an extended piece of writing on the topic of work experience.

1 Du bist Nils. Beantworte die Fragen.
Students answer the questions as if they were Nils.

Answers

1 Ich bin morgens um halb sieben aufgestanden. 2 Ich bin mit dem Bus zum Geschäft gekommen. 3 Die Arbeit hat um um 8 Uhr angefangen. 4 Ich habe mit dem Computer gearbeitet. 5 Ich bin um 16 Uhr nach Hause gegangen. 6 Ich habe Butterbrote für meine Kollegen geholt. 7 Ich habe fünf Tage im Geschäft gearbeitet. 8 Ich habe mich am letzten Tag ein bisschen traurig gefühlt. 9 Ich habe meinen Kollegen eine Schachtel Pralinen geschenkt. 10 Ich habe viel bei meinem Praktikum gelernt.

2 Beantworte diese Fragen über *dein* Praktikum. Schreib die Antworten in einer logischen Reihenfolge.
Students answer the questions about their own work experience, writing their answer in a logical order.

3 Schreib jetzt ein Tagebuch über dein Betriebspraktikum.
Students now write a diary about their own work experience using the previous activities and the tips in the *Hilfe* column as support.

Hilfe
Tips for writing about work experience:
- using questions from exercise 2 as a guide to what to include
- including a form summarising your work experience
- using the present, perfect and future tenses
- including opinions and reasons for your opinions

Workbook (pp. 62–68)

p. 62

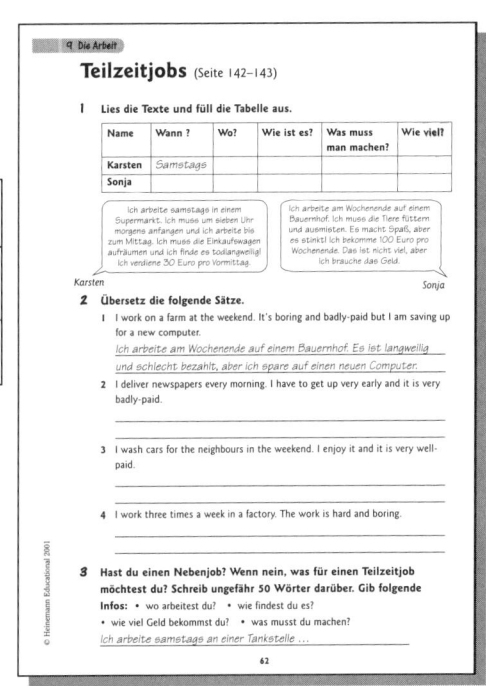

1

Name	Wann?	Wo?	Wie ist es?	Was muss man machen?	Wie viel?
Karsten	Samstags	Supermarkt	Todlangweilig	Einkaufswagen aufräumen	€ 30,00
Sonja	Wochenende	Bauernhof	Macht Spaß, aber es stinkt	Tiere füttern / ausmisten	€ 100,00

2 **1** Ich arbeite am Wochenende auf einem Bauernhof. Es ist langweilig und schlecht bezahlt, aber ich spare auf einen neuen Computer. **2** Ich trage jeden Morgen Zeitungen aus. Ich muss sehr früh aufstehen und es ist sehr schlecht bezahlt. **3** Ich putze am Wochenende Autos für die Nachbarn. Es macht Spaß und es ist sehr gut bezahlt. **4** Ich arbeite dreimal in der Woche in einer Fabrik. Die Arbeit ist schwer und langweilig.

3 open-ended: overlook minor errors

p. 63

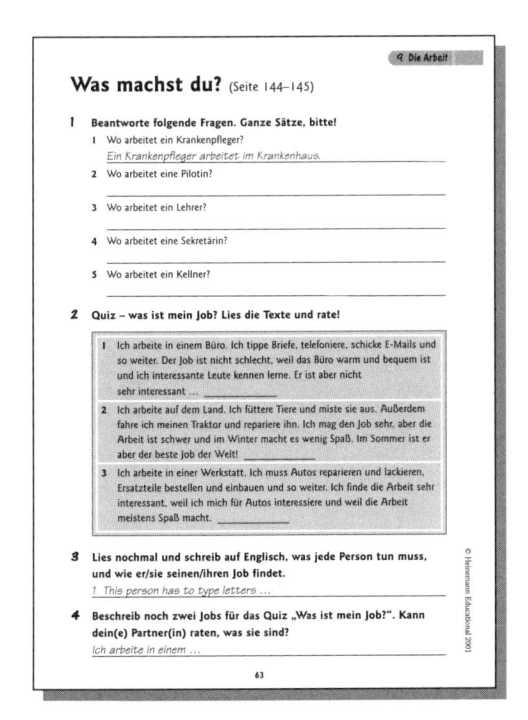

1 **1** Ein Krankenpfleger arbeitet im Krankenhaus. **2** Eine Pilotin arbeitet in einem Flugzeug. **3** Ein Lehrer arbeitet in einer Schule. **4** Eine Sekretärin arbeitet in einem Büro. **5** Ein Kellner arbeitet in einem Restaurant.

2 **1** Sekretär(in), **2** Bauer (Bäuerin), **3** Mechaniker(in)

3 open-ended

4 open-ended: overlook minor errors

p. 64

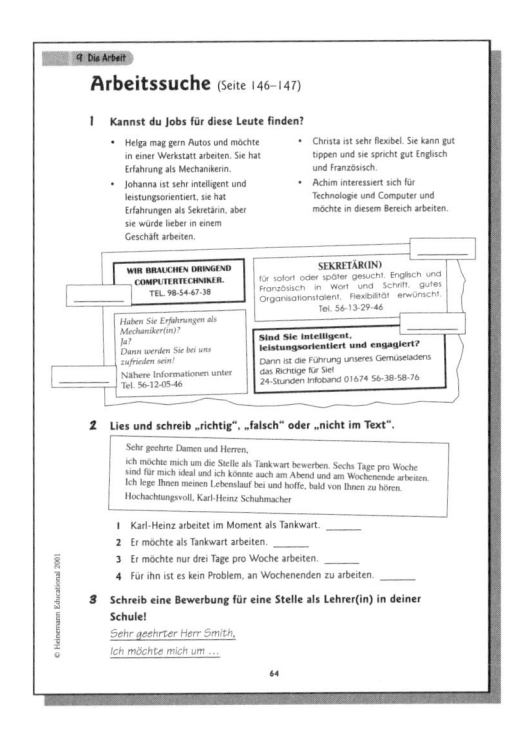

1

Achim	Christa
Helga	Johanna

2 **1** Falsch. **2** Richtig. **3** Falsch. **4** Richtig.

3 open-ended: overlook minor errors

p. 65

1 **1** Null fünf sechs sieben drei – fünfundvierzig – siebenundsechzig – dreiundzwanzig – fünfzehn, **2** Null eins fünf sechs sieben – fünfunddreißig – zweiundsiebzig – einundsechzig – neunzehn, **3** Null drei sieben acht zwei – siebenundzwanzig – zwölf – Null vier – siebenundsechzig, **4** Null eins drei sieben acht – zweiundfünfzig – achtundzwanzig – fünfzig – neunundvierzig

2 A: Guten Tag! Ist das die Firma Hackenschmidt?
  B: Ja, hier ist die Firma Hackenschmidt.
  A: Kann ich bitte Frau Becker sprechen?
  B: Es tut mir Leid, Frau Becker ist nicht hier. Kann ich etwas ausrichten?
  A: Ja. Mein Name ist Naumann. Heinrich Naumann.
  A: Meine Telefonnummer ist 38-92-12-78. Können Sie Frau Becker bitten, mich zurückzurufen?
  B: Ist in Ordnung, Herr Naumann. Auf Wiederhören.

3 open-ended, as long as the information given is conveyed accurately

p. 66

1 **1** In a factory. **2** By bus. **3** Very slow. **4** Any two of: clean up, make coffee, work in the office. **5** Not bad. **6** It was too long.
2 Er ist mit <u>dem Bus</u> zur Arbeit gefahren. Er ist um <u>sieben Uhr</u> angekommen, aber der <u>Arbeitstag</u> hat erst um acht Uhr begonnen. Die Arbeit war um <u>vier Uhr</u> zu Ende. Er hat <u>sauber gemacht</u>, im Büro <u>gearbeitet</u> und Getränke vorbereitet. Das Personal <u>war</u> <u>freundlich</u>, aber die Fahrt hat keinen <u>Spaß</u> gemacht und die Arbeitsstunden waren zu <u>lang</u>.
3 open-ended

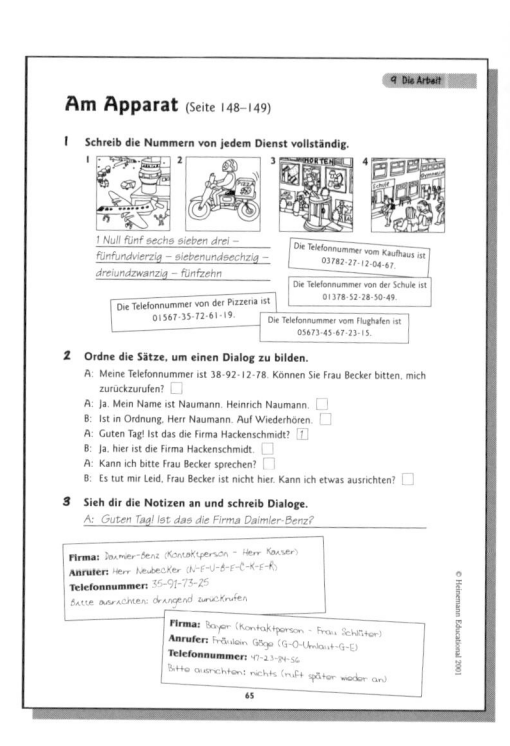

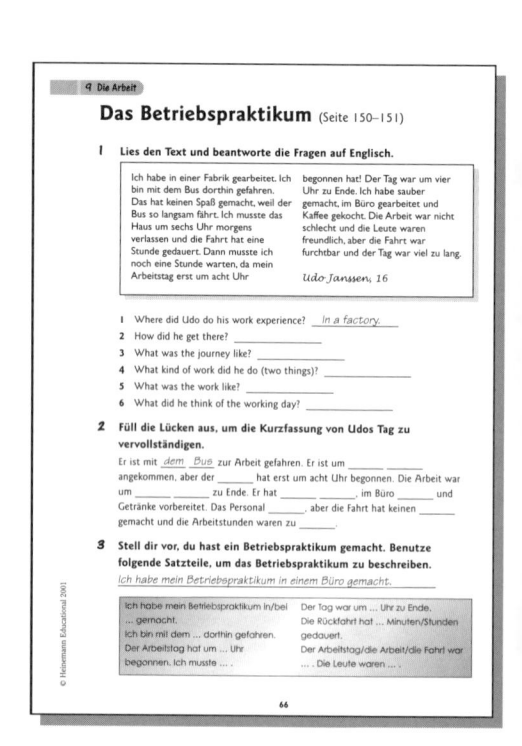

p. 67

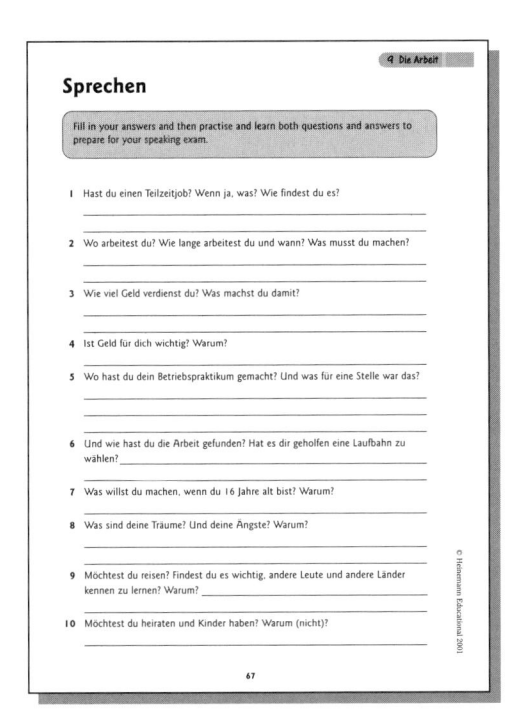

no answers – *Sprechen*

p. 68

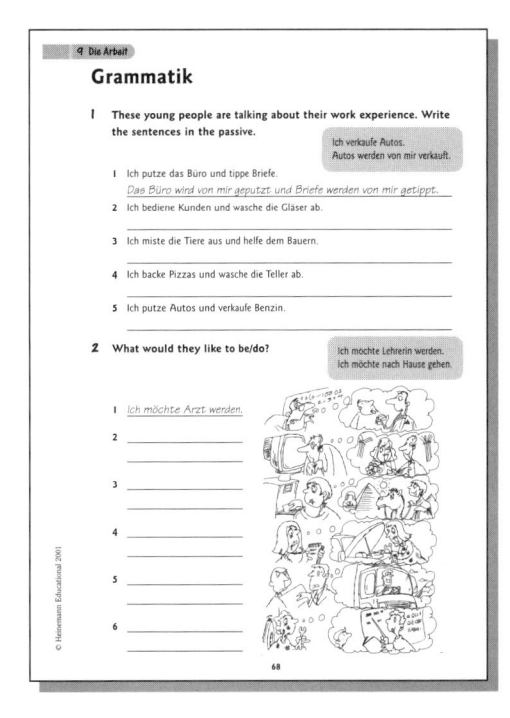

1 **1** Das Büro wird von mir geputzt und Briefe werden von mir getippt. **2** Kunden werden von mir bedient und die Gläser werden von mir abgewaschen. **3** Die Tiere werden von mir ausgemistet und der Bauer wird von mir geholfen. **4** Pizzas werden von mir gebacken und die Teller werden von mir abgewaschen. **5** Autos werden von mir geputzt und Benzin wird von mir verkauft.
2 **1** Ich möchte Arzt werden. **2** Ich möchte heiraten. **3** Ich möchte reisen. **4** Ich möchte Mechanikerin werden. **5** Ich möchte Lastwagenfahrer werden. **6** Ich möchte Lehrerin werden.

10 Teenies! (Student's Book pp. 158–175)

Topic area	Key language	Grammar	Skills
10.1 Charakter (pp. 158–159) Talk about personalities	*Ich bin … Mein Vater ist … Meine Freundin ist … oft / manchmal / sehr / ziemlich / immer launisch / streng / nett / laut / ruhig / fleißig / intelligent / faul / freundlich / lustig / doof / nervig. Er / Sie ist größer / kleiner / schlanker / dicker / älter / jünger / intelligenter als …* *Meine Schwester, die nett ist …* *Ich bin nicht so klein wie er / sie.*	Pronouns: *er, sie, ihn, sie* The comparative Relative clauses	Using different tenses and opinions in written work
10.2 Familienprobleme (pp. 160–161) Family relationships	*Ich wollte (ins Kino gehen), aber ich durfte es nicht.* *Mein Problem ist, dass ich einen Hund möchte / die Wohnung zu klein ist. Ich verstehe mich (nicht) sehr gut / ziemlich gut / gut / nicht besonders gut / gar nicht gut / mit meinem Bruder / meiner Schwester.*	Imperfect of *wollen, dürfen (ich, er / sie, wir* forms) *dass* clauses with relative clauses *sich verstehen mit …* + dative	Matching the tense of an answer to the tense of the question Useful structures for describing family members
10.3 Das ist ungesund! (pp. 162–163) Health matters	*Rauchen ist nicht gut für die Gesundheit.* *Tabak ist schlecht für die Lungen.* *Er raucht … Zigaretten pro Tag. Drogen sind gefährlich.* *Er nimmt Heroin / Haschisch / harte Drogen.* *Er trinkt (nicht) viel Alkohol. Man sollte viel Sport treiben / gesund essen / oft zu Fuß gehen.*	*Man sollte …*	Reading strategies Adjectives with their opposite meanings
10.4 Die Umwelt (pp. 164–165) The environment	*der Verkehr, Abfall, Lärm, die Umwelt, Luft* *Autos produzieren viele Abgase.* *atmen* *Es gibt (nicht) viele Obdachlose.* *gut / schlecht für die Umwelt* *eine Fußgängerzone bauen* *öffentliche Verkehrsmittel einführen* *Abfall mit nach Hause nehmen*		
10.5 Rettet die Umwelt! (pp. 166–167) Helping to save the environment	*Ich könnte … zu Fuß gehen / mit dem Rad fahren.* *Elektrogeräte ausschalten.* *duschen statt baden.* *zur Mülldeponie gehen.* *Paper, Plastik, Getränkedosen und Glasflaschen recyceln* *Autos produzieren Schadstoffe.* *das Loch in der Ozonschicht* *mit öffentlichen Vekehrsmitteln fahren* *Benzin sparen*	Conditional of *können*	
Prüfungstipps (pp. 170–173)			Tips for all parts of the exams

- The vocabulary and structures taught in Chapter 10 are summarised on the *Wörter* page of the Student's Book, 168.
- Further speaking practice on the language of this chapter is provided on p. 175.
- Further reading and writing practice on the language of this chapter is provided on pp. 204–205.
- For a selection of assessment tasks for Chapters 9 and 10, please refer to the separate Assessment Pack for your chosen examination board: AQA, OCR or Edexcel.

Logo! 4   10 Teenies!

1 Charakter (pp. 158–159)

Students will learn how to:
- talk about personalities

Key language
Ich bin …
Mein Vater ist …
Meine Freundin ist …
 oft / manchmal / sehr /
 ziemlich / immer …
 launisch / streng / nett /
 laut / ruhig / fleißig /
 intelligent / faul /
 freundlich / lustig /
 doof / nervig.
Er / Sie ist größer /
kleiner / schlanker /
dicker / älter / jünger /
intelligenter als …
Meine Schwester, die
nett ist …

Ich bin nicht so (klein)
wie er / sie.

Grammar focus
- pronouns: *er, sie, ihn, sie*
- the comparative
- relative clauses

Skill focus
- using different tenses and opinions in written work

Resources
- Cassette C, Side B
- Workbook p. 69

Start this spread by asking students how many adjectives they can remember which could describe people's personalities.

1a Hör zu und schreib in der richtigen Reihenfolge auf, wer die Personen sind und wie sie sind. (Listening / Writing)

Students listen to a tape of a young man leafing through a photo album and talking about his relations. In simple German sentences, they note down what he says about their personalities.

Answers
1 Ulis Vater ist intelligent. 2 Ulis Bruder ist laut. 3 Ulis Onkel ist lustig. 4 Ulis Oma ist ruhig. 5 Ulis Schwester ist faul. 6 Ulis Freundin ist launisch. 7 Ulis Mutter ist fleißig. 8 Ulis Lehrerin ist streng.

Interview mit Uli

Hallo! Also, jetzt möchte ich euch meine Familie und meine Freunde vorstellen. Hier in meinem Fotoalbum habe ich allerlei Fotos von Familienmitgliedern und anderen Leuten, die ich kenne.

Hier auf der ersten Seite ist mein Vater. Er heißt Hans und er ist Arzt. Ich finde, er ist sehr intelligent und wir verstehen uns sehr gut. Aber mein Bruder Markus – hier ist er – nervt mich. Er ist so furchtbar laut! Er spielt den ganzen Tag CDs in seinem Zimmer! Aber keine normalen CDs, sondern schreckliche amerikanische Metal-Bands mit doofen Namen. Nein, oh nein!

Okay … Das ist mein Onkel Rüdiger. Ich verstehe mich sehr gut mit ihm, weil er so lustig ist. Er interessiert sich für Theater und auch für Tiere und die Umwelt. Manchmal wandern wir zusammen im Schwarzwald.

Wen haben wir hier? Ach, wie niedlich. Meine Oma Mathilde ist schön ruhig. Sie ist die Mutter von meinem Vater und sie wohnt allein, weil ihr Mann vor einigen Jahren gestorben ist. Sie ist zweiundachtzig.

Aber die hier mag ich überhaupt nicht. Das ist meine Schwester Ulrike. Ulrike ärgert mich, weil sie unheimlich faul ist. Sie macht nie ihre Hausaufgaben, aber, was noch schlimmer ist, sie wäscht nie ab und ich muss es immer machen. Das ist echt unfair.

Aaaaah … Das hier ist meine Freundin Annette. Annette mag ich natürlich sehr gern, aber manchmal ist sie ein bisschen launisch. Wir treiben zusammen Sport und gehen manchmal ins Kino. Wir sind seit zwei Jahren zusammen.

So, und die nächste Seite … Ach ja, das hier ist meine Mutter. Ich mag meine Mutter auch sehr gern. Sie ist eine sehr fleißige Dame. Eigentlich arbeitet sie viel zu viel, denn sie macht die meiste Hausarbeit und hat auch eine Stelle in einer Bank.

Und zum Schluss noch, meine Schulklasse mit meiner Lehrerin Frau Franke. Ich habe ein bisschen Angst vor Frau Franke, weil sie so streng ist. Sie ist eine ganz gute Lehrerin – sie unterrichtet Deutsch.

1b Hör nochmal zu und notiere auf Englisch mehr Informationen über die Personen. (Listening)

Students listen again and note down, in English, as much extra information as they can gather about each person.

Suggested answers

1 His father, Hans, is a doctor. They get on well together. 2 His brother Markus annoys him by making such a row playing CDs by terrible American heavy metal bands with stupid names in his room. 3 Uncle Rüdiger is a good laugh and they get on well. He is interested in the theatre as well as animals and the environment. Sometimes they go walking together in the Black Forest. 4 His granny (his father's mother) is called Mathilde. She is widowed and lives alone. She's 82 and very quiet. 5 His sister Ulrike annoys him because she is so lazy. She never does her homework and leaves him to do all the washing up. 6 His girlfriend Annette can be moody. They have been going out for two years, mostly doing sport and going to the cinema. 7 He likes his mother, who is very hard-working. As well as working in a bank, she also does most of the housework. 8 Uli is a bit scared of his German teacher Frau Franke. She is quite a good teacher but strict.

Grammatik: Pronomen (pronouns)
Er and *sie* change to *ihn* and *sie* in the accusative. Practice of this point is provided in exercise 2.

2 Partnerarbeit. Partner(in) A (▲) stellt Fragen über andere Personen oder Familienmitglieder. Partner(in) B (▲) antwortet. (Speaking)
Students practise using the accusative forms *ihn* and *sie* by asking and answering questions about people, based on the prompts provided.

Grammatik: Relativsätze (relative clauses)
How to use a relative clause (examples with *der* and *die*). Students practise this in exercise 3a.

3a Partnerarbeit. (Speaking)
Students practise comparatives and relative clauses by following the example provided and making up similar dialogues based on the picture prompts. Students should take it in turns to ask and answer questions.

Grammatik: Der Komparativ (comparison)
Examples of the comparative used to compare people. The new element here is how to say 'not so ... as ...' as well as '...er than ...'

3b Erfinde eine Familie, wie die Familie in Übung 3a. Beschreib die Familie. Welche Personen gibt es? Wie ist ihr Charakter? Wer ist größer / dicker / nicht so groß usw.? (Writing)
Students should make up a family similar to that in exercise 3a and describe them in German.

3c Beschreib deine eigene Familie (Writing)
Students then go on to describe their own families. Encourage them to include as much detail about the people as possible.

4a Lies Manjas Homepage und beantworte die Fragen (ganze Sätze, bitte!).
(Reading / Writing)
Students read this homepage and answer questions about it in full German sentences.

Answers
1 Nein, sie wohnt in einer Wohnung. 2 Sie wohnt seit zehn Jahren da. 3 Sie versteht sich nicht gut mit Boris (, weil sie ihn doof findet). 4 Nein, sie ist geschieden. 5 Sie ist sehr freundlich und lustig. 6 Er ist ganz nett, aber manchmal streng. 7 Er hat einmal gesagt, dass Manja nicht so viel fernsehen soll. 8 Sie versteht sich jetzt ganz gut mit ihm. 9 Sie hat ihre Katze seit zwei Jahren. 10 Sie ist sehr niedlich.

4b Lies die Homepage in Übung 4a nochmal und schreib eine E-Mail an Manja. Schreib so viele Informationen über deine Familie wie möglich: Charakter, Größe usw.
(Writing / Reading)
In reply to the information on Manja's homepage, students must write out a detailed description of their own families, including appearance and personality, how they get on, etc. This is an extremely common GCSE topic, so must be corrected and learnt by heart.

Tip box
A reminder to students to use different tenses and to express their opinions when doing written work.

Further practice of the language and vocabulary of this unit is given on the following page.
Workbook: p. 69

Logo! 4 10 Teenies!

2 Familienprobleme
(pp. 160–161)

Students will learn how to:
- talk about family relationships

Key language
Ich wollte (ins Kino gehen), aber ich durfte es nicht.
Mein Problem ist, dass …
  ich einen Hund möchte.
  die Wohnung zu klein ist.
Ich verstehe mich (nicht) sehr gut / ziemlich gut / besonders gut / gar nicht gut mit meinem Bruder / Stiefbbruder / Halbbruder / Vater / Stiefvater / meiner Schwester / Stiefschwester / Halbschwester / Mutter / Stiefmutter.

Grammar focus
- imperfect of *wollen*, *dürfen* (*ich*, *er* / *sie*, *wir* forms)
- *dass* with relative clauses
- *sich verstehen mit* + dative

Skill focus
- matching tense of answer to tense of question
- useful structures for describing family members

Resources
- Cassette C, Side B
- Workbook p. 70
- Sprechen p. 175, Gespräch I
- Lesen / Schreiben A p. 204

Start this spread by brainstorming, in English, the sorts of problems that can occur within families.

I Lies den Brief und beantworte die Fragen auf Deutsch (ganze Sätze, bitte!).
(Reading / Writing)
Students read a letter from Dennis describing a family problem he has and answer questions about it in German.

Answers

I Er hat in der Stadt gewohnt. 2 Er hat das gut gefunden. 3 Er wohnt jetzt auf dem Land / auf einem Bauernhof. 4 Weil sein Stiefvater einen Bauernhof hat. 5 Er wollte gestern in die Disco gehen. 6 Weil der letzte Bus um neun Uhr fährt.

Tip box
A reminder to students to make sure that the tense of their answer matches the tense of the question. This is particularly important to remember in the exam.

Grammatik: wollen und dürfen (Imperfekt) (to want to, to be allowed to – imperfect)
The *ich, er / sie* and *wir* forms of *wollen* and *dürfen* in the imperfect with examples of their use.

2 Schreib Sätze. (Writing)
Based on the example and the prompts provided, students construct sentences using the imperfect of *wollen* and *dürfen*.

Answers

I Ich wollte ins Kino gehen, aber ich durfte es nicht. 2 Leo wollte rauchen, aber er durfte es nicht. 3 Wir wollten Whisky trinken, aber wir durften es nicht. 4 Ich wollte ein Motorrad kaufen, aber ich durfte es nicht. 5 Ich wollte ins Restaurant gehen, aber ich durfte es nicht.

3a Hör zu und schreib „richtig" oder „falsch".
(Listening)
Students listen to Manja describing her problem on a radio phone-in, look at the sentences provided and decide whether they are true or false.

Answers

I Falsch. 2 Falsch. 3 Richtig. 4 Falsch. 5 Richtig.

> Susi: Hallo, Manja. Hast du ein Problem?
> Manja: Ja, Susi. Ich wohne in einem Wohnblock in der Stadtmitte. Mein Problem ist, dass ich eine Katze habe, aber ich möchte auch einen Hund haben. Aber das andere Problem ist, dass meine Mutter „nein" sagt. Sie sagt, dass die Wohnung zu klein ist. Ich sage, dass ich Katzen und Hunde liebe. Was sagst du denn, Susi?
> Susi: Hmm, das ist oft ein Problem in der Stadt. Vielleicht ist die Wohnung wirklich zu klein. Du hast schon Glück, dass du eine Katze hast. Ich glaube, dass deine Mutter Recht hat. Vielleicht könntest du einen Hamster kaufen? Ich glaube, dass das eine bessere Idee ist. Viel Glück!

Grammatik: Relativsätze (relative clauses)
This explains how to use *dass*: put a comma in front of it and put the verb at the end of the sentence. Practice is provided in exercise 3b.

3b Verbinde die Satzteile aus dem Gespräch in Übung 3a und schreib sie auf.
(Writing / Listening)
Students listen once more, then link the half sentences to make correct answers using *dass*.

Answers

I e Mein Problem ist, dass ich einen Hund möchte. 2 f Aber das andere Problem ist, dass meine Mutter „nein" sagt. 3 d Sie sagt, dass die Wohnung zu klein ist. 4 c Ich sage, dass ich Katzen und Hunde liebe. 5 a Du hast schon Glück, dass du eine Katze hast. 6 b Ich glaube, dass deine Mutter Recht hat.

Grammatik: mit (with)
Examples of how to use *sich verstehen mit* with the dative to say how you get on with different family members. Practice is provided in exercise 4.

4 Lies die E-Mail. Was sagen die Personen? (Reading / Writing)
Students read an e-mail and then fill in the information using the *sich mit ... verstehen* construction.

Answers
1 Ich verstehe mich nicht mit meinem Mann. 2 Ich verstehe mich nicht mit meiner Mutter. 3 Ich verstehe mich nicht mit meinem Vater. 4 Ich verstehe mich nicht mit dem Hund. 5 Ich verstehe mich nicht mit meiner Schwester.

5 Partnerarbeit. Partner(in) A (▲) stellt fünf Fragen über Familienmitglieder von Partner(in) B. Partner(in) B (●) antwortet. (Speaking)
Students ask and answer questions about their relations with other family members. The answers must be true ones, as there are no prompts. Students should take it in turns to ask and answer questions.

6 Schreib so viel du kannst über deine Familie. Lass deinen Aufsatz von deinem Lehrer / deiner Lehrerin korrigieren und lerne ihn auswendig! (Writing)
This is an opportunity for students to prepare a large-scale essay about their families. This will have been tackled many times over the course, but now they are armed with much more to say in the way of descriptions of personalities, relationships, etc. They should include as many tenses, details, reasons and opinions as they can. This work must be taken in and marked.

Tip box
This lists useful structures when describing family members.

Further practice of the language and vocabulary of this unit is given on the following pages.
Speaking: p. 175, Gespräch I
Reading and Writing A: p. 204
Workbook: p. 70

Logo! 4 10 Teenies!

3 Das ist ungesund!
(pp. 162–163)

Students will learn how to:
- talk about health matters

Key language
Rauchen ist nicht gut für die Gesundheit.
Tabak ist schlecht für die Lungen.
Er raucht … Zigaretten pro Tag.
Drogen sind gefährlich.
Er nimmt Heroin / Haschisch / harte Drogen.
Er trinkt (nicht) viel Alkohol.
Man sollte viel Sport treiben / gesund essen / oft zu Fuß gehen.

Grammar focus
- *man sollte …*

Skill focus
- reading strategies
- adjectives and their opposites

Resources
- Cassette C, Side B
- Workbook p. 71

Introduce this spread by conducting a (confidential!) poll on the smoking and drinking habits of the class. Explain that laws in Germany are slightly different, in that drinking alcohol and smoking are permitted from the age of 16. In general, smoking is more common among German teenagers than their English counterparts, with many schools having a smoking area. There are drug problems in German schools, just as there are in any European country.

1 Lies den Text. Wer ist wer? Schreib Sätze über Werner, Sonja, Udo oder Udos Bruder (im Präsens). (Reading / Writing)

Students read a magazine review of a TV programme, then look at the pictures, work out who is who and write down their names.

Answers
1 Sonja raucht nicht. 2 Werner raucht täglich 20 Zigaretten. 3 Udo raucht nicht. 4 Sonja trinkt manchmal ein Glas Wein. 5 Udo trinkt nie. 6 Werner trinkt Bier. 7 Sonja raucht manchmal Haschisch. 8 Udos Bruder nimmt Heroin.

Tip box
This gives some reading strategies which will prove useful in the exam. Students should be reminded not to be put off if they don't know every word. They should pick out the words from the text that they need and also look for words which are similar to the English. Imperfect verb forms are used when relating what people said.

2 Hör zu und beantworte die Fragen. (Listening)

Students listen to young people talking about their habits and answer questions using a couple of German words. The more able can be asked to provide their answers in full sentences.

Answers
1 vierzig Zigaretten pro Tag, 2 Wein, 3 sie sind zu gefährlich, 4 nein, 5 Heroin, 6 sie ist Sportlerin, 7 nein, 8 er nimmt Haschisch, 9 nein, 10 nein

> **Moderator:** Hier sind wir wieder bei „Jugend heute". Und heute haben wir ein hartes Thema: Drogen, Alkohol und Tabak. Wer raucht? Wer trinkt? Und wer nimmt Drogen? Hallo, wie heißt du?
> **Christoph:** Ich heiße Christoph.
> **Moderator:** Rauchst du, Christoph?
> **Christoph:** Ja, ich rauche 40 Zigaretten pro Tag. Leider!
> **Moderator:** Um Gottes Willen! Und trinkst du auch Alkohol?
> **Christoph:** Ja, aber nur Wein. Harte Sachen wie Whisky trinke ich nicht.
> **Moderator:** Und hast du je Drogen genommen, Christoph?
> **Christoph:** Ich habe einmal Haschisch geraucht, aber heute interessiere ich mich nicht mehr für Drogen. Sie sind ja viel zu gefährlich.
> **Moderator:** Danke, Christoph. Und du, wie heißt du?
> **Bärbel:** Mein Name ist Bärbel.
> **Moderator:** Na, Bärbel? Nimmst du Drogen?
> **Bärbel:** Nein, ich nehme keine Drogen und ich würde es auch nie machen. Eine Freundin von mir hat Heroin genommen. Sie war sehr krank, das war furchtbar.
> **Moderator:** Trinkst du Alkohol?
> **Bärbel:** Nein. Ich trinke nicht, ich rauche nicht und ich nehme keine Drogen. Ich bin Sportlerin. Ich spiele Federball für Frankfurt.
> **Klaus:** Hallo, ich bin der Klaus.
> **Moderator:** Und wie ist es mit dir?
> **Klaus:** Also, ich persönlich rauche keinen Tabak, aber ich trinke manchmal ein Glas Wein. Und in den Ferien rauche ich manchmal Haschisch mit meinen Freunden.
> **Moderator:** Du rauchst Haschisch? Aber das ist doch illegal!
> **Klaus:** Ich weiß, aber für uns ist es normal.
> **Moderator:** Nimmst du auch harte Drogen?
> **Klaus:** Nein, das würde ich nicht tun.
> **Moderator:** Hmm … Danke, Klaus.

3a Schau das Poster an. Das stimmt alles nicht! Schreib die Wahrheit. (Reading / Writing)

Students look at a spoof poster making wild claims about the alleged benefits of smoking. They then write sentences which actually tell the truth! They should use the Tip box, which provides adjectives with their opposites.

Answers

Teachers may allow other answers.
1 Rauchen ist schlecht für die Gesundheit. **2** Tabak ist schrecklich für Sportler. **3** Zigaretten sind schlecht für die Umwelt. **4** Mädchen finden Raucher furchtbar. **5** Tabak ist schlecht für die Lungen. **6** Zigaretten riechen schlecht. **7** Rauchen ist teuer. **8** Rauchen ist schlechter als essen!

Tip box
Adjectives with their opposites to help with exercise 3a.

3b Partnerarbeit. Partner(in) A (▲) stellt Fragen über Übung 3a. Partnerin B (●) antwortet. (Speaking)
Working in pairs, students ask and answer questions based on the poster in the previous exercise. A detailed example is provided, showing how to answer using the *dass* construction.

3c Benutze deine Antworten aus Übung 3a, um ein ANTI-Rauchen-Poster zu machen. Mach auch Poster gegen Alkohol und Drogen. (Writing)
Now students must design a poster condemning smoking. They can also make similar advertisements against alcohol and drugs.

Tip box
The conditional form of *sollen* is introduced. The infinitive goes to the end of the sentence. Practice of the point is provided in exercise 4.

4 Ein gesundes Leben. Was sollte man machen, um gesund zu bleiben? (Writing)
Following the prompts provided, students write information about what one should and shouldn't do in order to remain healthy. They can also think up more examples of their own.

Further practice of the language and vocabulary of this unit is given on the following page.
Workbook: p. 71

Logo! 4 10 Teenies!

4 Die Umwelt (pp. 164–165)

Pupils will learn how to:
- talk about the environment

Key language
der Verkehr, Abfall, Lärm
die Umwelt, Luft
Autos produzieren viele Abgase.
atmen
Es gibt (nicht) viele Obdachlose.
gut / schlecht für die Umwelt
eine Fußgängerzone bauen
öffentliche Verkehrsmittel einführen
Abfall mit nach Hause nehmen

Resources
- Cassette C, Side B
- Workbook p. 72

Introduce this spread by explaining that the topic of the environment is an integral part of the GCSE syllabus and therefore very likely to crop up in the exam. There is a certain amount of specialist vocabulary involved, and that is what is being presented on this spread.

1a Lies den Artikel. Finde diese Ausdrücke im Wörterbuch oder in der Vokabelliste. Wie heißen sie auf Englisch? (Reading)

Students read a Greenpeace-style article about the state of the environment and use the glossary or a dictionary to translate German expressions from it into English.

Answers

1 traffic, 2 environment, 3 litter, 4 exhaust gas, 5 noise, 6 air, 7 breathe

1b Finde Sätze im Text aus Übung 1a für jedes Bild. (Reading)

Students look at a set of pictures, all of which represent one German sentence from the text. They should find the sentences and write them down.

Answers

1 Wir verpesten die Luft mit Autoabgasen. 2 Wir fordern: normale Teller und Tassen, keine Plastikteller und Pappbecher. 3 Es gibt so viel Lärm, dass die Leute kaum noch miteinander sprechen können. 4 Auch sehr schlecht für die Umwelt ist der Abfall, den wir täglich auf die Straße schmeißen. 5 Wir bei der Grünen Gruppe haben schon oft Proteste vor Hamburger-Restaurants durchgeführt, weil sie alles in Papier und Pappe einwickeln.

2 Hör zu und schreib Notizen auf Englisch: Welche Umweltprobleme gibt es in Wurmhausen? Welche Lösungen schlägt der Reporter vor? (Listening)

Students listen to the TV reporter Jürgen Schiller describing the alleged environmental problems in Wurmhausen and make notes in English to describe the problems and the suggested solutions.

Suggested answers

Problems: noise caused by traffic, lots of litter, homelessness, pollution
Possible solutions: build a pedestrian zone, introduce public transport, take litter home

> Guten Tag, meine Damen und Herren. Hier spricht Jürgen Schiller aus Wurmhausen. Wie Sie hören, ist es hier sehr laut! Es gibt sehr viel Verkehr. Autos, Motorräder und Busse fahren durch die Stadt. Es ist furchtbar, es gibt viel zu viel Lärm. Das ist ein großes Problem.
>
> Schauen Sie mal. Auf der Straße liegt ein armer junger Mann. Er ist leider obdachlos. Die jungen Leute hier essen in Hamburger-Restaurants. Sie werfen das Papier einfach auf die Straße. Deswegen gibt es sehr viel Abfall hier und die Luft ist sehr schlecht, die kann man nicht gut atmen.
>
> Was können wir tun? Wir müssen:
> - eine Fußgängerzone bauen;
> - öffentliche Verkehrsmittel einführen;
> - Abfall mit nach Hause nehmen.

3 Lies den Text und wähle die richtige Antwort. Schreib die Sätze auf. (Reading)

Explain that the people of Wurmhausen are furious about Jürgen Schiller's allegations. This is an article in the local paper, setting out their grievances. Students read the article and then select from multiple-choice answers.

Answers

1 a Wurmhausen hat eine Fußgängerzone. 2 a Abfall auf der Straße gibt es in jeder Stadt. 3 c Der junge Mann ist obdachlos. 4 c Die Abgase kommen von Autos. 5 a Die Luft in Wurmhausen ist besser als in der Großstadt. 6 b In Wurmhausen gibt es weniger Obdachlose als in Hamburg.

4 Beschreib deine Stadt vom Gesichtspunkt „Umwelt". (Writing)

Students follow the prompts and write a paragraph about environmental aspects of where they live. This work, which is suitable for homework, should be collected in and marked.

Further practice of the language and vocabulary of this unit is given on the following page.
Workbook: p. 72

5 Rettet die Umwelt!

(pp. 166–167)

Students will learn how to:
- talk about measures to save the environment

Key language
Ich könnte …
zu Fuß gehen / mit dem Rad fahren
Elektrogeräte ausschalten
duschen statt baden
zur Mülldeponie gehen
Paper, Plastik, Getränkedosen und Glasflaschen recyceln
Autos produzieren Schadstoffe.
das Loch in der Ozonschicht
mit öffentlichen Vekehrsmitteln fahren
Benzin sparen

Grammar focus
- conditional of *können*

Resources
- Cassette C Side B
- Workbook p. 73
- Sprechen p. 175, Gespräch 2
- Lesen / Schreiben B p. 205

Start the unit by brainstorming, in English, the general world problems which threaten the environment. Explain that this spread will teach some vocabulary to help deal with this topic in German. Remind students that Germany is, in general, an extremely environmentally conscious country, with low levels of litter and a sophisticated recycling system.

1a Lies die Tipps. Schreib auf Englisch, was wir alles machen könnten, um unsere Umwelt zu schonen. (Reading)

Students read a leaflet setting out ways of preserving the environment. They write down, in English, what advice is given in the text.

Suggested answers

We could walk or cycle to school (because it is better for the environment and our health). We could turn off appliances we are not using (to save energy). We could have showers instead of baths (a bath uses ten times more water than a shower). We could recycle paper, plastic, cans and glass bottles (to save energy).

Grammatik: Der Konditional (conditional)

The conditional of *können* is shown *(ich, du* and *er / sie* forms) along with examples of use. Practice of this point is provided in exercise 1b.

1b Was könnte man machen? Vervollständige die Sätze. (Writing)

Using the information provided in the text, plus the conditional format described in the Grammar box, students construct sentences saying what one could do in order to protect the environment.

Answers

1 Statt alles in den Mülleimer zu werfen, könnte man zur Mülldeponie gehen. 2 Statt mit dem Auto zu fahren, könnte man zu Fuß gehen oder mit dem Rad fahren. 3 Statt Geräte anzulassen, könnte man sie ausschalten. 4 Statt zu baden, könnte man unter die Dusche gehen.

2 Hör zu, lies den Text und verbinde die Satzteile. Schreib die Sätze auf. (Listening / Reading)

Students listen to an interview with a university professor, read the text of the interview and then link parts of sentences to make correct answers. The more able are welcome to attempt this exercise without looking at the script on the page.

Incidentally, scientific opinion may differ as to exact causes of global warming. These are only the opinions of Professor von Glühstein!

Answers

1 d Schadstoffe verursachen das Loch in der Ozonschicht. 2 c Fahren Sie bitte nur mit öffentlichen Verkehrsmitteln. 3 a Autofahrer sollten langsamer fahren. 4 e Die Globalerwärmung verursacht schlechtes Wetter. 5 f Langsam fahren spart Benzin. 6 b Radfahren ist gesünder als Autofahren.

Interview mit Professor Otto von Glühstein von der Universität Heidelberg.
Interviewer: Herr Professor, Sie sind doch Umweltexperte. Können Sie uns bitte Tipps geben, wie wir die Umwelt retten können?
Professor: Ist es Ihnen aufgefallen, dass in den letzten Jahren das Wetter immer schlechter geworden ist? Das hat alles mit Globalerwärmung zu tun.
IInterviewer: Woher stammt das Problem? Und was können wir dagegen tun?
Professor: Nun ja, das Problem stammt von uns Menschen. Wir sind faul und wollen überall hin mit dem Auto fahren. Aber Autos produzieren Schadstoffe und diese Schadstoffe haben das Loch in der Ozonschicht verursacht.
Interviewer: Aber was können wir dagegen tun?
Professor: Regel Nummer eins: nur Auto fahren, wenn es unbedingt nötig ist. Gehen Sie zu Fuß oder fahren Sie Rad. Das ist alles viel besser für die Gesundheit. Wenn Sie fahren müssen, dann fahren Sie bitte mit öffentlichen Verkehrsmitteln, zum Beispiel mit der Straßenbahn. Und wenn Sie unbedingt Auto fahren müssen, dann fahren Sie bitte langsam. Das macht weniger Lärm, stößt weniger Schadstoffe aus und spart Benzin.

3 Lies die Texte aus Übung 1 und 2 nochmal. Schreib eine Liste von Sachen, die gut für die Umwelt wären. (Writing / Reading)

Students reread both the main texts on this spread and write down as many environmental tips as they can, following the format in the examples.

Suggested answers

Man könnte zu Fuß in die Schule gehen / mit dem Rad fahren. Man sollte duschen statt baden. Man sollte elektrische Geräte ausschalten. Man sollte viele Sachen recyceln. Man sollte mit öffentlichen Vekehrsmittel fahren. Man sollte mit dem Auto nur langsam fahren,

4 Partnerarbeit. (Speaking)

Students create conversations about the environment, following the pattern suggested and insert their own ideas and opinions.

Further practice of the language and vocabulary of this unit is given on the following pages.
Speaking: p. 175, Gespräch 2
Reading and Writing B: p. 205
Workbook: p. 73

All the vocabulary and structures from this chapter are listed on the *Wörter* page (p.168). This can be used for revision by covering up either the English or the German. Students can check here to see how much they remember from the chapter.

For more speaking practice to do with this chapter, use p. 175.

Further grammar and speaking practice on the language of this chapter is provided on pp. 74–75 of the Workbook.

Assessment materials for Chapters 9 and 10 and an end-of-course assessment are available at this point.

Prüfungstipps (pp. 170–173)

These pages contain a selection of tips to help students to get a high mark in their exams. These tips home in on the typical errors that students are likely to make and the kinds of trap that they sometimes fall into in exams. So they need to be studied carefully, as they could make the difference between a good grade and a very good one.

Further suggestions:

- Ask students to identify themselves the things which they find most difficult in exams (especially after the mocks). Suggest ideas for avoiding the most common errors.

- Brainstorm, in English, things which individual students have found helpful in exams and which might aid others.

- Select several students' pieces of written work and demonstrate how often just one or two repeatedly made errors can make a piece of work seem poor, and that just removing those few errors can turn it into an excellent piece of writing.

Workbook (pp. 69–75)

p. 69

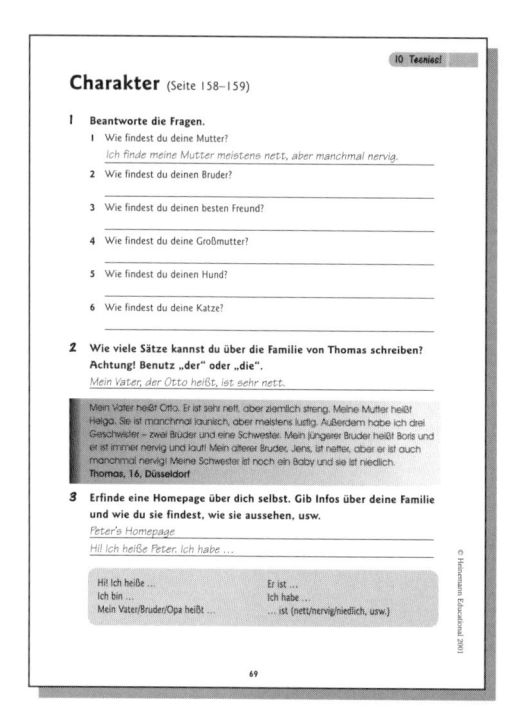

1.
   1 open-ended
   2 open-ended
   3 open-ended

p. 70

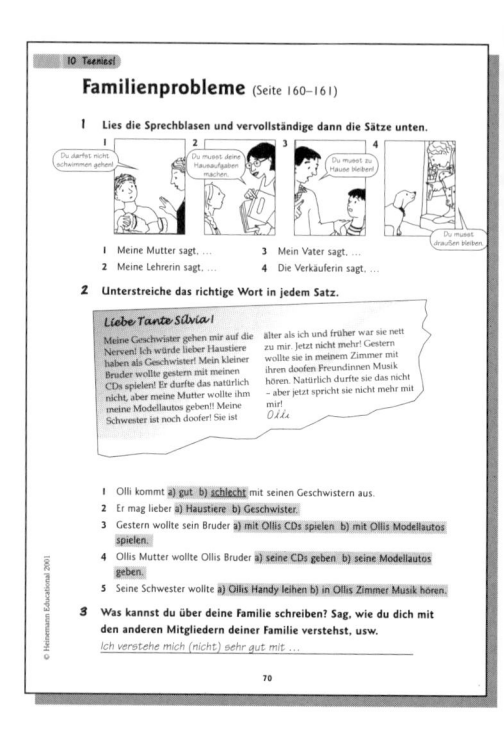

1 1 Meine Mutter sagt, dass ich nicht schwimmen gehen darf. 2 Meine Lehrerin sagt, dass ich meine Hausaufgaben machen muss. 3 Mein Vater sagt, dass ich zu Hause bleiben muss. 4 Die Verkäuferin sagt, dass ich draußen bleiben muss.
2 1 b, 2 a, 3 a, 4 b, 5 b
3 open-ended: overlook minor errors

p. 71

1 1 b, 2 c, 3 a, 4 d

2

	Bier	Wein	Whisky	Zigaretten	Drogen
Andrea	Ja	Ja	Nein	Nein	Nein
Hugo	Nein	Nein	Nein	Ja	Nein

3 open-ended: as long as students convey a 'fit' message which covers the issues mentioned, they can express this how they wish

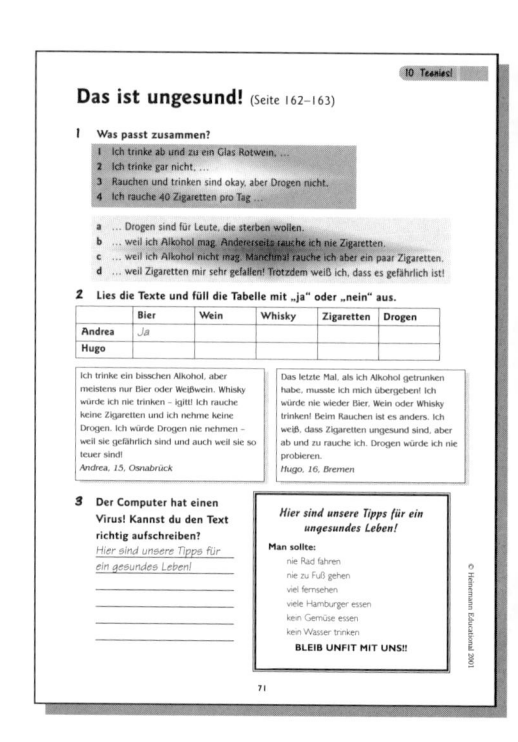

178

Logo! 4 10 Teenies!

p. 72

1 1, 4, 6

2

Gut
Es gibt relativ wenig Verkehr.
Es gibt fast keine Obdachlose.
Eine Hilfsorganisation gibt den Obdachlosen Unterkunft und Suppe.

Schlecht
Es gibt keine Fußgängerzone.
Es gibt viel Müll.
Viele Jugendliche werfen ihre Plastikteller weg.

3 open-ended: overlook minor errors

p. 73

1 1, 2, 5, 6, 7, 8, 10, 11, 12, 13, 14
2 open-ended
3 open-ended

p. 74

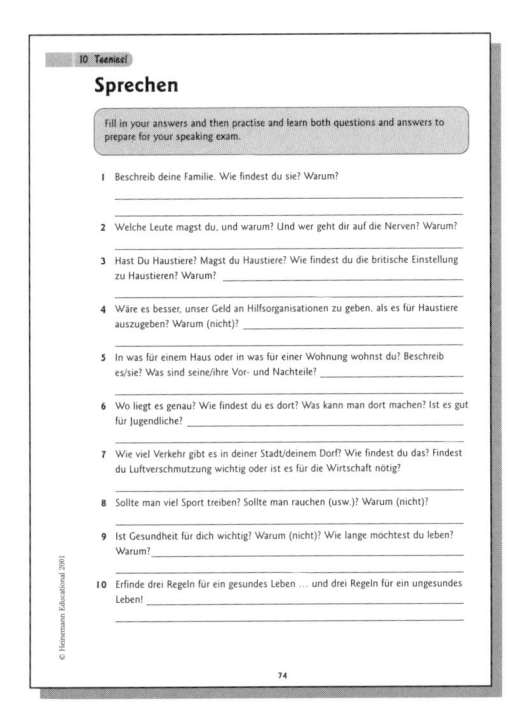

no answers – Sprechen

p. 75

1 **1** Sie ist intelligenter als er. **2** Er ist kleiner als sie. Sie ist größer als er. **3** Er ist älter als sie. Sie ist jünger als er.
2 **1** Man sollte nicht rauchen. **2** Man sollte nicht immer Auto fahren. **3** Man sollte oft Rad fahren. **4** Man sollte keine Drogen nehmen. **5** Man sollte nicht viel Alkohol trinken. **6** Man sollte gesund essen. **7** Man sollte Glasflaschen zum Recyclingcontainer bringen.

179

Lesen / Schreiben

1A Hallo! Ich bin's! (p. 186)

This page is best used at any point after pp. 10–11 of the Student's Book.

1 Lies den Artikel. Wer ist das? Was ist die *beste* Antwort? Schreib Frank, Daniela, Ebru oder Alexander. (Reading)
Students read the article and the sentences and say who each sentence refers to.

Answers
1 Frank, 2 Ebru, 3 Alexander, 4 Ebru, 5 Alexander, 6 Daniela, 7 Daniela, 8 Frank, 9 Ebru, 10 Daniela

Tip box
Use the questions from exercise 1 to adapt for exercise 2, remembering to change the pronoun where necessary.

2 Was für Freunde und Freundinnen hast du? Schreib drei kurze Absätze über sie. Benutze „Er sagt" / „Sie sagt" wie oben. (Writing / Reading)
Students write a short paragraph about two or three of their friends, using the texts as models.

3 Schreib einen Bewerbungsbrief für einen Freund oder eine Freundin an „Big Brother". Lies die Sätze 1–10 aus Übung 1 nochmal! (Writing)
Students write a letter to Big Brother, putting forward one of their friends as an applicant.

1B Hallo! Ich bin's! (p. 187)

This page is best used at any point after pp. 12–13 of the Student's Book.

1 Lies den Text. Welcher Satz ist richtig? Wähle a, b oder c. (Reading)
Students read the text and choose the correct alternative from the three given in the sentences below.

Answers
1 a, 2 c, 3 a, 4 b, 5 b, 6 a

Tip box
Students should use the wrong answers from exercise 1 as a basis for writing the answer to exercise 2.

2 Du bist Journalist/in für die Zeitung „Morgen!" Schreib einen Artikel „Der Skandal von Big Brother!" mit den *falschen* Sätzen aus Übung 1. (Writing)
Students use the wrong sentences from exercise 1 to write an article about a scandal from the Big Brother house.

2A Schulstress (p. 188)

This page is best used at any point after pp. 32–33 of the Student's Book.

1 Zwei Schüler sprechen über ihre Schulen. Wer ist das? Sven oder Lothar? (Reading)
Students read the sentences and say whether each refers to Sven or to Lothar.

Answers
1 Lothar, 2 Sven, 3 Lothar, 4 Lothar, 5 Sven, 6 Sven, 7 Sven, 8 Sven, 9 Lothar, 10 Lothar

2 Was ist richtig? Wähle a, b oder c. (Reading)
Students choose the correct answer from the three provided.

Answers
1 a, 2 a, 3 b, 4 c, 5 a, 6 c

Tip box
Students are advised to use Sven's text as a basis for their letter, remembering to write in the third person.

3 Schreib einen Brief an Svens Eltern von seinem Klassenlehrer. (Writing)
Students write a letter to Sven's parents from his teacher.

2B Schulstress (p. 189)

This page is best used at any point after pp. 34–35 of the Student's Book.

1 Lies den Artikel von Brian Halse und füll die Lücken aus. Es gibt mehr Wörter als Lücken. (Reading)
Students read the article and the copy and complete the gaps in the passage below.

Answers
1 immer, 2 Sprachlehrer, 3 seinem, 4 zufrieden, 5 nachmittags, 6 viel, 7 anders

Logo! 4 Lesen / Schreiben

2 Lies die folgenden Satzteile. Was passt zusammen? (Reading)
Students read the phrases and match the two sentence halves to make complete sentences.

Answers
1 g, 2 a, 3 e, 4 f, 5 d, 6 b, 7 c

Tip box
This provides advice to students to reuse the material from exercises 1 and 2 in their writing activity.

3 Was meint ein Deutscher / eine Deutsche, der / die als Lehrer / Lehrerin in Großbritannien arbeitet? Schreib einen Artikel über ihn / sie. (Writing)
Students write an article about what a German teacher who is working in a British school thinks about the school system.

3A Wir haben frei! (p. 190)

This page is best used at any point after pp. 42–43 of the Student's Book.

1 Was könnte man empfehlen? Welche Internet-Adresse könnte interessant sein? (Reading)
Students pick out the internet addresses which would be suitable for the people listed.

Answers
1 dasding.de, 2 vatican.va/news_service, 3 bloomberg.com, 4 disney.go.com/radiodisney, 5 zdnet.com/zdtv/radio, 6 dwelle.de

2 Und wo findet man das? Schreib eine (oder zwei) richtige Internet-Adresse(n) auf. (Reading)
Students pick out the possible internet addresses to find the information listed.

Answers
1 bayern3.de, 2 vatican.va/news_service, 3 dasding.de, 4 dwelle.de, 5 disney.go.com/radiodisney, 6 bloomberg.com

3 Wer findet diese Webseiten interessant? Geschwister? Eltern? Freunde? Lehrer? Schreib fünf Sätze. (Writing)
Students write sentences about people they know who would find these internet addresses interesting.

3B Wir haben frei! (p. 191)

This page is best used at any point after pp. 46–47 of the Student's Book.

1 Was machen die meisten? Richtig oder falsch? (Reading)
Students read the text and the sentences and say whether each is true or false.

Answers
1 Richtig. 2 Falsch. 3 Falsch. 4 Richtig. 5 Richtig. 6 Richtig.

2 Beantworte die Fragen auf Englisch. (Reading)
Students answer the questions in English.

Answers
1 meeting friends, sport, listening to music, 2 watch TV, 3 spending time on the computer, 4 environmental groups, sportsmen and women, 5 parents and friends, 6 politicians

3 Was meinst du? Was ist für dich im Leben wichtig? Schreib Sätze. (Writing)
Students write a short passage saying what is important to them. The Tip box reminds them to use sentences from exercise 1.

4A Urlaub (p. 192)

This page is best used at any point after pp. 66–67 of the Student's Book.

1 Lies den Text. Welche Sätze sind richtig? Hake nur *fünf* Sätze ab. (Reading)
Students read the text and pick out the five true sentences from those listed below.

Answers
richtige Sätze: 1, 3, 4, 6, 9

2 Beantworte die Fragen (ganze Sätze, bitte!). (Reading / Writing)
Students answer the questions in full sentences.

Answers
1 Die Donau ist ein Fluss. 2 Die Donau fließt durch Österreich. 3 Man kann von Passau bis nach Wien mit dem Rad fahren. 4 Wien ist die österreichische Hauptstadt. 5 Autos sind auf dem Weg nicht erlaubt. 6 Weil der Weg autofrei ist. 7 Kleine Kinder fahren hier ganz sicher. 8 Man findet Gaststätten alle zehn Kilometer. 9 Man kann in Gasthäusern und auf Campingplätzen gut übernachten. 10 Die Campingplätze sind modern. 11 Die Fahrt von Passau nach Wien dauert eine Woche.

Tip box
This provides reminders about the perfect tense: the past participle goes to the end and verbs of movement use *sein*.

3 Du hast mit Familie und Freunde sehr schöne Ferien an der Donau gehabt. Beschreib, was ihr gemacht habt. (Writing / Reading)
Students write about a holiday they had on the Danube.

4B Urlaub (p. 193)

This page is best used at any point after pp. 68–69 of the Student's Book.

1 Lies die Berichte. Wer spricht? Axel, Katrin oder keiner von beiden? (Reading)
Students read the report and then say who is saying the sentences below.

Answers
1 Katrin, 2 Axel, 3 keiner von beiden, 4 Axel, 5 Katrin, 6 keiner von beiden, 7 Katrin, 8 Katrin, 9 Katrin, 10 Axel, 11 Axel

2 Was haben sowohl Katrin als auch Axel gemacht? (Reading)
Students complete the passage with the correct words.

Answers
1 c, 2 a, 3 e, 4 d, 5 f, 6 b, 7 g

Tip box
This provides advice to students to use information from Axel's account, but to make sure that they use the perfect, present and future tense.

3 Axel schreibt eine Postkarte an Katrin. Was schreibt er? (Writing / Reading)
Students write a postcard to Katrin as if they were Axel.

5A Meine Stadt (p. 194)

This page is best used at any point after pp. 86–87 of the Student's Book.

1 Was weißt du über die Geschichte Berlins? Lies den Text und beantworte die Fragen. (Reading / Writing)
Students read the text and answer the questions below.

Answers
1 1961, 2 Präsident Kennedy, 3 am 9. November 1989, 4 mehr als 28 Jahre, 5 nach Ostberlin, 6 zehntausende von Ostberlinen

2 Richtig, falsch oder nicht im Text? (Reading)
Students read the sentences and say whether they are true or false or not in the text.

Answers
1 Richtig. 2 Falsch. 3 Richtig. 4 Richtig. 5 Richtig. 6 Falsch.

Tip box
Students should look at the text and exercise 2 to help them write their diary entry for exercise 3.

3 Was hat ein/e Ostberliner/in in ein Tagebuch geschrieben? Vervollständige die Sätze. (Writing)
Students complete the diary of an East-Berliner.

5B Meine Stadt (p. 195)

This page is best used at any point after pp. 80–81 of the Student's Book.

1 Auch in Deutschland sind nicht alle mit der Bahn zufrieden. Lies den Zeitungsartikel. Welcher Satz ist richtig? Wähle a, b oder c. (Reading)
Students read the article and then choose the correct ending for the sentences below from the three alternatives given.

Answers
1 c, 2 c, 3 a, 4 c, 5 b, 6 a

Tip box
This provides advice about using the model letter and thinking carefully about what to add to it.

2 Du bist mit dem ICE nach Würzburg gefahren, aber der Zug hatte drei Stunden Verspätung! Schreib jetzt einen Brief an die Zeitung. (Writing)
Students write a letter to a paper about a train journey, using the details given and adding to them.

Tip box
Advice to students to use the gapped letter from exercise 2 as a basis for exercise 3, but changing the mode of transport.

Logo! 4 Lesen / Schreiben

3 Schreib jetzt über eine schlimme Reise, die hier in England passiert ist. Das kann mit dem Bus, mit dem Auto oder mit dem Flugzeug gewesen sein. (Writing)
Students write about a bad journey in England using any mode of transport.

6A Einkaufen (p. 196)

This page is best used at any point after pp. 98–99 of the Student's Book.

1 Lies den Artikel. Richtig, falsch oder nicht im Text? (Reading)
Students read the article and say whether the statements below are true or false or not in the text.

Answers
1 Richtig. 2 Falsch. 3 Richtig. 4 Falsch. 5 Falsch. 6 Falsch. 7 Richtig. 8 Falsch.

2 Beantworte die folgenden Fragen auf Englisch. (Reading)
Students answer the questions in English.

Answers
1 She was too tired to go into town. 2 Two (for her brother and sister). 3 It is possible to get items at very good prices. 4 You have to wait to see who submits the highest bid. 5 She waited for six days and her bid was the highest.

Tip box
This provides advice for students to write one paragraph for each friend (exercise 3).

3 Du kaufst auf dieser Seite *zwei* Geschenke für Freunde. Schreib, was du gekauft hast. (Writing)
Students write two paragraphs about presents they have bought from the internet site (one for each person).

6B Einkaufen (p. 197)

This page is best used at any point after pp. 102–103 of the Student's Book.

1 Lies den Artikel und bring die Sätze in die richtige Reihenfolge. (Reading)
Students read the article and put the sentences below in the correct order.

Answers
g, f, b, e, c, i, a j, d, h, k

2 Beantworte die Fragen (ganze Sätze, bitte!). (Reading / Writing)
Students answer the questions in full sentences.

Answers
1 Sie sind in Dudelstadt angekommen. 2 Sie wohnen in Schottland. 3 Sie hatten das Auto im Parkhaus geparkt. 4 Sie wollten einen Einkaufsbummel durch die Altstadt machen. 5 Sie haben im Kaufhof eingekauft. 6 Als sie im Kaufhof an der Kasse waren. 7 Er ist draußen auf der Straße hingefallen. 8 Er war vier Stunden lang im Krankenhaus. 9 Das Parkhaus war in der Poststraße. 10 Der Autoschlüssel war im Portemonnaie. 11 Ihr Auto war nicht im Parkhaus.

3 Frau Sinclair muss eine kurze E-Mail an ihre Freundin in Luzern schreiben. Sie erzählt ihr, was passiert ist, aber sie hat nicht viel Zeit. Was schreibt sie? (Nicht mehr als 70 Wörter!) (Writing)
Students write an e-mail as Frau Sinclair to her friend.

4 Ein schweizerischer Tourist ist mit seinem Motorrad in deiner Stadt in Großbritannien angekommen. Er hat da auch Pech gehabt. Schreib einen Artikel auf Deutsch für eine schweizerische Zeitung! (Writing)
Students write an article for a Swiss newspaper about a Swiss tourist who has arrived in their town on his motorbike and has had some bad luck.

7A Freizeit und Urlaub (p. 198)

This page is best used at any point after pp. 116–117 of the Student's Book.

1 Lies den Artikel. Welcher Satz ist richtig? Wähle a, b oder c. (Reading)
Students read the article and say which of the three alternatives in the following sentences is correct.

Answers
1 c, 2 b, 3 c, 4 a, 5 c, 6 a, 7 b

Tip box
This provides advice for students when choosing the words to fill the gaps in exercise 2.

2 Was hast du neulich im Kino gesehen? Schreib eine kurze Kritik von einem Film. (Writing)
Students write a short critique of a film they have recently seen, using the outline provided.

7B Freizeit und Urlaub (p. 199)

This page can be used at any point after pp. 120–121 of the Student's Book.

1 Bring die folgenden Sätze in die richtige Reihenfolge. (Reading)
Students read the text and put the sentences in the right order.

Answers
d, c, e, f, b, g, a

Tip box
This provides a reminder to students that the past participles of verbs are different to the infinitive that they will find in the dictionary.

2 Vervollständige diesen Bericht eines katastrophalen Maitags. (Writing / Reading)
Students complete the report with the words in the boxes below.

Answers
gegangen, getrunken, gefunden, gedauert, gefällt, gebracht, gefunden, geklopft, gewartet, geschlafen, gerufen, geweckt, aufgemacht, angeschrieen

Tip box
Students may be able to think up some or their own reasons to use in exercise 3.

3 Und du? Was hältst du von dieser Tradition? Warum würdest du das vielleicht *nicht* machen? Schreib noch drei Sätze. (Writing)
Students write about what they think of this tradition using the sentences provided and writing more of their own.

8A Mein Leben zu Hause (p. 200)

This page is best used at any point after pp. 128–129 of the Student's Book.

1 Ein Ernährungswissenschaftler ist mit den Zeitungsüberschriften nicht einverstanden. Ordne die Sätze 1–5 den Texten a–e zu. (Reading)
Students match up the sentences with the five texts.

Answers
1 b, 2 e, 3 d, 4 c, 5 a

Tip box
This provides advice to students to use the texts a–e from exercise 1 answers as a basis for exercise 2.

2 Wie stehst du zu den Texten a–e aus Übung 1? (Writing)
Students complete the sentences using the texts a–e above to help.

Tip box
This provides helpful structures for students to express their own opinion in exercise 3.

3 Was glaubst du? Hat der Ernährungswissenschaftler aus Übung 1 Recht? Oder bist du nicht so sicher? Schreib ein paar Sätze. (Writing)
Students write about whether they think the nutrition expert from exercise 1 is right. Some helpful phrases are provided in the Tip box.

8B Mein Leben zu Hause (p. 201)

This page is best used at any point after pp. 136–137 of the Student's Book.

1 Lies den Artikel und füll die Lücken aus. (Reading)
Students read the article and complete the gaps in the sentences.

Answers
1 heute, 2 Umwelt, 3 kein, 4 Politik, 5 möglich

2 Wen oder was beschreibt man? Finde einen Ausdruck im Text, der am besten zum Satz passt. (Reading)
Students pick out an expression in the text which best fits the sentences listed.

Answers
1 Eltern oder Lehrer, 2 der Krieg, 3 Arbeitslosigkeit, 4 Umweltkatastrophen, 5 Einsamkeit, 6 Umweltzerstörung

Tip box
This provides advice to students to check the genders of the words they insert in exercise 3.

3 Und du? Was ist für dich wichtig oder nicht wichtig? (Writing)
Students complete the gapped text about what is important or not important to them.

Logo! 4 Lesen / Schreiben

9A die Arbeit (p. 202)

This page is best used at any point after pp. 146–147 of the Student's Book.

1 Schau die Stellenbeschreibungen an. Wo werden die Arbeitnehmer arbeiten?
Students match the workplaces to the texts.

Answers
1 d, 2 a, d, 3 b, 4 d, 5 c

2 Welche Stelle aus Übung 1 würdest du diesen Leuten empfehlen? (Reading)
Students match the sentences to the texts.

Answers
1 d, 2 b, 3 a, 4 c, 5 c

3 Welche Stelle aus Übung 1 würdest du wählen? Schreib einen Bewerbungsbrief. (Writing)
Students write a letter of application for one of the jobs using the outline provided.

Tip box
Advice to students to use an advert from exercise 1 and the sentences from the adverts to help them write their own advert.

4 Was ist dein Traumjob? Schreib eine Anzeige wie in Übung 1. Benutze die Wörter aus den vier Anzeigen a–d: Firmenprofil, Jobprofil usw. (Writing)
Students write an advert for their dream job.

9B Die Arbeit (p. 203)

This page is best used at any point after pp. 154–155 of the Student's Book.

1 Lies das Interview. Richtig, falsch oder nicht im Text? (Reading)
Students read the interview and say whether the sentences are true, false or not in the text.

Answers
1 Nicht im Text. 2 Falsch. 3 Richtig. 4 Richtig. 5 Falsch. 6 Richtig. 7 Falsch. 8 Nicht im Text. 9 Falsch.

2 Schreib für eine Schülerzeitung einen Artikel über Heike (70 Wörter). (Writing / Reading)
Students complete the gapped text to write an article on Heike.

Answers
Buskraftfahrerin, zehn, Friseurin, ins, gegangen, Spanien, gearbeitet, fünf, Deutschland, Annonce, Zeitung, zwei, schwer, Buskraftfahrerin

Tip box
This provides advice for exercise 3: put verbs in perfect tense, use structures from exercise 1 with *ich* form of verb, use some time phrases at the beginnings of sentences.

3 Wie alt bist *du* in fünfzehn Jahren? Was für einen Beruf wirst du dann haben? Schreib, was dir in den fünfzehn Jahren passiert ist. (Writing)
Students imagine themselves in 15 years' time and write about what they have done and what work they have had.

4 Kennst du jemanden, der älter (30? 40? 50?) ist und viele Jobs gehabt hat? Was hat er / sie gemacht? Wo? Wann? Warum? Was macht er / sie jetzt? Schreib Sätze. (Writing)
Students write about someone else and what work they have done.

10A Teenies! (p. 204)

This page is best used at any point after pp. 160–161 of the Student's Book.

1 Lies den Artikel und füll die Lücken aus. (Reading)
Students read the article and write out the sentences below, completing the gaps.

Answers
1 Amerikaner, 2 den Vereinigten Staaten, 3 fast nichts, 4 deutsches, 5 Surfen, 6 sehr oft

2 Lies die folgenden Satzteile. Was passt zusammen? (Reading)
Students match up the two halves of the sentences.

Answers
1 e, 2 f, 3 a, 4 b, 5 d, 6 c

Tip box
This provides advice to students to use the bulleted questions in exercise 3 as the basis of their writing. The text from exercise 1 can also be adapted.

3 Schreib jetzt einen kurzen Bericht über einen Engländer / eine Engländerin, der / die jetzt in Deutschland wohnt und gern britisches Radio im Internet hört! (Writing)
Students write a short article about an English person who lives in Germany and likes to listen to British radio on the internet.

10B Teenies! (p. 205)

This page is best used at any point after pp. 166–167 of the Student's Book.

1 Lies den Artikel und beantworte die Fragen kurz auf Deutsch. (Reading)
Students read the article and answer the question with short German phrases.

Answers
1 von Nottingham, 2 Bobbys, 3 Drogenhändler, 4 eine Pistole, 5 50% (halb so hoch wie in Berlin)

2 Beantworte die Fragen mit „ja" oder „nein". (Reading)
Students answer each question with *ja* or *nein*.

Answers
1 nein, 2 ja, 3 nein, 4 ja, 5 nein, 6 ja

Tip box
Students don't need to use all of the words provided to fill the gaps for exercise 3, but they need to take care to have a consistent opinion.

3 Was meinst du? Ist das eine gute oder eine schlechte Initiative? Schreib diesen Absatz ab und füll die Lücken aus. (Writing)
Students complete the gapped text to express their opinion for or against policemen carrying guns.

Solutions to *Grammatik* exercises

(Student's Book pp. 206–227)

1 1 Der, 2 die, 3 den, 4 Die, 5 Die, 6 das

2 1 Ein, 2 eine, 3 eine, 4 Eine, 5 ein, 6 ein

3 1 der, 2 der, 3 einem, 4 einer, 5 dem, 6 einem

4 1 neue, 2 alte, 3 grünen, 4 schwarze, 5 braune, 6 rote, 7 kleines, 8 englischer, 9 großer, 10 junges, 11 deutsche

5 1 billige, 2 deutsche, 3 alten, 4 krankes, 5 intelligente, 6 hübsche

6 1 neuen, 2 alten, 3 englischen, 4 armen, 5 guten

7 1 meine, 2 Ihre, 3 meinen, 4 Ihre, 5 Sein, 6 unserer

8 1 ihn, 2 uns, 3 sie, 4 Sie, 5 euch, 6 mich

9 1 uns, 2 ihr, 3 ihm, 4 ihnen, 5 Ihnen, 6 mir

10 1 ihn, 2 sie, 3 Es, 4 ihm, 5 er, 6 es

11 1 gehen, 2 finden, 3 trinken, 4 komme, 5 liegt, 6 Schwimmen, 7 Gehst, 8 singt, 9 Kommt, 10 machen, 11 höre

12 1 fährt, 2 schlafen, 3 Nimmst, 4 esse, 5 Seht, 6 vergisst, 7 sprichst, 8 singen, 9 liest, 10 helfen, 11 trifft

13 1 Wir steigen am Hauptbahnhof aus. 2 Der Zug fährt um 9 Uhr ab. 3 Wir stehen sehr früh auf. 4 Er sieht jeden Abend fern. 5 Der Film fängt um 18 Uhr an. 6 Ich ziehe einen Pulli an.

14 1 Wir kaufen nur bei Aldi ein. 2 Dieser Hund geht nie weg! 3 Sie steigen in den Bus ein. 4 Wann kommen sie zurück? 5 Wir ziehen am 15. Dezember um. 6 Du steigst am Rathaus aus.

15 1 Ich will heute Abend fernsehen. Ich muss heute Abend fernsehen. 2 Ich will meine Hausaufgaben machen. Ich muss meine Hausaufgaben machen. 3 Ich will Radio hören. Ich muss Radio hören. 4 Ich will in die Disco gehen. Ich muss in die Disco gehen. 5 Ich will zu Hause bleiben. Ich muss zu Hause bleiben. 6 Ich will Tischtennis spielen. Ich muss Tischtennis spielen.

16 1 Ich muss in die Stadt gehen. 2 Wir wollen zu Hause bleiben. 3 Du musst deine Hausaufgaben machen. 4 Ich kann nicht ins Kino gehen. 5 Sie dürfen hier nicht rauchen. 6 Sie mag eine Cola trinken. 7 Er will Tennis spielen. 8 Ich muss jetzt nach Hause gehen. 9 Ihr könnt morgen zu mir kommen. 10 Wir dürfen unsere Hefte nicht vergessen. 11 Magst du ein neues T-Shirt kaufen?

17 1 mich, 2 sich, 3 sich, 4 mich, 5 dich, 6 uns

18 1 Ich verspreche, meine Schulaufgaben zu machen. 2 Kann ich dir helfen, den schweren Koffer zu tragen? 3 Sie hat vor, im Sommer nach Berlin zu fahren. 4 Er hat vergessen, an seine Oma zu schreiben. 5 Wir haben angefangen, Spanisch zu lernen. 6 Sie sollten aufhören, so viel fernzusehen.

19 1 Bleib hier im Zimmer! 2 Fahr mit dem Bus! 3 Nimm die zweite Straße links! 4 Geh um die Ecke! 5 Ruf die Polizei an! 6 Trink nicht so viel!

20 1 Bleibt / Bleiben Sie hier im Zimmer! 2 Fahrt / Fahren Sie mit dem Bus! 3 Nehmt / Nehmen Sie die zweite Straße links! 4 Geht / Gehen Sie um die Ecke! 5 Ruft / Rufen Sie die Polizei an! 6 Trinkt / Trinken Sie nicht so viel!

21 1 Ich mache heute Abend meine Hausaufgaben. 2 Ich gehe nächste Woche ins Theater. 3 Wir fahren nächstes Jahr nach Amerika. 4 Meine Freundin kommt nächsten Monat zu Besuch. 5 Er bleibt in den Sommerferien in Köln. 6 Sie feiert Ende Mai ihren Geburtstag.

22 1 Ich werde den ganzen Tag schwimmen. 2 Sie werden viel arbeiten. 3 Er wird nicht studieren. 4 Werdet ihr nach Deutschland fahren? 5 Wir werden den Wagen reparieren. 6 Werden Sie einen Schlips tragen? 7 Die Kinder werden auf den Spielplatz gehen. 8 Wirst du die Zeitung lesen? 9 Sie wird das Geschenk bringen. 10 Ich werde mich nicht ausziehen.

23 1 Ich würde den ganzen Tag schwimmen. 2 Sie würde viel arbeiten. 3 Er würde nicht studieren. 4 Würdet ihr nach Deutschland fahren? 5 Wir würden den Wagen reparieren. 6 Würden Sie einen Schlips tragen? 7 Die Kinder würden auf den Spielplatz gehen. 8 Würdest du die Zeitung lesen? 9 Sie würde das Geschenk bringen. 10 Ich würde mich nicht ausziehen.

24 1 gelesen, 2 gegessen, 3 gesehen, 4 gekauft, 5 gespielt, 6 getrunken

25 1 Sie hat ein Buch gelesen. 2 Sie hat Pommes frites gegessen. 3 Sie hat einen guten Film gesehen. 4 Sie hat zwei CDs gekauft. 5 Sie hat Karten gespielt. 6 Sie hat eine Cola getrunken.

26 1 Wir haben ein Buch gelesen. 2 Wir haben Pommes frites gegessen. 3 Wir haben einen guten Film gesehen. **4** Wir haben zwei CDs gekauft. **5** Wir haben Karten gespielt. **6** Wir haben eine Cola getrunken.

27 **1** Ich habe eine Cola getrunken. **2** Ich habe meine Hausaufgaben gemacht. **3** Sie hat ein neues Computerspiel gekauft. **4** Wir haben Fußball gespielt. **5** Er hat immer Radio gehört. **6** Du hast die Zeitung gelesen. **7** Ich habe bis 11 Uhr geschlafen. **8** Sie haben ihre Mutter gesehen. **9** Wir haben keinen Kuchen gegessen. **10** Ihr habt zwei Tassen Tee getrunken. **11** Hast du eine Postkarte geschrieben?

28 **1** Ich bin ins Kino gegangen. **2** Wann ist er nach Hause gekommen? **3** Sie sind mit dem Zug nach London gefahren. **4** Sie ist jeden Tag im See geschwommen. **5** Wir sind nach Rom geflogen. **6** Ich bin den ganzen Tag im Bett geblieben. **7** Du bist schnell zum Supermarkt gelaufen. **8** Mein Hund ist gestorben. **9** Bist du zur Schule gegangen? **10** Wir sind am Sonntag im Wald gewandert. **11** Die Kinder haben auf den Baum geklettert.

29 **1** Ich habe mich jeden Morgen gewaschen. **2** Wir haben uns umgezogen. **3** Ich habe mich auf den Stuhl gesetzt. **4** Er hat sich jetzt hingelegt. **5** Sie hat sich immer aufgeregt. **6** Du hast dich hier erkältet.

30 **1** Er ist am Bahnhof ausgestiegen. **2** Der Zug ist um 9 Uhr abgefahren. **3** Wir sind sehr früh aufgestanden. **4** Er hat jeden Abend ferngesehen. **5** Der Film hat um 18 Uhr angefangen. **6** Ich habe einen Pulli angezogen.

31 **1** Ich haben ihren Namen vergessen. **2** Sie hat die Woche 7 Euro Taschengeld bekommen. **3** Wir haben den Text nicht verstanden. **4** Sie haben ihre Verwandten in Australien besucht. **5** Er hat das Problem erklärt. **6** Du hast immer dasselbe Getränk bestellt.

32 **1** Ich wollte / musste heute Abend fernsehen. **2** Ich wollte / musste meine Hausaufgaben machen. **3** Ich wollte / musste Radio hören. **4** Ich wollte / musste in die Disco gehen. **5** Ich wollte / musste zu Hause bleiben. **6** Ich wollte / musste Tischtennis spielen.

33 **1** Ich musste in die Stadt gehen. **2** Wir wollten zu Hause bleiben. **3** Du musstest deine Hausaufgaben machen. **4** Ich sollte nicht ins Kino gehen. **5** Sie durften hier nicht rauchen. **6** Sie wollte eine Cola trinken.

34 **1** konnten, **2** könnten, **3** könntest, **4** konnte, **5** könnte

35 **1** Sie schlief ein, denn sie hatte den ganzen Tag gearbeitet. **2** Wir waren enttäuscht, denn unsere Freunde hatten uns nicht besucht. **3** Sie waren verärgert, denn der Zug war schon abgefahren.

4 Er ging nach Hause, denn er hatte sein Geld vergessen. **5** Sie langweilte sich, denn sie war den ganzen Abend zu Hause geblieben. **6** Mir war kalt, denn ich hatte keinen Pulli angezogen.

36 **1** Ich sehe durch das Fenster. **2** Ich kaufe ein Geschenk für den Lehrer. **3** Gehen Sie um die Ecke. **4** Ich komme durch die Fußgängerzone. **5** Er geht ohne das Mädchen. **6** Wir spielen gegen die beste Mannschaft.

37 **1** Ich spreche mit dem Lehrer. **2** Ich fahre mit der Bahn in die Stadt. **3** Sie ist seit dem Wochenende hier. **4** Das ist das Auto von dem Arzt. **5** Wie kommt man zu dem Bahnhof? **6** Sie gehen nach der Mittagspause zum Café.

38 **1** Der Hund liegt unter dem Tisch. **2** Der Junge wohnt in einem großen Haus. **3** Sie geht in den Supermarkt. **4** Sie stehen vor dem Kino. **5** Er hängt das Bild an die Wand. **6** Ingrid legt die Teller auf den Tisch. **7** Sie sitzt auf meinem Mantel. **8** Er besuchte uns vor einem Monat. **9** Gehen wir in das Theater? **10** Stell die Schuhe hinter den Stuhl. **11** Wir wohnen in einer Stadt.

39 **1** Spielst du gut Tennis? **2** Bleibt mein Freund zu Hause? **3** Kommt das Mädchen aus Griechenland? **4** Läuft sein Bruder gern Ski? **5** Gehen Sie auf die Party? **6** Trinkt er Kaffee ohne Milch?

40 **1** Ich mache heute Abend meine Hausaufgaben. **2** Sie geht jeden Tag ins Schwimmbad. **3** Er arbeitet samstags in einer Drogerie. **4** Sie spielen am Sonntag gegen Stuttgart. **5** Wir haben vor drei Wochen einen neuen Wagen gekauft. **6** Ich bin letzten Sommer nach Frankreich gefahren.

41 **1** Heute Abend mache ich meine Hausaufgaben. **2** Jeden Tag geht sie ins Schwimmbad. **3** Samstags arbeitet er in einer Drogerie. **4** Am Sonntag spielen sie gegen Stuttgart. **5** Vor drei Wochen haben wir einen neuen Wagen gekauft. **6** Letzten Sommer bin ich nach Frankreich gefahren.

42 **1** Wir gehen am Freitag zusammen ins Theater. **2** Sie wohnt seit drei Jahren mit ihrer Schwester in Dortmund. **3** Sie spielen am Wochenende mit ihren Kindern im Garten. **4** Ich fahre jeden Tag mit der Bahn zur Schule. **5** Er bleibt bis November bei seiner Tante in Hamburg. **5** Wir fahren im Sommer mit dem Zug nach Frankreich.

43 **1** Am Freitag gehen wir zusammen ins Theater. **2** Seit drei Jahren wohnt sie mit ihrer Schwester in Dortmund. **3** Am Wochenende spielen sie mit ihren Kindern im Garten. **4** Jeden Tag fahre ich mit der Bahn zur Schule. **5** Bis November bleibt er bei seiner

Tante in Hamburg. **6** Im Sommer fahren wir mit dem Zug nach Frankreich.

44 1 Ich bin immer sehr müde, weil ich spät ins Bett gehe. **2** Sie geht gern zur Schule, weil der Unterricht immer interessant ist. **3** Er hört gern Musik, wenn er allein ist. **4** Ich esse gern Pizza, wenn ich in die Stadt gehe. **5** Wir mögen Mathe nicht, weil der Lehrer zu streng ist. **6** Jürgen hat Kopfschmerzen, weil er zu viel Bier getrunken hat.

45 1 Sie fährt nach Frankreich, um den Eiffelturm zu sehen. **2** Er ruft den Arzt an, um einen Termin zu machen. **3** Ich bleibe in der Schule, um mit meinem Lehrer zu sprechen. **4** Wir fahren nach Hamburg, um unsere Mutter zu besuchen. **5** Sie trainieren jeden Tag, um das Turnier zu gewinnen. **6** Du solltest viel Gemüse essen, um gesund zu bleiben.

46 1 Er kam ins Zimmer, ohne zu klopfen. **2** Sie ging nach Hause, ohne den Brief zu lesen. **3** Er war den ganzen Abend in der Kneipe, ohne Bier zu trinken. **4** Ich suchte überall im Haus, ohne meinen Reisepass zu finden. **5** Du gehst immer aus, ohne einen Mantel zu tragen. **6** Wir sprachen mit dem Mädchen, ohne ihren Namen zu wissen.

47 1 Karsten hat einen Bruder, der in München wohnt. **2** Ich fahre mit der Straßenbahn, die über Nollendorf fährt. **3** Sie wohnen in dem Haus, das auf dem Hügel liegt. **4** Fahren Sie mit dem Bus, das dort anhält. **5** Ich habe eine Katze, die auf meinem Bett schläft. **6** Kennst du den Lehrer, der nur freitags arbeitet?

Photocopiable grids

Kapitel 1
Page 8, 2a

	Wohnort	Geschwister	(Stief)Vater?	(Stief)Mutter?	Haustiere?
Anja					
Peter					
Sylvia					

✂ -

Chapter 3, Unit 5,
p. 48, Ex. 2a

	Wohin?	Wann?	Wo treffen sie sich?
Birgit / Rosita			
Robert / Uli			
Petra / Felix			
Isabell / Michael			

✂ -

Chapter 5, Unit 6,
p. 84, Ex. 1a

	Auf dem Land	In der Großstadt	In einem Dorf	In einer Kleinstadt	Gern	Nicht gern
1 Matthias						
2 Irena						
3 Ricky						
4 Viktoria						